ASIATIC STUDIES

RELIGIOUS AND SOCIAL

ASIATIC STUDIES

RELIGIOUS AND SOCIAL

By

SIR ALFRED C. LYALL

K.C.B., D.C.L.

SECOND SERIES

GYAN

Published by

GYAN

Gyan Publishing House
5, Ansari Road
Daryaganj, New Delhi-110002
Phone: 011-47034999, 9811692060
E-mail: books@gyanbooks.com

Distribution Network
gyanbooks.com
India, USA, Canada, UK, Australia, France

ISBN : 978-81-212-6208-8 (PB)
First Published, 1899

2nd Impression 2022

Printed at: Gyan Press, Delhi.

ASIATIC STUDIES
Author: Sir Alfred C. Lyall

ASIATIC STUDIES

RELIGIOUS AND SOCIAL

By SIR ALFRED C. LYALL
K.C.B., D.C.L.

SECOND SERIES

1899

PREFACE

THE single volume of "Asiatic Studies" published in 1882 has been for some years out of print. In preparing a fresh edition, with some necessary revision, I have thought it might be worth while to add a second volume containing a few selected essays and dissertations, chiefly on the subject of Asiatic religions, that have been written by me at different times in recent years. In order to bring together two essays upon the same subject—the relations of the State with Religion in China—I have transferred to this new volume chap. v. of the original Studies.

The first chapter of the second volume contains three letters which were originally published under the signature of Vamadeo Shastri. In these letters I ventured upon the attempt to represent, or at least to throw light upon, certain religious views, feelings, and opinions which I believe to exist, not without considerable influence, among the conservative classes of India, but which are apt to escape the attention of Englishmen, whether at home or in that country. For this purpose the assumption of a pseudonym was convenient, and, I hope, excusable. It has been chosen to denote an orthodox Brahman, versed in the religion and philosophy of his own people, and to some extent in the literature of the West, who is chiefly interested, like all Indians of the old schools, in the religious situation, and who surveys from that standpoint the moral and material changes that the English rule is producing in India.

In two chapters (iii. and iv.) I have ventured to criticise the use of evolutionary principles for the explanation of certain primitive customs and beliefs. I agree that the psychology of primitive man exhibits general tendencies, and follows broad lines of direction, that ideas and ritual can be traced through connected stages of development. But it seems to me doubtful whether the evidence of folklore, ancient and modern, can be so handled as to establish the origin and filiation of a particular rite or legend, or to justify a positive demonstration of the precise order and sequence that govern the formation and modification of some widespread religious beliefs. The field of exploration has been enormously enlarged of late, by travellers, by missionaries, by the extension of civilised dominion over the outlying parts of the earth; and the customs, traditions, and superstitions underlying the great religions, or outside their sphere, have been laboriously investigated. An immense miscellany of facts and observations has been thus collected for systematic examination and assortment, with the important result that we have now a much wider knowledge and clearer comprehension of natural religion. But

I think that one effect of this accumulation of materials has been to encourage speculative generalisation, because it has provided a repertory out of which one may make arbitrary selection of examples and precedents to suit any theory. So many strange customs, rites, and legends, ancient and modern, are susceptible of different interpretations, their exact meaning is often so enigmatic and hard to ascertain, that they may be fitted into one hypothesis as well as another, according to the point of view or the drift of the argument. They can certainly be explained in a single, straightforward fashion, as generated by man's varying conditions and circumstances, by the necessity that is the prolific mother of invention; or they can be scientifically grouped to show the general procession of early thought and culture. But when we come to the deciphering of some particular fable, or to providing a triumphant solution of some recondite anthropological problem, I own that I distrust the method of resorting to a vast storehouse of complex data which would supply evidence for many more than a single conclusion.

The chapter upon History and Fable has been added because I conceive it to have some bearing upon those general views regarding the elementary commixture of fable and fact in ages that may be called prehistoric, and the great difficulty of disentangling them, which have been suggested in several of the essays that are contained in these two volumes.

A. C. LYALL.

March, 1899.

CONTENTS.

CHAPTER I.

LETTERS FROM VAMADEO SHASTRI.

CHAPTER II.

ON THE RELATIONS BETWEEN THE STATE AND RELIGION IN CHINA.

CHAPTER IV.

ORIGINS AND INTERPRETATIONS OF PRIMITIVE RELIGIONS.

CHAPTER V.

NATURAL RELIGION IN INDIA.

CHAPTER VI.

HISTORY AND FABLE.

CHAPTER VII.

PERMANENT DOMINION IN ASIA.

Socrates.—Then when does the soul attain truth?—for in attempting to consider anything in company with the body she is obviously deceived.

Yes; that is true.

Socrates.—Then must not existence be revealed to her in thought, if at all?

Yes.

And thought is best when the mind is gathered into herself and none of these things trouble her—neither sounds nor sights nor pain nor any pleasure—when she has as little as possible to do with the body, and has no bodily sense or feeling, but is aspiring after being?

That is true.

—*The Phædo of Plato—Jowett's Translation.*

ASIATIC STUDIES:

RELIGIOUS AND SOCIAL

CHAPTER I.

LETTERS FROM VAMADEO SHASTRI.

I.

MORAL AND MATERIAL PROGRESS IN INDIA.

It is natural that much diffidence should be felt by a Hindu, with somewhat conservative and old-fashioned Brahmanic ideas, in venturing, even with the aid of kind English friends, to place before an English public some expression of the perplexities and forebodings which beset him. Several Indian gentlemen have latterly written excellent papers in the London reviews that have met with a generous reception; but I think these have been mostly young men belonging to the latest school of advanced practical reformers; they have been carefully educated in England, or in Anglo-Indian colleges, and their writings are in the tone and upon the subjects that suit the sanguine humour of the day They slash away in good democratic style at the Indian Government and its measures; they deal usually with such questions as the disestablishment of English chaplains in India, tenant-right, the representation of the people, and official incompetence generally. No one would be surprised if, instead of an Asiatic name, these articles bore some ordinary English signature; but although such consummate imitation may flatter your national self-esteem, I find myself, regretfully, unable to share the gratification with which my English acquaintances discover that a young Bengalee can be trained to write almost exactly like a Londoner.

My own position is different; and I have neither the capacity nor the taste for venturing into this field of political discussion. I have had a good English education, but it was given to me at Benares, where the study of Sanskrit classics still survives; and though I have looked into the current literature of Europe, I have never been able, even by crossing the seas, to escape beyond the deep shadow that has been cast over my ideas and feelings by the climate, the religious practices, and the philosophy of my own country. The enfranchised Hindu, who is attracted by the luxurious and (perhaps I may say) the sensual side of European life, contrives to make merry after the hearty manner of Englishmen, enjoys wine and women's society, and rejoices loudly in the rapid material development of his people. I do not undervalue the benefits of railways, sound finance, and an efficient police; but I confess myself to be not profoundly interested in the spread of European comfort, or in the accumulation of riches and luxuries among the commercial and the professional classes in India. One of your cynical writers has observed that we can see what the Christian God thinks of wealth by marking the kind of people on whom He bestows it; and in my own country those popular deities do not bear a very high character who are propitiated merely for the acquisition of riches. But the truth is that I am rather of a melancholy and vaguely speculative temperament. I come from that part of India which is the home of Brahmanic theosophy, and where a few lean Pandits still continue puzzling themselves over the mystery of existence, and are less interested in making the best of this sensational world than in making their escape from it. Such persons are undoubtedly the product of their environment, as yet undisturbed by exotic influences. English gentlemen who have endured many hot seasons in the Gangetic plains, especially when cholera is raging, will understand why the philosophy of life that I have received from my forefathers is not a very cheerful one. I have been told that some sixty years ago the English officers at a large station in those parts formed themselves into what they called a Hellfire Club, and proceeded to adapt their mode of life to the diabolical despair thus indicated. The incident perhaps illustrates the religious despondency generated in those latitudes; and it also betrays your English impatience of uncomfortable existence, and your characteristic hurry to reach the end of a tiresome journey. For it is to me remarkable that, while your people are full of restlessness and irritability over the ennui and vexations of their present life, they seem nevertheless very well reconciled to the prospect of one single hasty run through the visible world, ending with sudden and final precipitation into an abyss just beyond it. This reminds me sometimes of your rapid tours through India, when, after much hurrying to and fro in steamers and on railways the traveller's journey closes abruptly with the rush of an express train into some gloomy London terminus, whence he is borne off into the midst of a yellow fog and disappears. We Indians endure life more patiently, journey through it more quietly; we do not first accept existence as eternal, and then stake our whole future on one desperate race; but we cherish the hope that, after many stages and diverse trials, we shall at last slip altogether outside the pains and penalties of existence. We think that by putting all the suffering of future life into the state of penal existence you may leave nothing but ennui for the state that is expected to be one of blessedness; that no such division of sensations into absolute happiness and absolute misery is conceivable; and that consequently we are right in holding that the final stage of rest, the real journey's end, must be absorption and unconsciousness.

But it is of no use to debate whether the eastern or the western solution of the great problem of a future life be the more satisfactory. Your missionaries will never convince us, and we do not seek to convince you. My present concern is with the immediate future, in a phenomenal sense, of that ancient and unfortunate people to whom I belong: unfortunate because with all their intellectual depth they have inherited little political capacity, and because, under the impulse and influence of what you call civilisation, they seem to be on the way towards cutting loose the mainstay and chief bond of their society, Religion. I see all round me in India signs of the disintegration of the old caste system and regulative rituals, which have grown up in this climate and country; and I can perceive that the next generation may need an entirely fresh set of authoritative rules of conduct and belief. And as I must admit that the Indian gods (in whom I have, secretly, no great confidence) do not seem to be coming forward with any new revelation for our guidance, I have been looking, as we Asiatics are apt to do, for assistance to the English government and the English nation. I have heard, moreover, that your people are not unacquainted with similar difficulties connected with a perceptible decline of religious belief. And, therefore, since I reached England, I have been glancing over the latest books and articles on ethical questions, in the hope, now that the lights of Asia are burning low, of gaining something by the exchange of old lamps for new.

I have not as yet found much solace from considering the ways of your government in India. In Asia, no serious person expects much from rulers, especially in the way of moral instruction or example: yet, considering that it is the English administration of India which has turned all our religious ideas upside down, and remembering that spiritual anarchy is of serious concern to any government, I am inclined to doubt whether your official views and proceedings are quite up to the level of your own situation. The India Office periodically issues a Blue Book purporting to describe the Moral and Material Progress of India under British rule. Material progress is easily demonstrated: there can be no doubt that trade is flourishing, cultivation extending, and that all the industrial pursuits have increased and multiplied, while we have been taught many things that our fathers never knew. I am not so sure, by the way, whether progress is demonstrable in Art, and I fear that you have not enhanced the poetical aspects of things in India. Art in its higher orders has hitherto, like morality, preferred a religious to an obviously utilitarian motive; and when utility comes too obtrusively into the foreground, the artistic, like the religious, spirit becomes depressed and loses grasp of its principle. At this hour a Hindu sculptor in outlying places will execute temples beautiful in design and details, because the subject not only inspires and exalts his imagination but leaves it quite free. The introduction of your European patterns is confusing to the spiritual instinct as to form and colour; the imaginative faculty becomes superfluous; and then the immense European demand for the finer handiwork of India has demoralised our artisans, who, instead of endeavouring to express the multiform religious idea, however grotesque, are now employed in executing wholesale commercial orders according to sample. However, let us give up Art as probably doomed, and admit that Material Progress in the more solid sense is undeniable; the chapter in your Blue Book which purports to register India's Moral Progress is still rather disappointing to me.

I find that in this official volume Moral Progress signifies, generally, the spread of primary and middle-class instruction in the Government schools and colleges. This public instruction is necessarily utilitarian and secular; and the English text-books are full of outlandish and unfamiliar allusions; but the course of teaching gives much serviceable information, and is therefore becoming very popular with the great and growing class of those who learn in order to earn. I have nothing to say against this kind of education, nor against the higher university examination—except this, that I am not at ease about its eventual effect, taken alone, upon Moral Progress. It seems to me doubtful whether, according to the Blue Book classification, the words moral and material do not practically mean the same thing; and I fear that among Indians educated under your system there is a distinct leaning toward this interpretation. We are also parting rapidly, under the influence of this Public Instruction, with our religious beliefs; they were never of much ethical use to the people: but at any rate, they provided certain authoritative theories of conduct and social obligation. And now that the whole form and character of our society are changing, and western civilisation, applied suddenly like a galvanic battery, is waking us up into a new state of life, we may naturally, if unreasonably, expect the English, to whom we owe all this material advancement, to help us forward also in the readjustment of our moral ideas upon a new foundation. That this expectation is not entirely unreasonable is indeed admitted by the government, for the problem has been recently stated, and even some solution of it attempted, in a voluminous report of the Education Commission that was issued in 1884. This Commission, in the course of an elaborate enquiry into the method of public instruction in India, came inevitably upon the difficulty of religious instruction in State schools, and having adroitly rounded this point by declaring that the State offers no such instruction, found themselves brought up in front of the much wider and deeper problem of moral teaching.

> "If we may judge by the utterance of the witnesses" (says the Report), "there is in the North-Western Provinces and the Panjáb a deep-seated and widespread feeling that discipline and moral supervision require to be supplemented by definite instruction in the principles of morality. The feeling seems not to be so strong in the provinces where Western education has been most firmly established."

It will be noticed, in the first place, that this solicitude about morality prevails chiefly in the old-fashioned and less Anglicised provinces; and, secondly, that, since in almost all our schools and colleges the pupils attend by the day, it seems to be assumed that the principles of morality will not be learnt at home. And the Commission, acknowledging the inherent instability of "a morality based to a large extent upon considerations of prudent self-interest," recommends "that an attempt be made to prepare a moral text-book, based on the fundamental principles of natural religion, such as may be taught in all Government and non-Government colleges."

It must be admitted that this is but a weak and hesitating treatment of the problems which beset the moral progress of our rising generation, and which disquiet Hindus like myself. You English are aware, I presume, that you have made yourselves responsible for the destinies of about two hundred and fifty millions of people, most of whom are, morally as well as materially, in a rather primitive condition. Among most of these millions the religious conception has not yet reached that particular stage at which the main object of divine government is understood to be the advancement of morals. On the other hand, there is a considerable minority whose ideas have passed beyond this stage, and who conceive their Divinity as supremely indifferent to all things, material as well as moral; but on the whole the popular divinities are supposed to follow very much the same policy as that of the British Government in India; they superintend material interests in this world, and do not profess to prescribe in moral cases, except by attaching penalties to disregard of certain unintelligible laws. Moreover, we Hindus have never constructed any positive dogmatic creeds or commandments for general use: the common polytheism has grown up out of the nature of things, and out of observations, exceedingly inaccurate and short-sighted, of phenomena; so that our natural theology is a sort of rudimentary utilitarianism. We have for ages been groping about to ascertain by experience what is the will of the gods and of the government; just as your government now goes about hazily seeking to discover what suits the people. Of such theology, however, so far as it prevails among the more intelligent classes, it is to be expected that scientific education and moral aspirations will make short work; and indeed idolatry is to many of us merely traditional symbolism, useful to simple-hearted devotion. For this superficial polytheism is after all nothing more than a fantastic mystery play, exhibiting under various figures and disguises the marvellous drama of Nature; it is the only form in which the Pantheistic principle of a divine omnipresent energy can be interpreted to the people. And as for our high ritual, with its elaborate forms, its severe penances, and the fantastic posturing of our ascetics, all this is only self-discipline for wrestling with or appeasing the unknown but ubiquitous Forces that press round on the soul in its passage through diverse existences. As the Sankhya philosophy represents matter acting a pantomime before the soul, like a dancing-girl before some prince, so do our Hindu worshippers and devotees take up positions, strike attitudes, and recite sacred verses; and I suppose something of the kind goes on in every liturgy. It is the secret of the few in India, as possibly in other countries, that nothing of the kind will really avail, that the Supreme Being is not to be bribed or flattered, that He is a legislator who issues hard laws without deigning to explain them except by the consequences, an Artist who disdains to introduce His own personality into the story of human destinies, but who leaves men to find out the plot and the moral through the dramatic evolution of His works.

And, therefore, when your missionaries and philologists expound to us that the Hindu mythology is mere imagination, and that the popular gods are fanciful creations, we of the priesthood can only reply mournfully that we have known it for some thousand years: the divinities are shadows and signs of the incomprehensible. The vanishing of polytheism will simply clear away a harmless illusion, as when on a stage actors take off their masks and costumes, and speak with their natural voice; it will uncover Nature working according to regular laws to be understood of any one, and beyond Nature there will be nothing sensibly visible at all, except the dark stage curtain. I have little hope that the disappearance of our popular superstitions will leave any solid platform for the development of a superior religion. We Indians are not barbarous tribes who can be lifted up by missionaries from a lower to a higher grade of supernatural conceptions; nor is the world now in the same condition as when in Europe the old pagan statues were unearthed and set up again with new names. For the real substance of my country's religion, the mainspring that moves the puppet-show of popular idolatry, is Pantheism; and it is with Pantheism, not Polytheism, that a rising morality will have to reckon. If any Hindu desires to go behind the ordinary rites of worship and propitiations, and to understand the inner nature of divine government, he learns that the Deity pervades and is immanent in all forces and forms, and that the gods whom he has been adoring are mere embodiments of, or emanations from, the universal energy. Very many enquirers go thus far, and here most of them stop; but those who, perceiving that the identity of God with the material universe cannot be an ultimate idea, ask what is beyond, may be told that there is somewhere an Infinite Being, unconditioned and unconscious, to whom object and subject present no duality. Such a Being can have no interest in the cosmic evolution; it acknowledges no liability for the facts or results of the soul's existence, or for the ills that have inevitably followed the clothing of the soul's integument with sensation. To escape from corporeal fetters, out of the endless desert of ignorance and delusion, is the soul's concern; the Spirit, calm and still, regards its struggles, looking on at the fantastic play of forces set in motion by some secondary Demiurge.

We may assume, then, that polytheism will gradually subside, and we have to enquire whether the essence of the Brahmanic theology offers any material for a religious reformation of the kind suitable to an enlightened and practical people. I am afraid that the only point, in all our theology, of direct interest to humanity in regard to its future destiny, is the process of the soul's transmigration through incessant births and deaths, until at last it becomes absorbed in the totality of existences. As the accomplishment of this journey depends more or less upon a balance of merits and demerits, the conception might possibly be developed into an ethical doctrine; though how far the rate of progress depends upon works, and how far upon a deep subjective realisation of divine attributes, has always been a matter for scholastic dispute. On the whole, however, the predominating influence is that of a creature's own deeds; and here the practical common sense and experience of mankind, transfigured into a transcendental idea, is to be detected in the belief that each generation fares according to the sins or well-doing of its predecessor. And perhaps the notion that at each death consciousness is so interrupted, that the precise sins or successes of a previous existence are not remembered, but can only be guessed at by their effect, merely indicates that the real morality of our actions cannot be properly determined at all in a single life. Here we may trace an analogy with the modern scientific theory of hereditary transmission of experiences; and the doctrine also contains some elements of practical morality. The Western creeds seem to regard eternal punishment as mainly retributive, while the metempsychosis may be thought to have a nearer affinity with reformatory discipline, which in your latest administrative systems is taken to be the higher method of dealing with offenders. On the other hand, the ethical defect of our doctrine, as a working scheme of moral government, is that it relieves both gods and men of individual responsibility, in any single existence, either for the justice of the sentences or for the offence found. It is as if men were taught to expect, after innumerable periods of probation, and upon a most complicated balance of countless transactions, a final judgment-day at which they should be absolved or condemned without the faintest recollection of what they had done, and without any explanation or summing up on the part of a presiding Power. I admit that such a process would be not unlike the manner in which we occasionally suffer on earth, as when one is seized and suddenly executed by a despotic ruler, or as when an aerolite kills one dead; but these are just the incidents that make some Indian philosophers doubt all theories of a watchful Providence; and the natural consequence has been a strong tendency toward fatalism. If it be true, as English judges have said, that in India evidence given *in articulo mortis* is far less trustworthy than in Europe, I should take this to be a minor symptom of the inadequacy of our transmigration dogma as a moral restraint.

To all this it may be objected, by those who are superficially acquainted with India, that recondite and abstruse theologic doctrines are wide apart from the popular religion. But nothing is more certain than that for centuries the prevailing beliefs of all Hindus who form any definite ideas on questions touching God and immortality have been coloured and moulded by Pantheism. And if there is one metaphysical dogma that has taken a kind of physical shape, and has thus impressed itself on the multitude, it is the belief in metempsychosis, *i.e.* in the scheme of future existence regulated, not according to the decision of a Supreme Judge in faith and morals, but by the spontaneous and as it were natural operation of a soul's experiences.

This is, as I have said, the one element of some ethical promise that can be extracted from the mass of our traditional beliefs. Otherwise the transmigration is only one series in the shifting exhibition of Pantheism; an incessant change of form and habitation without any moral evolution; and the prospect of such an illimitable journey toward the infinite only extinguishes human sympathy for the individual by minimising the importance of a single life. The Supreme Intelligence, if it interferes at all, does not go beyond awarding marks at successive examinations. It may condescend to award marks and confer degrees, but does not enforce discipline or exercise personal supervision—the system is that of our Indian Universities, or rather of the London University compared with Oxford and Cambridge—and I have heard that the latter system is better for morals. In short, we Hindus have the doctrine of future rewards and punishments, but no judge to pass and execute decrees; and the divine law exists rather in the scientific sense of invariable consequences, than in that of stern commandments supernaturally delivered. I do not allege that our sacred Scriptures are incapable of being treated as Revelation; but I fear the message is not precise enough to be of much practical weight in shaping and informing the mind of a vast population. Some of us are now endeavouring to find in these ancient writings a warrant for the recognition of a Supreme Moral Ruler, such as is required (perhaps unphilosophically) by ordinary minds as soon as their natural religion begins to fade away. Many centuries ago, indeed, we Hindus, in our desire to refine and clarify the primitive Vedic utterances into something like a formal theology, had set to work upon similar speculations. But the deplorable subtlety and inquisitiveness of the Indian intellect always led us to overshoot the mark; our researches took us straight into the labyrinth of Pantheism, or beyond in pursuit of mirages in the Transcendental desert. Our Supreme Being disappeared beyond Space and Time, leaving the world of experience without a responsible government. And although the teaching of Sakhya Muni, our greatest heretical reformer, set up the lofty doctrine of Righteousness as the only true Way of deliverance, yet he abolished even such a vague entity or unity as Brahma, into whom the Hindu hopes to be finally absorbed, and substituted Nirvana, or Nonentity, as the ultimate goal. There can be little doubt that this, and his scorn of prayer and sacrifices, must have been the main reason why the Brahmans have so completely recovered their dominion; and the expulsion of Buddhism from India was probably due to the immense difficulty of establishing the purest morality without some system of spiritual sanctions and of salvation by supernatural grace.

And now that Brahmanism is in its turn threatened with slow dissolution, the result of our searching after some ultimate religious authority fails to indicate some fresh resting-place, or to show us how out of the old materials we may hope to build up some consistent and reputable system of belief, acceptable of the people, such as in Christianity and Islam a man must either accept and repose upon, or reject and wander abroad at his peril. No sooner do we embark upon a fresh voyage of discovery, in quest of the promised land, than we are carried off into some current of interminable speculation, drawing us back again into the open sea of Pantheism, or in hopeless quest of the Unknowable. All that we bring with us out of the old faiths is the doctrine of the soul's immortality, that its nature is something different from that of mere illusive phenomena, and that somehow our hope of release from misery depends on what is done in this sensual existence. I do not undervalue this residuum, for metempsychosis, thus understood, keeps alive a sense of responsibility and an anxiety about our unknown future. The doctrine is, moreover, to some degree an explanation of the unequal distribution of good and evil in the world, that problem which has in all ages haunted and disturbed the reflective mind. It is therefore of the highest importance, if our future religion is to maintain any effective connection with morals, that this doctrine, or some refined form of it, shall survive. No one can as yet distinctly foresee the effect that will be produced on morals by a widespread conviction, such as that which

Positivism accepts with such equanimity, that beyond this visible world there is nothing; we can only perceive clearly that this conviction, once firmly established in the popular mind, will finally close the great procession of religious ideas, from the ghosts to the gospels; and that a mere "subjective incorporation" of the dead will never take among future generations the mighty part hitherto played in religion by deified humanity. For this reason I trust that some distinct belief in a future existence will develop out of our ancient idea of the purifying transmigration of souls; although it is still questionable how far this belief will be useful to morals, unless supplemented and administered by the conception of a Supreme Ruler of human action. If, again, all theories of the persistence of the soul's life must be treated as mere guess-work, then it is questionable whether the monotheistic conception, if we can manage to develop it, will not have reached us too late to serve us as an efficient moral basis.

This is the situation that fills me with apprehensions. I fear that, whatever may be the new form of religion worked out of their old materials by the coming generation of Hindus, it must at best represent a political constitution of which only the theory is settled while the functions and mechanism of practical, every-day administration are ill-defined. The divine executive will be weak, because it will stand, like the Deity of our modern Brahmoism, upon an abstract principle, a mere notion of the divine nature, not upon some right or authority palpably exercised in this world or another. It may be right for Europe to insist upon the vast importance of separating spiritual from temporal jurisdiction; but in Asia we find that, when divine interference in the visible world ceases, the spiritual sanction loses its popular authority. And, therefore, I think it on the whole unfortunate for my countrymen at large that they have never attained the imperial conception of a paramount, omnipotent, actively governing Power, like the commanding personalities of Christianity and Islam. The absence of the simple monarchical idea of such a Ruler is one reason why the Hindus are wanting in the concentrated religious enthusiasm so valuable to races in their early world struggles, before they get banded together as nations; and it has left them little of that incentive to strenuous exertion which is supplied by the sense that the present life, passed under the watchful eye of an omniscient judge, is all important to the immediate future beyond death. It is true that our notions of an indefinite succession of innumerable existences have a closer analogy to the evolutionary course of nature suggested by modern science, than a doctrine that stakes everything on a single existence; and I admit that the dogma of eternal torments shocks a people that is less practical, though perhaps more delicate intellectually, than the European. Nevertheless, I must confess that Christianity and Islam are the religions that have trained and led the conquering nations of the world; and it is becoming plain to me that a few simple, uncompromising ordinances, backed by the sternest of divine sanctions, are of excellent service to mankind during the rough and fierce periods of history, in critical times when the Unknowable is not to be found, and when Humanity is behaving very inhumanly.

I need not go beyond India to show, if proof is needed,

how powerfully religious ideas act on the character of a people. It is illustrated by the remarkable difference still perceptible between Hindus and Mahomedans born and bred for generations in the same country and climate; and here I am merely giving the Mahomedans due credit for some of the stronger qualities they have derived from their painfully unphilosophical creed. If there is any state of mind in which popular feeling comes out characteristically, it is in the spirit with which religion and poetry (the same thing in Asia) confront war; for the battle-field provides the vantage ground upon which religion seizes to command the wild enthusiasm of the fighting man, and to pose as the supreme arbiter of his destiny in decisive moments. We Hindus know to our cost that the God of Islam, though the conception is open to much intellectual criticism, is nevertheless (or has been) a mighty conquering Divinity, who can persuade his votaries to throw away life in his cause, by promising to transport them at once into a second and superior existence. This is the essential spirit of Islam, and some of your readers may be interested in comparing it with the much deeper Hindu feeling that inspired the opening of that great and popular Indian poem, composed long before the Arabian prophet upset Asia, the Bhagavadgíta, or the Divine Lay. It represents Arjuna, the hero, fully armed and ready to lead his host to the attack, surveying on the battle-ground his nearest kinsfolk and relatives arrayed in opposing ranks for mutual slaughter. He hesitates to take part in the carnage, which must be bloody, and must destroy many noble and beloved persons. "Even if I conquer," he says, "I shall lose all pleasure in life when these my friends and kinsfolk have been slain; grief will cloud my triumph." He shows, in fact, a compunction that early poets and divines have usually thought too weak a feeling for warriors about to engage. I have read somewhere, by the way, that Xerxes the Persian had a similar weakness when surveying his army; but I am doubtful whether this may be ascribed to his profound Asiatic sense of the transitoriness of things, or merely to the elegiac strain that ran through the imagination of his Greek annalist. Your western hero, at any rate, is usually full of poetic ardour or of sombre fanaticism on such occasions; and your western divinities have generally taken sides with great vigour. Very remarkable, therefore, is the contrast between the traditional tone of divinities, or their embodiments, present at a western battle, and the language of the Hindu deity to whom Arjuna turns for advice.

Says the god, who accompanies Arjuna in the shape of his charioteer—"You are grieving for those who deserve no grief; the wise man does not mourn for those that are dead, or for those who are not dead. Neither I nor thou wast at any time non-existent, nor is there any time when we shall not be. . . . What is not, can never be; what really is, never ceases to be. . . . The spirit neither slays nor is slain, nor is killed with the slain body; the spirit merely changes bodies, as a man doth a garment; fire nor sword touch it. And all that is born dies; all that dies is born; the living nature is senseless at its beginning and senseless at its departure; only a sensitive state between entry and exit. What cause is here for grief? Wherefore arise, and go to battle with a firm mind. For to one that is born death is certain, and to one that dies, birth is certain." From this follows a long discussion between Arjuna and the deity as to esoteric truths and in regard to the comparative efficacy, in liberating the soul from illusions, of Devotion and Works; touching also the real occult nature of the world, the divine essence underlying all phenomena, and the way of escaping from a return to life "which is transient, the home of woes." Arjuna's doubts are eventually cleared away, and he proceeds to fight with a reasoned conviction of the utter baselessness of any apparent distinction between killing and being killed.

Now it should be understood that this is not merely a recondite philosophic treatise put into verse, like the poem of Lucretius, but also a poem that is still universally read, praised, and quoted in educated Hindu society, as a famous episode of the national Hindu epic of the Mahabharata. And I would ask, where else in poetry, or in religious legend, will you find a hero communing with divinity on the brink of a desperate battle, who is persuaded that he does well to fight, not by promise of victory or sanction of the justice of his cause, but by a demonstration that life and death, the slayer and the slain, are philosophically indistinguishable? That the incongruity of such dissertations in the very poise and imminent collision of battle should not have damaged the great popularity of the poem shows, I would point out, what repose the Hindu mind has drawn, at all times and in all places, from the solace of Pantheism. Indeed, the central idea of Hinduism, the mysticism and quietism, seems to be purposely brought into strong relief, and its force intensified by the dramatic surroundings given to it in this poem. I have seen something like it in your Shakespeare, whose poetry has strange flashes into the depths of mysticism, but nowhere else among the English. To a Hindu Shakespeare's finest effects of light and shade are produced by contrasts of this kind, when, in the midst of some highly-wrought delineation of the tragic crisis, the supreme struggle of his heroes, comes in a sudden touch of mystery, a half-veiled hint that the whole scene and movement are illusory, may be all a dream. When Macbeth's purpose is shaken by the horror of the deed he is contemplating, Lady Macbeth tells him that the sleeping and the dead are but as pictures, a thoroughly Indian sophism; and to our minds nothing is more striking than the tone in which Macbeth, hemmed in by his foes, and hopelessly at bay, falls suddenly musing upon to-morrow and yesterday, and reflects that life is after all full of sound and fury signifying nothing. But then these are low chords just touched in momentary pauses between the high organ notes of violent action; whereas our Hindu artist preludes with his war-notes and battle-pieces by way of overture to a dialogue upon the true knowledge that is attainable by complete mental abstraction from the world of sense.

I am afraid that Arjuna has led me into digression. But I wished to illustrate the ideas and conceptions upon which the Hindu people have been mentally nourished for centuries; and for popular ideas one must always go to religion and poetry. The Hindu habit of thought has been really and deeply moulded and shaped by these views of human existence, its state and prospect, underlying and springing up through the loose and superficial formations of mythology and idolatry. Upon such a people comes a wide and rapid flood of national and intellectual change. The whole accumulated results of the experiences and researches of Europe are thrown at the Hindu's feet; the complete apparatus of modern civilisation is placed at his disposal; he is summoned to join a citizenship which he has not inherited, neither has he obtained it by a great sum. His consent has not been asked; he has simply been included within the dominion of a busy, roving, casteless nation, with ideas and habits totally incongruous to his own. And now that you English are taking possession of the country spiritually as well as materially, now that you are destroying our temples more effectively, if more slowly, than ever did the Moghuls—the point that interests us is whether you will be able to help us to build again, whether you will put an end to the spiritual anarchy that is coming, as you have pacified India politically. I see that our popular beliefs are losing their credibility, and that even the Bhagavadgíta may hardly comfort us much longer; but after some examination of your literature, sacred and profane, I am inclined to conclude, regretfully, that the one commodity we shall never be persuaded, even by its cheapness, to import from Europe, is a Religion. It is true that your missionaries offer it to us, gratis, on the spot; whereas we find all your other importations rather costly; while I admit that the English and American Protestantism so freely expounded in our bazaars is a stout useful doctrine, making undoubtedly for morality. It may not be picturesque, it is certainly not philosophical; but it is distinctly suited to the intellectual and material needs of a practical race that has made a figure in history, and will leave its mark on the earth. Nevertheless, I fear that neither are we likely to adopt, nor are you disposed very confidently to recommend, this or any other form of the western creed; because, although your creeds unquestionably inculcate very high morality, they are beginning to fail in the element of *à priori* certainty. The Protestant, indeed, appears to regard morality as the essence of his religion, and to try every doctrine by a simple ethical test, as when your once favourite philosopher, Mr J. S. Mill, declared he would go to Hell rather than obey divine commands that in his judgment should be immoral. But this peremptory exercise of the right of private judgment seems to us Hindus to lead back into a kind of intellectual polytheism, bearing the same relation to primitive polytheism as in the arts literature does to architecture. For idolatry came because unlettered man carved in stocks or stones his particular imagination of a god; whereas in these latter days, when men write their thoughts instead of carving them, and are more hasty with the pen than formerly with the chisel, we have innumerable and fantastic images of the Supreme Being delineated in books. And I think our highest divinities, the supreme personifications of Energy, would prefer, like your Catholic Church, to abdicate at once rather than be reduced to mere ethical teachers, tolerated so long as they satisfy the changeful moral feelings of the time, but overruled or dismissed whenever they presume to disregard the dictates of public opinion, or to set up as independent authorities. Vishnu and Siva will not descend to the level of ministers of Public Instruction. In short, I do not at present discern how either the English or the Indian theology is to be easily and rapidly adjusted to suit impending circumstances and the general environment in India.

Meanwhile, the attitude of the British Government in India affords, as I have already hinted, little help toward the solution of these problems; unless the legal Codes are to be taken as superseding and repealing all other commandments, human and divine. It is the Government that has created all these bewildering changes of moral, political, and social circumstance, and it is the Government that sits apparently indifferent, holding no form of creed, but contemplating all—an attitude which, though correct if you are figuring in the character of a mere embodiment of intelligent Force, is from the religious standpoint somewhat disappointing. For your old philosopher, Hobbes, was right when he wrote that the religion of the Gentiles is a part of their policy; and although in Asia there are no separate spiritual jurisdictions in the legal sense, the spiritual sanction has always been assumed to be necessary to acts of State. But the contrary proposition, that the art of politics is completely utilitarian, and excludes theology, is your principle in India. You have not only placed the temporal power above all spiritual jurisdictions, but the spiritual sanction your rulers formally decline to invoke. On this principle you have undoubtedly succeeded in establishing a very efficient administrative system, which, so long as you are dealing with material interests, enables you to avoid or simplify many difficulties. Many of us Hindus, to whom the system appears superficial, are inclined to suspect that it is really founded upon some esoteric philosophy, unknown to the vulgar, which rejects every kind of revelation, and teaches that the world has somehow been launched into space and left to govern itself by the laws of Nature. This would of course explain the complete exclusion of religion from the sphere of your politics, in England as well as in India; but then it is quite certain that the great majority of your countrymen hold no such philosophy as that conjectured; and here comes in my difficulty. For the complete disconnexion of government from religion suggests to an Asiatic the inference that the collective State has no need of divine guidance, although it is generally admitted to be necessary for individuals. This is a point that lies rather outside the ordinary arguments over such matters as the relations between religion and temporal government; and it does not seem to have been exhaustively treated in Macaulay's brilliant essay upon Church and State, which, like all his essays, is very widely read in my country by the educated class, and which, like Mr Gladstone's book that it reviews, draws various striking illustrations from India.

Now, I do not pretend to revive, or fully to understand, an extinct controversy over terms that have no accurate meaning in Asia, where the antithesis between temporal and spiritual in the historic European sense is hardly comprehended. Mr Gladstone's argument seems to have been that since governments have the highest moral duties and responsibilities, they must possess religion, and that this religion must be that of the conscience of the governor, must be professed by the governing body in their public and collective character. Macaulay shows easily enough that since men differ widely, and are hard to convince on religious questions, while they find no trouble in uniting in practical business and politics, no association of men, from a government to a gas company, could work together if the articles of the association required religious uniformity. For their strongest illustrations both Mr Gladstone and Macaulay went, as I have said, to India, which afforded Macaulay a ready example of a country that could not be governed if Church were put by the English above State; though he forgets that the Mahomedans did somehow set up a great empire in India upon Mr Gladstone's principle that a government, in its collective capacity, should profess and propagate a religion. And he is quite mistaken in arguing, from the false analogy of an eighteenth-century battle-field in Europe, that religious uniformity can be of no advantage, but the contrary, to an army. In the absence of patriotism, it has often provided the common cause for which men fight and die together. The Mahomedans, indeed, would probably side theoretically with Mr Gladstone; and if we Hindus prefer Macaulay's view that a government should mind its own business of governing, it is only because our thinkers doubt whether the efficient Cause of the world whatever It may be, is concerned at all with the ups and downs of human affairs.

In other respects Macaulay's conclusion adds to our

present difficulties, for it offers no guidance, and is indeed rather embarrassing to those who, like myself, have come to England to find out how religion may still be adjusted so as to form an authoritative rule of conduct. For the proposition that governments have nothing whatever to do, as such, with the profession of a religion, does appear to me to rest ultimately upon the principle of regarding morality as entirely independent of dogmatic theology. At least the proof of any necessary and indisputable connection between morals and religion is to our minds much weakened if a government can only prosper by carefully avoiding the reference of its acts and motives to any definite religious sanction. For morality is indisputably the essence of a strong and civilised government, and yet it appears that State morality forbids a governing body to act upon the dictates of any form of theology, because to do so would be to appeal to an authority strenuously denied by one section or another of its subjects. In fact, neither the State nor its subjects are allowed to plead a religious command in justification of acts ordered or prohibited. I understand that in England it is now unanimously held to be wrong for a statesman to allow his public acts to be influenced by his creed, except of course where articles of belief are indistinguishable from rules of positive morality; and Macaulay's position, that a government has no more to do with theology than a gas company, is commonly allowed to be impregnable. But since he would have agreed that morality is of prime importance both to gas companies and to governments, I do not perceive how he would have opposed the inference that theology and morality have very little necessary connection with each other. His proposition amounts, in fact, to an entire substitution of the rule of expediency for the dictates of religion in dealing with the most important human concerns; for the plain reason that since in religion conclusions are variable and hard to verify, it is not the State's business to decide among them. In fact, neither the State nor its subjects are allowed to plead a religious command in justification of acts publicly ordered or prohibited. Yet the position that religious belief has everything to do with the conduct of individuals, and nothing to do with the conduct of governments, is foreign to the traditions of Asiatic kingcraft, and would in India be thought hard to defend.

I am afraid it is clear that a government which is thus sailing under the bare poles of utilitarianism can afford us Hindus small aid or encouragement toward a suitable adjustment of our ancient faiths to what your Blue Books style Moral and Material Progress. Nevertheless, I do not argue that the English governors of India are wrong, as practical administrators, in discarding the aid and sanction of theology: I only observe that this goes some way, for good or ill, in the direction of displacing all morality from its religious basis, because the spectacle of State morality improving and extending, yet formally parted from religion, is undoubtedly suggestive. It seems certain to me that your government, by thus disowning dependence on any creed for guidance or authority, has dealt a palpable blow against Indian religions generally. Whether this blow will tell, in the long run, for or against the development of morality in India, whether our future ethical system will be founded upon some religious reformation, or upon the utilitarianism that our English pastors and masters so vigorously practise and preach by example, is to me a deep and most interesting question. All that you undertake to provide for us is this practical demonstration of the advantages of morality backed up by good laws; and though I am far from despising this very material contribution to the matter, since undoubtedly statutes fortify ethics, yet I confess I should like to see the moral progress of India less closely bound up with the latest edition of the Penal Code. The great political changes recorded in history have usually been in some way coincident with a change, generally an advance, in religion: and the two motive forces have been so interlaced, that it has been difficult to distribute between them the proportion of the main onward impulse. At any rate, so far as I can understand the earlier history of your own great religion, a dispassionate observer may be permitted to doubt whether Christianity would have become an Universal Faith if the powerful rulers who latterly swayed the destinies of the Roman world had not lent all their political strength to help the construction of an organised system of belief and morals. In these days when, instead of Europe being overrun from the East, it is the turn of Asia to be thrown into confusion by the irruption of powerful barbarians from the West, a sort of chance medley and conflict among old and new faiths is again supervening. If at this epoch those who are reconstituting fundamentally the polity of India decline to concern themselves with its religion, I own that to a Hindu, whose life has hitherto rested upon religious associations, the moral and religious future seems clouded. On the other hand, since you are quite resolved that the State of the future shall take no account of the old creeds, I would not advise you to attempt teaching us a new one that you yourselves do not hold to be essentially necessary; and therefore I fervently deprecate setting up official professors to lecture us on Natural Religion, as has been somewhat hastily proposed by the Educational Commission.

It seems, then, that we must accept the situation likely to be presented to us under the new order of things, and that we may be content, like the Ephesians in your Holy Writ, to be referred to the law courts if we fancy that anything is going wrong with our divinities. I do not blame your Government for this; I see that you are compelled to manage India upon English principles, and that the English themselves are relegating dogmatic religion beyond the sphere of practical politics, are evidently determined to try the experiment of a society upon an independent ethical basis. It seems to me as if your interest in the question of a future life were gradually decaying, and you were becoming reconciled to the idea that civil society, properly organised, can dispense with religion as the ground-work of morals. Since I came to England I have, as I mentioned before, been looking up the latest ethical books in order to understand the course you are taking. The number of these books, and their diverse drifts, appear to betoken the temporary indecision and unsteadiness caused by the parting of the old theologic cables and by the sense of casting about for fresh anchorage. But this haven has hitherto proved undiscoverable philosophically; not a single writer, of those who discard theology, can propound to you anything beyond some variation, more or less disguised, of the theory of refined and far-seeing utilitarianism. In the long run, they say, the tendency of evolution is toward more general happiness: evil will turn itself into good if you only give things time, and you may console yourself for your personal sufferings and despair by confidence in the bright Future of Humanity. As for the old religions, whatever was not myth and illusion was ordinary utilitarianism divinely transfigured; natural laws working under the disguise of supernatural acts and design. These ideas have not yet prevailed among you, and you listen reluctantly, but they are circulating. In the meantime I notice that your people mostly transact necessary business by a sort of double standard, sometimes referring to religion, sometimes to utility, and paying with the coin that suits best the occasion. Of course this produces some confusion in your moral currency; nevertheless I observe that either standard, boldly presented, is taken as a legal tender on a demand for one's motives; though possibly the utilitarian standard may show a tendency toward superseding all others, as I observe that the earlier coin is largely exported by missionaries for circulation in Asia and Africa. It is credible that the English may take no harm by following, like their Government, the dry light of experience and attention to consequences; they are a firmly-seated nationality, with very definite notions of making themselves strong and comfortable in the world, with properly verified perceptions of what is good or bad for the community, and a capacity for united action thereupon. Moreover, the English have firmly grasped the dominant idea of a Supreme Almighty Ruler, who decides, once for all, whether a man has merited reward or punishment in the next existence. Whereas I am not sure whether we Hindus, overtaken as we are by a sudden flood of new knowledge, shall have time to reform and close up our popular beliefs on any such central position. The notion of a just and incorruptible Sovereign Power, sternly executing laws, has been so unfamiliar to us phenomenally, that we have never framed our speculative conceptions upon this model. It is true that in India, as elsewhere, the idea of one Supreme Being, vaguely imagined, stands behind all the phantasmagoria of supernatural personages. The perpetual flux and change of things suggest a cause, and as intelligence grows the chain of causality lengthens, for polytheism only satisfies the most simple enquiries. But in India this feeling of a necessary and ultimate idea upon which all lines converge is met, not by Monotheism, but by Pantheism, which, as a vague deification of Nature acting freely and universally, may slide very easily into your modern materialism by dropping the abstract notion of all-pervading divinity. And I admit that I fail at present to see how Pantheism is to help us when the times comes, among our people at large, for seeking not only an explanation of phenomena, but a basis of morals.

That the decay of religious beliefs is a matter interesting to practical administrators, your Government in India already discerns faintly; you are beginning to perceive that where no other authority is recognised, the visible ruler becomes responsible for everything. You consequently endeavour by various devices to shift off upon the people themselves the burden of their immense responsibility for their own destinies, and to stir them up into accepting it by spirited appeals to their independence, their progress in education, and their duty of self-help. In vain, for the mass of the Indian people, like the creature to whom Frankenstein gave life, impute to the English Government all the confusion and disquietude that have accompanied their sudden introduction, unprepared, into a world of new and strange desires and difficulties, the discontent and distress of the peasants, the economic changes affecting all the old society, the displacement of classes and breaking up of castes, the general unrest produced by the subsidence of old landmarks, religious, social, and political. They say that your civilisation and education were none of their seeking, but have been forced upon them from the other end of the earth; and that foreigners who set up in India the rushing and screaming locomotive that typifies what you call Progress, must drive it themselves.

One word more. The virtue chiefly inculcated by our own sages, and divines has been asceticism, which of course your modern spirit of material progress is doing its best to deride, and if possible to destroy—very successfully, so far as the rising generation of Young India is concerned. We Brahmans have been for ages teaching the Hindus the way and means of speedy escape from the world of restless strife and effort; you English are turning the popular mind in the contrary direction of multiplied desires, and an incessant energetic struggle against the physical and climatic impediments to a pleasurable existence in this country; your doctrine is that even in India life can and should be made comfortable. I myself am personally inclined to hold, with my forefathers, to the opinion that this temporary habitation of consciousness is not, in India at any rate, worth expending much labour upon in the way of improvements, or for the purpose of prolonging one's lease of it. I prefer the simple life and a speedy departure to another tenement; but this is a matter of taste, and all I remark is that with you lies the responsibility of leading Indians to adopt the western theory of existence. The old faiths, which all came from Asia, all proceed upon the contrary theory that, for the majority of human beings, life is hardly worth living in this world, and that man must look to Hereafter either for an escape from suffering, as we Hindus believe, or for an eventual compensation for it, which is the Christian view. In India our ultimate ideal has not been beatification, for which, judging by the analogy of Nature, we had no warrant, but absorption; and if you can convince us that existence in an Indian climate can be made enjoyable to most of us, it is manifest that this may in time affect our customary point of view. I own that you are doing a good deal to soften and enliven material existence even in this melancholy, sunburnt country of ours, and certainly you are so far successful that you are bringing the ascetic idea into discouragement, and, with the younger folk, into contempt. It remains to be seen whether you will be able to guide the impulse that you are giving us toward a scramble for sensuous enjoyment, and what principles you can suggest to us for controlling it. It seems quite possible that among the steady, well-disciplined races of the West, whose development has proceeded in an orderly and natural course, the principle of automatous moral evolution will be justified by results; but I am not so confident about us Asiatics. Although I have the greatest respect for Mr Herbert Spencer's writings, which are very well known and much read by those Hindus who study English literature, yet I doubt whether his ethical system is strong enough, of itself, to bear the strain of the fierce longings and blind rage for animal pleasures that come over hastily civilised people in the earlier phases of their development. We of the old school, who are possessed by the traditional despondency about this world, fear that evolution may be baffled and thrown off its line by the strong appetites and the sensual curse of man's nature. These impulses the philosopher would leave to self-regulation and the force of environment; while the Christian would mortify, and we think safest to extinguish them. If the Hindus are encouraged by European education and example too precipitately to discard asceticism, which is just the quality you English least understand, it may follow that morals in any highly spiritual sense will part company with material progress in the Blue Books of the future.

Nothing indeed depresses me more, as I survey the triumphant advance of material prosperity, than the gradual discovery that the English, while they are involuntarily undermining the whole fabric of our religious convictions, have nothing to offer that is likely to be accepted by the coming generation in India, to replace that which is passing away. Europe presents to me an arena of contending speculations; and among the more brilliant notions that are dancing like fire-flies over the morass of general scepticism, Hindus recognise with mingled amazement and despair their own chimeras. Some of the latest conclusions of your metaphysical theology and of your philosophy bear a disheartening likeness to the ultimate ideas reached by our people many centuries ago. Mr Mansel's Bampton Lectures seem to me impregnated with an odour of Oriental speculation—I could quote passages that might have been taken almost textually from the Vedantists—while the German school of pessimism openly acknowledges the influence of Indian thought; and many eyes are looking back beyond Christ and Mahomet to the figure of Buddha, standing alone in the remote background of religious history. These tendencies, this inclination to revert toward earlier types, produce in my mind an apprehension that the essential sources of religion are drying up, that the conditions are unfavourable to its further development, or even to its prolonged existence. When we see, in Art, that an age has ceased to be productive, and is only reproductive, that the old styles are imitated, the antique studied and worshipped, while, as in the case of your Church architecture, the modern design is quite destitute of originality, then we begin to fear that the real artistic spirit in this form is passing away. And so with Religion; you are either rejecting the primitive masterpieces, or you are trying to imitate and adapt them, not very skilfully, to a changing world. Those who reject, say Religion is tending toward extinction; those who would adapt, say its tendency is toward transformation.

Now this transformed religion, according to one of your

philosophic thinkers, "instead of proclaiming the nothingness of this life, the worthlessness of human love, and the imbecility of the human mind, will proclaim the supreme importance of this life, the supreme value of human love, and the grandeur of human intellect."* If this, as seems likely, is the only religion that you have to offer to us Indians, the transformation will certainly be complete; for the innermost religious idea of the Hindus has for ages been the supreme unimportance, if not the nothingness, of this particular stage of existence, and they have lapsed into a deep indifference for humanity at large, a feeling that is probably as much the product of their environment as are their dark skins and physical delicacy. The lords of life may be pleasure and pain; but though we have deified them under various symbols, we have always sought to escape from the servitude of their dominion, believing that the soul's true liberty lay beyond their realm. And the truth seems to be that Religion thus transformed will be Religion extinguished; it may haunt the world long after its death, sitting like a ghost upon the ruins of the ancient faiths; but religion as now felt and visibly seen by Hindus will have then vanished, like a lost art, or a primeval age, or a planet burnt out. The foundations of a creed, says the writer just quoted above, can rest only upon the known and knowable; and it is true that all our popular Asiatic religions rest upon rude guesses at the Unseen, accepted by the people as known and sufficiently verified in some unintelligible way; but this is an entirely different conception from that of scientific knowledge. So soon as a thing can be demonstrated the whole flavour of

---

* Lewes, "Problems of Life and Mind."

religion leaves it, and the mystery retires one step backward into the shadow of the incomprehensible; so that all religion is like that untravelled world, seen afar through the arch of experience, whose margin is for ever fading as we move toward it. And thus your transformed religion will only throw us all back upon the finally Unknowable, with whom, if the paradox may be pardoned, we Hindus have long been philosophically acquainted. For the rest we shall apparently have to trust to Leviathan to make us keep our compacts and develop our sociology.

Lastly; while the somewhat arrogant materialism of Europe is exploding our popular superstitions, a bigoted Hindu might observe with some excusable satisfaction that the subtle opiate of Indian pessimism is operating upon the energy, if not the vitality, of the great European religions. You are undermining the external fabric of Brahmanism; but we are aiding, I fear, to sap the foundations of Christianity. I regret this sincerely, for Christianity, whatever may be its philosophic basis, does at least come armed with an imperative mandate that is totally wanting in Brahmanism. "Vengeance is mine, saith the Lord, and I will repay it"—is just the kind of bold authoritative declaration that I wish the fine-drawing Hindu brain could ever be got to accept without argument or analysis. It is therefore saddening, if not maddening, to find Schopenhauer, who is drugged with all the drowsy syrups of the East, explaining this text as delivered out of the deeper knowledge that "allows eternal justice to proceed in the sphere of the thing-in-itself, which is different from that of the phenomenon." In other words, instead of the avenging personal God, we have to "recognise how in themselves the inflicter of suffering and the sufferer are one;" and this deeper knowledge is proved by Schopenhauer to contain a truth of much higher ethical significance. It is indeed the very language of our Bhagavadgíta; and he further prophesies that "Indian philosophy, streaming back to Europe, will produce a fundamental change in our knowledge and thought." Undoubtedly it will; for if the Oriental essences ever come into general use among you, they may revive a new species of Gnosticism and Mysticism, and the effect upon your moral constitution will certainly be laxative. I attach no importance to such vagaries as those of the Theosophists; though you will have noticed how a slight dabbling in the occult practices of Indian Yogis has turned a few honest English proselytes into poor demented gentlemen. Nevertheless, the incident is significant; and I am afraid that if you Europeans ever take seriously to importing from India our religious phantasies and patterns, you will find yourselves well requited, in the sphere of morals, for any material mischief you may have done us by your exportation to India of aniline dyes, cheap cotton goods, and other deleterious articles of your insatiable commerce. I can only hope that the exchange of our spiritual products for your material manufactures may not be a kind of free trade that augurs small advantage to the future ethical development of either nation.

II.

BRAHMANISM AND THE FOUNDATIONS OF BELIEF.

SOME time ago you were good enough to publish a communication in which I told you of my disappointment, as a philosophic Brahman of the old school, at the very moderate assistance obtainable from English sources by those who desire to exchange their old lamps for new ones, so far as this may enable them to adjust the traditional religion of India to its changing intellectual environments. I was then unwillingly forced to the conclusion that we had very little to learn from you in the matter of profound theology, and that the system of Christianity—a faith for which my practical understanding has the most sincere respect—could not satisfy the restless inquisitive Hindu mind. Its moralising tendencies seemed to me to cloud and distract the true spiritual vision; and the narrow range of its conceptions regarding the soul's destiny in a future life appeared out of scale and incomplete. There was something, I observed, shortsighted and abrupt in a programme of heaven and hell as the immediate and yet interminable consequences of conduct in a single brief, almost momentary, existence; while the danger of resting a vast scheme upon such ephemeral and movable foundations as historical evidences, miracles, final causes, or the testimony of human understanding in any form, appeared to me to be serious. Upon that field you were necessarily exposed to rationalistic attacks; and if instead of holding aloof from materialistic science you attempted a reconciliation with it, you found yourself slowly sinking into a mechanical interpretation of the universe, leading surely to the conclusion that the destinies of mankind are ordered by nothing higher than evolutionary determination. In your search for an underlying principle you discovered only Darwinism, or selection by death; and you were driven to the conception of the Deity as a constitutional monarch ruling a vast kingdom by unchangeable laws. It seemed to me that religion thus transformed would be shifted from its essential foundations, and would before long lose its hold upon the reverence of humanity.

I perceive now that I was too easily depressed, and that I had underrated the recuperative power of your religion. It is with surprise and pleasure that I have read Mr Balfour's book on "The Foundations of Belief." With surprise, I say, because according to our notions the γνῶσις, or knowledge of divine things, can only be attained by ascetic exercises, by secluded meditation in an atmosphere untroubled by activity of any sort. But here is one of your leading statesmen, ever foremost in debate, who finds time in the pauses of argumentative strife to demonstrate the ultimate fallibility of all reasoning, and who can simulate admirably an eager interest in the phenomena of politics, although he knows them to possess no more substance than any other spectral illusion. It reminds me of the scene at the opening of our great poem, the "Bhagavadgíta," where two mighty armies are facing each other on the battle-field, and the leader of one army, Arjuna, seizes the moment before the actual shock of war to enter into a profound pantheistic discussion on the identity of the slayer with the slain.

But to proceed—it is with pleasure that I have read

this book, because the strain of thought and the dialectical methods tally so remarkably with our Indian tastes and traditions. If it does not provide any complete solution of our difficulties, and I must confess that now and then the author seems to be proving too much, it certainly helps us in putting our enemies to confusion. Mr Balfour is an adversary of mere Naturalism; so are we. He is determined, if it be possible, to keep physical science from trespassing upon and insulting theology; that is our desire. How can observation and experiment, the mere grouping and classification of recurrent appearances, be in any way connected with questions regarding origins and essences, the creative reason, the moral law, and the divine nature? Uniformity of nature, cause and effect, these phrases involve either a fallacy or an assumption of the point to be proved; and Darwinism seems to us very little better than an interesting collection of anecdotes. I entirely assent to the statement that "a purely empirical theory of things, a philosophy which depends for its premises in the last resort upon the particulars revealed to us in perceptive experience alone, is one that cannot be rationally accepted." Of course we Brahmans have known this for many centuries, but it is very useful to find it repeated in modern language on such excellent authority. For we recognise but too clearly the urgent need of protecting our august beliefs from the corrosion of naturalistic tendencies, and especially of protesting against the pretensions of that half-educated class which in India, as presumably in England, seems to imagine that a wider acquaintance with the structure of the visible world can have some kind of bearing upon our intuition of things supra-sensual. To those who are concerned in resisting such errors this book brings solace and timely succour.

In India, the most conservative of countries, there has latterly been serious embarrassment about assimilating what you English worship under the name of Progress with our traditional ideas, social and religious. It is, therefore, not unpleasant to discover that even in England a conservative philosopher finds it necessary to clear for his religion a road out of similar difficulties. You will be none the worse for being reminded that your phenomenal activities, which have upset the contemplative quietude of India, must not attempt to push their way into the higher regions of thought, and that your immemorial experiences lose all meaning and coherence under the stroke of philosophic analysis. And there is something almost comical in the lesson read to you by this book, that what most of you fancied to be intellectual emancipation —the exact and extended comprehension of natural processes—does in reality prolong man's servitude by blocking up the gates of the spiritual knowledge with a heap of disorderly and obstructive facts. We also despise and denounce the presumption with which Naturalism, as the author calls the empiric method, pretends to invade the dominion of Theology, to molest her ancient solitary reign, and almost to annihilate her peculiar jurisdiction. So long as empiricism confines itself to the sphere of sense-perceptions, it is legitimately and perhaps harmlessly employed, and in reward for its humility it may be dignified by the title of Science. It is welcome to continue taking notes as a spectator of the fantastic nature-play; it may go on making dim uncertain conjectures about the plot and the probable ending of the terrestrial drama; it may even amuse itself by tracing a moral purpose. But when empiricism ventures to set up a kind of spiritual court, and attempts to pass judgment on some deep intuition of divinity that does not accord with a very finite range of sensation, then it is justly labelled Naturalism, baseborn, purblind, and fundamentally irrational. In India when a low-caste preacher or a petty god of the jungles becomes popular and prosperous, and rebels against the hierarchy, the Brahmans disclose his mean origin to the world at large, which usually turns against the parvenu unless he is remarkably successful. If he sets up as a reformer, they ask how an insignificant upstart can know anything of the divine counsels. After the same fashion does the book wisely deal with the pretensions of naturalism, notably with such assertions as that a lofty morality can have been evolved out of the slow purification of primitive instincts and bestial appetites, that hideous noises have developed into musical modulations, and that reason can have had an unconscious irrational origin. To a refined and cultivated temperament, the theory that moral sentiment and noble emotions could have been reared by that homely nurse Nature out of "the complicated contrivances, many of them mean and disgusting, wrought into the organism by the shaping forces of selection and elimination," must, I agree, be intolerably repulsive.

Moreover, since with nine-tenths of average Englishmen the moral working of a religion seems to be the test of its truth, I quite comprehend that any attempt to class morality as a terrestrial product, with roots in our common earth, must be promptly disowned and defeated. In this latter respect, however, our Indian position is not precisely coincident with that of the Christian apologist, since we have avoided entanglement with ethical considerations, and have never yet pledged ourselves to the postulate that the universe is morally governed. We yield to no one in our recognition of the beauty of Virtue; but we nevertheless conceive that any theology which stakes its credibility on a moral criterion is unstable at base, because a rising morality may force the religious sovereignty into undignified compromises with unphilosophic public opinion. Yet since our support is due to anything that encourages distrust and contempt of mere common sense applied to spiritual mysteries, we may fairly join hands against naturalism; and it suits us very well to lay bare the inadequacy of a physical basis for Ethics. We can therefore admire freely the eloquent description given in this book of the demoralising effects likely to flow out of the discovery that, since all animated existence will cease totally on this planet within a calculable period, the whole question of human origins and destinies must in time dwindle, on the naturalistic theory, into supreme unimportance. The chapter on Naturalism and Ethics ends thus:—

> "It cannot, therefore, be a matter to us of small moment that, as we learn to survey the material world with a wider vision, as we more clearly measure the true proportions which man and his performances bear to the ordered whole, our practical ideal gets relatively dwarfed and beggared, till we may well feel inclined to ask whether so transitory and so unimportant an accident in the general scheme of things as the fortunes of the human race can any longer satisfy aspirations and emotions nourished upon beliefs in the everlasting and the Divine."

Now, so far as this really fine peroration is likely to

intimidate your countrymen, to deter them from facing with intrepidity the prospect of a ruined and silent world, from looking steadily at the calm impassive face of Nature, I quite appreciate its effectiveness. Such considerations depreciate the influence of empiricism by reminding every one that it can only deal with very ephemeral things. Let Science prove that the earth is rolling surely toward universal death, and then what matters Science unto men? The picture is well calculated to turn the masses in alarm towards some religion that purports to stand clear of the earth's road to ruin; the lower minds will cling more closely to superstition; the higher will seek refuge in the transcendental regions of sublime theosophy. This, indeed, is a situation not unlike that which in India we have already attained, though we have no objection to be fortified in it by western skill; so that for us the despairing prophecies of science have little terror. Our higher intelligences did not need the arguments in this book to convince us that the whole phantasmagoria of sense-perceptions is essentially deceptive and illusory, insomuch that whether it disappear to-morrow or after many million years is profoundly immaterial; if indeed time has any meaning in relation to such a passing dream. Nor will even the simple Indian folk be much interested by the news that the whole order of creation to which they belong is to be annihilated within a measureable period. They have never set an inordinate value on the short and sorrowful days passed under this burning sun; while for heaven or hell they have little care, desiring only to be rid of sensitive existence in any shape. Nevertheless the influx of western ideas is affecting all classes, even in India, wherefore I am in accord with any salutary warning to our weaker brethren against following any such vain and transitory ideal as the perfectibility of mortal man.

When such fallacies are abroad, it is high time that the Naturalists should be desired to practise their mechanical dexterities altogether outside the domain of religion. Within it their method can produce nothing but confusion. For any one can see that the positive beliefs, the accumulation of traditions, divine myths, and visible thaumaturgy, which empiricism directly attacks, are the rough outworks that everywhere surround the inner citadel of theology. And these must be founded on something impervious to discussion, because a worshipping people places little trust in a religion that goes upon reason, or in morality that is subject to the evolutionary law. Men worship the sun and the wind, because there is no arguing with them; and so soon as you begin to question the morality of a deity, you are on the brink of doubting his credibility. Our Indian multitude, at any rate, desire something or somebody that will not parley, will not condescend to moralise, and listens without answering except by deeds—in short, a Divinity, arbitrary, immutable, whose works are the index of his will. Vainly would the scientists allege that such a Divinity is only the abstract impersonation of inscrutable energies, "the Sunday or red-letter name of gravitation"—since no one can adore blind Force. What mankind has always worshipped is the manifestation of intelligent though irresponsible Power. Although Natural Selection may be a grand hypothesis, as a dogma it is very disputable, and as a process it is automatic, having its metaphysical prototype in the Buddhistic doctrine of Karma, whereby the soul rises higher or falls lower in successive existences according to merit or demerit. But it becomes a mighty influence in the sphere of religion when it is embodied in the conception of our great god Siva, who presides autocratically over the issues of life and death, over the eternal striving of the soul upward through innumerable forms and existences.

It will thus be understood why we Brahmans are in close sympathy with your distinguished countrymen in rebuking the arrogant encroachments of empiricism, with its pitiable groping by the light of the senses after ultimate ideas. For ages we ourselves have maintained that of all false guides perceptive experience is the most fallible, that it carries no guarantee whatever of its veracity, and that for any one to throw ridicule at a prodigy or a dogma because it is contrary to inductions from experience is a mere confession of ignorance. The short method with such sciolists, Mr Balfour remarks with unanswerable lucidity, is to ask them to compare "the causal movement from object to perception, with the cognitive leap through perception to object." As sources of information, he adds truly, our perceptions are habitually mendacious; and what can be more hollow than the attempt to construct any reality out of such unsubstantial image-making? The deeper you delve the less chance there is of finding a bottom; you only unearth greater perplexities and contradictions. And it is knowledge of this sort that tampers with articles of religion! So long as empiricism keeps to its own superficial level and does not dabble in higher things, we need not dispute its every-day usefulness. The naturalist is like any other collector of samples and specimens, good enough for the market or the museum. But when he undertakes not only to invent a scheme of faith and morals, but also to dictate terms of surrender to every other system, we must turn round and expose his own essential futility. If he objects to any theologic truth that it is not verifiable by his instruments, we can prove to him that his own so-called verification of the simplest assertion (as, for instance, that the sun shines) is radically untrustworthy. This, said one of your sages more than a century ago, is a reason why "with such imperfect faculties, narrow reach, and inaccurate observation, we should never go beyond such subjects as are best adapted to human understanding. While we cannot give a satisfactory reason why we believe, after a thousand experiments, that a stone will fall or fire will burn, can we ever satisfy ourselves concerning any determination which we may form with regard to the origin of worlds, and the situation of nature from and to eternity?" This, says Mr Balfour, is a reason why we need not be surprised "that we do not adequately comprehend God, seeing that we can give no very satisfactory account of what we mean by 'a thing.'" Although Mr Balfour's scepticism is quite as destructive as Mr Hume's, the inferences that follow are diametrically opposed; for I observe with complacency that at the point where these two Scottish gentlemen part company, while the latter sits down contentedly within the strait limits of ordinary human comprehension, the former sets out boldly upon a metaphysical path leading very much in the direction of India.

In the chapter on "Philosophy and Naturalism," for example, the argument is all on our side. "What," he asks, "is Rationalism? Some may be disposed to reply that it is the free and unfettered application of human intelligence to the problems of life and the world, the unprejudiced examination of every question in the daylight of emancipated reason." Well, this is just what it is, a very troublesome and pernicious notion when it degenerates into Naturalism, and still insists on trespassing within the theologic domain, where it should have no admittance, because it can have no business on those premises. I cannot agree unreservedly with Mr Balfour's statement that "rationalists as such are not philosophers," for all the deepest speculations, like the Neo-platonism of old, are pursued by the light of pure reason. But your modern rationalists are of another and a lower order. They were formerly content with skirmishing on the frontier between science and theology, with defending their own territory, vindicating what they called common sense, and occasionally attacking preposterous ritualistic extravagances. This kind of criticism has often been rife in India; it did us no harm, and was even laudable in some practical ways; it kept our pundits in training, just as your army is exercised by petty warfare against barbarians across the Indian frontier. But this book truly points out that as an organic system it had neither a solid base nor a binding cement; its professors talked of consecutive argument and consistent principles, when they were unconsciously working among insoluble perplexities and contradictions. And yet they are now proposing to apply these "rationalising methods with pitiless consistency to the whole circle of beliefs!" We Brahmans have rarely been accused, like your theologians, of persecution; nevertheless we are inclined to ask whether such presumption is not too tenderly dealt with in this admirable book. If, as the author proves, and as I agree, the attempt to determine the range of potential human knowledge by such short measurement is no better than blundering unreason, why allow credit to these people for any competency whatever? Why not declare at once, as we should be prepared to do, that no solid truth can rest on defective foundations, and that all this verbiage about emancipated reason and unfettered intelligence is the mere product of that ignorance which mistakes appearance for reality, and which is utterly incapable of comprehending Nature as the phenomenal veil of immanent divinity. The Naturalist is fighting with shadows, and building up lofty arguments on transitory impressions, which the true spiritual illumination dissolves at once into their fontal nothingness.

This is, indeed, the logical outcome of the book's destructive analysis. If it were pressed home the war might be carried victoriously into the territory of the assailant, and Naturalism's defeat might be turned into a disastrous rout. That one result might be the triumph of universal scepticism is no particular objection from our point of view; though I can easily understand that in your country the complete demolition of rationalising methods might be embarrassing, for an English philosopher has to reckon with a well-meaning but timorous public opinion. And the truth is that even your theologians have been for some time past tampering with the enemy; they have been attempting to settle a kind of concordat with the naturalist; a false and futile manœuvre to which we have never condescended in India. The consequence is that at this point of his argument Mr Balfour is hampered by the necessity of gently disentangling orthodoxy from her naturalistic connection before he can proceed to set her up again on clear philosophical foundations. Now, I shall explain presently why I fear that this operation may be encompassed by some important practical difficulties; but I may at once say that with the general drift of his chapter on rationalist orthodoxy I am thoroughly in concurrence. Assuming rationalist Orthodoxy to take its stand on the assertion "that our ordinary method of sense-perception, which gives science, is able to supply us also with theology," I readily agree with him that the proposition is hopelessly indefensible. For I understand from this book that the two pillars on which this system of orthodoxy relies in your country are Natural Theology and Revelation. The former is supported mainly by the argument for design; its inferences regarding the ways and intentions of Divinity are drawn from the course and constitution of the visible world. This, I may observe, has always been the true foundation and source of popular Hinduism, which detects everywhere the touch of a divine hand, and concludes empirically that prayers and sacrifice will propitiate rulers who are capricious because they are omnipotent. There is nothing in the argument that militates against the supposition that the course of nature is shaped and governed by many intelligent and powerful gods, nor does it contradict the pantheistic hypothesis that underlies the anthropomorphic polytheism. Nevertheless a theology which relies on inductions from sense-perceptions, even as a defensive outwork, is undoubtedly exposed to the increasing audacity of the scientific enemy who, being at heart irreconcileable, is only encouraged by weak overtures for a hollow truce. And when I hear of the popularity obtained in England by vague pseudo-scientific theories about natural law in the spiritual world, I can understand why Mr Balfour is inclined to prefer hauling down that flag once for all. "We are asked to believe the universe to have been designed by an architect for the same sort of reason that we believe Canterbury Cathedral to have been designed by an architect." It is because such a position is always liable to be turned metaphysically, having no finality whatever, that to the higher Hindu intellect, ever searching for ultimate ideas, the architectonic Providence has never brought rest or consolation. And even the more easily satisfied western mind must by this time be suspecting that the argument involves a confusion of the essential distinctions between Nature and Art. It may have some supplementary use as a buttress placed outside the main religious fabric: it can never serve as a foundation.

Nor can I withhold my assent from the remarks in this book, upon the disadvantage to the rationalising theologian of taking his stand upon the evidence of sacred history. We can easily appreciate the danger of leaning too heavily on historical proofs, or on any testimony that appeals to the senses; it is tantamount to accepting battle on the enemy's ground. So if, as seems to be intimated, the general field of natural theology is hardly tenable in controversy, the expediency of taking up a fresh position beyond the range of modern critical artillery is manifest. I understand that the leading purpose of this book is to construct some provisional entrenchment of the kind, and in principle this seems to me thoroughly sound, just as our own religion always keeps open a line of retreat upon transcendental fortifications. But the question of documentary evidence is probably much more important to your theology than to a religion like Hinduism, which has never professed to be historical, neither has it ever attempted to make compromises with scientific research. If this is so, the operation of withdrawal may in your case be troubled with greater practical difficulties than in ours.

Nor is it altogether our interest, from one point of view, to wish you well out of them, seeing that Christianity is one of the two religions which have taken up an active proselytising attitude against Hinduism. The attraction which any spiritual novelty presents to our people has induced me, on rare occasions, to listen with decorous curiosity to your Christian missionaries. I have found that they almost always employ against the Brahmanic teaching and tradition that very argument which in this book is termed rationalistic, touching the absurdity of our worships and beliefs, the incredibility of our miraculous narratives, the want of authenticity for our scriptures, and so on, with appeals to reason, sense-perception, and the new learning generally. Now in these controversies (which are always forced upon us) any admission that your own rationalistic orthodoxy is not unassailable would give us an effective rejoinder; while as to Islam, the other faith militant and aggressive, if any Mahomedan leader took to doubting his own historic evidences there would certainly be a mutiny in his camp. I make these remarks to prove that I am entirely disinterested in warning you

English to take care what you are about. There is in this book no avowal that the author has lost confidence in the orthodox evidences; he says they are good as far as they go. Yet the impression left upon an impartial reader is that the rationalising theologian, whether he relies upon the teleologic argument, or whether he stands by miracles, prophecies, and the authenticity of the inspired Scriptures, is in either case doomed to lose any pitched battle with thorough-going rationalism. And the ordinary bystander would probably conclude that neither the natural nor the revealed theology could bear close scientific handling. That a philosopher who is deeply tinged with mysticism should have attained this interior conviction is to me not in the least surprising; for we Brahmans long ago reached a similar end by a very different road; but then we kept the secret to ourselves. Now although I have no acquaintance with the "psychological climate" of England, it does appear to me strange that the very delicate operation of substituting a new Foundation of Belief for that which has hitherto upheld your whole religious edifice should be proposed and proclaimed in the ears of the general multitude.

In India, as every one knows, we have, first, our external forms, secondly, our inner, and lastly our innermost doctrines. The mystery play goes on in front of the stage, the esoteric interpretation, the keys to the mythologies, are kept by the spiritual teachers who lift the veil for the initiated, and for each man according to his capacity. As we do not aspire to any canon of consistency, as we have never committed ourselves to precise creeds, or submitted to the bondage of law, we can vary our external front according to circumstances; so when the time comes we can retire slowly and concentrate upon our unassailable possession of divine knowledge. But we do not invite general attention beforehand to the line of our possible retreat; nor, whenever the rationalist takes the field seriously against our theology, natural or revealed, shall we publish abroad our admission that the arguments available from those sources are practically inadequate for the effort of overthrowing him. This would be to cut deep into the core of popular religion, which is rooted in the certainty of positive and literal beliefs, and can never live in any other soil. It may be that in England you have attained a very different mental atmosphere; yet from what I have heard with my ears of the tone of Christian propagandism in India I should be inclined to judge otherwise.

The superiority of authority to reason is so paramount in India that one naturally marks with approval the high place allotted to the former in the chapter on "Authority and Reason." Nothing can be truer, for Asia as for Europe, than the statement that "to authority we owe in the main, not religion only, but ethics and politics." Obviously this must, or ought, always to be so; for the ordinary man can have neither leisure nor capacity for hunting up causes and origins; he accepts the dictates of what you call science as well as those of theology, so long as they suit his needs and accord with his standard of credibility. You will have observed that simple folk everywhere believe prodigies more readily than mere improbabilities; the latter are contrary to practical experience; the former, as they lie clear beyond the people's understanding, are easily classed as superhuman. A man will believe some explanation of a solar eclipse as a portentous miracle, when he will reject the story of a flying fish. It may be that some such kind of predisposition underlies the principle, which is cited in this book, that one may believe a dogma because it is impossible, and a very useful principle some of us have found it to be. But since Mr Balfour has so clearly exhibited the very important part played in human affairs by authority, I am somewhat dismayed at discovering that he is inclined to question its efficiency as a fundamental support of theologic systems. He does nevertheless rate authority very high when he says that the respect paid by mankind to authority is, much more than reason, the quality in which we most notably excel the brute creation. Yet this may be going rather too far, since authority has been defined in the book as a group of non-rational causes, and we know that the effect of such causes is to beget customs or habits, whereby animals are almost entirely governed. The same definition might almost be fitted to the word instinct; and there is certainly a strain of paradox in the statement that the superiority of man over brutes consists chiefly in his higher susceptibility to non-rational influences.

However, if authority is, as we agree, so enormously powerful, then I must venture once more to remonstrate with an influential and very attractive writer, who works out in public a line of reasoning that is plainly calculated to undermine it. Having proved (what is quite clear) that for the vast majority of us, religious belief does and must rest upon authority, he proceeds to declare that as one of the fundamental reasons for believing a creed authority is inadmissible. Here, again, I must remark that the point touches Christianity more nearly than Hinduism, for nowhere in India, or indeed in Asia, has authority become embodied in such an extreme and inflexible dogma as that of Papal Infallibility, yet this is the very dogma which is here shown to rest upon a circular argument, from the authority of a scriptural text to infallibility, and again from infallibility to the propositions deduced by Churchmen from the text. What, I must ask, is the use of exalting authority if it can be so easily abased? If all these anchors are to be drawn up, as not strong enough against the rising flood of naturalistic views, too many of your people will drift out into the open sea of private judgment, and in attempting to steer by mere reason and sense-perceptions they will run straight into that religious error from which this book, as I understand it, is intended to deter them. It has been reported to us, indeed, that one of your French philosophers has already set up a whole hierarchy on the basis of empiricism, from sheer despair of finding any solid bottom in metaphysical problems. Or else, if the people cannot discover a rational religion, they will fall back on one that is irrational, and rally again under the standard of any teacher who professes undoubting, though illogical certitude; they will fly to any superstition for protection against this ubiquitous scepticism, and will find shelter in the extravagant ritualism which, in India at any rate, the higher priesthood tolerates only as a concession to devout ignorance. In the name of all established religions I propound for consideration the expediency of carrying on these interesting researches in some private philosophical laboratory. Otherwise a profound analyst may be charged with subverting the authoritative foundations of popular religion everywhere; or on the other hand he may be accused of betraying a certain aversion to meeting in the open field of free independent discussion that same antagonist, naturalism, whom he heartily despises. I may perhaps venture to warn him against committing what seems to us Brahmans the grave imprudence of telling the people that the outer walls of the City of God are not impregnable, so that they should take refuge, before it is too late, within some inner sanctuary.

For is this sanctuary fit for the reception of a frightened crowd? and can we at least show them the way or promise them security within it? It is argued that "we need not be driven into a universal license of credulity by recognising that we must for the present put up with some working hypothesis which falls far short of speculative perfection." Far be it from us to deny that philosophic doubt is defensible. On the contrary, we sympathise heartily with a state of mind that has been fostered from time immemorial in India, where no one ever troubled himself to persecute a doubter until the advent of Islam introduced the precise creeds and peremptory legality of the West. We agree with the saying of that ancient Greek teacher, which inspired your early Apologists, that he should deem a coward the man who did not prove what is said about spiritual things to the uttermost, or whose heart failed him before he had examined them on every side. Yet these maxims are meant for enquirers who are beyond the danger of falling back into unlimited credulity, not for the multitude to whom a religion that is avowedly hypothetical is of no value at all. The strength of your western creeds has always, in our opinion, lain in this: that you have looked much more to a good working system, powerfully organised for the development of ethics, than to speculative perfection; you have insisted, in England at least, that the mere principles of reason, improved by consideration and experience, will support that natural religion, "which is indeed the foundation and the principal part of Christianity." And your writers have shown that between natural and revealed religion there is a strange undeniable analogy. We have never thought that the philosophical foundations of that analogy went very deep, yet we recognise the strength that it gave to your cardinal doctrine of the world's moral government; and we have often had cause to wish that Hinduism possessed any such excellent instrument for controlling the unruly affections of sinful men. But an unflinching belief in the exclusive truth of any particular religion, natural or revealed, is not, as we have seen, encouraged in this book. "To claim for any beliefs that they are wholly true, is the height of absurdity; it is indeed foolish, and even dangerous, when we are engaged on the deeper problems of science, metaphysics, or theology; when we are endeavouring in solitude to take stock of our positions in the presence of the Infinite." . . . "To describe any scheme of belief as wholly false which has imperfectly met the needs of mankind is the height of arrogance." Within the philosophic cenacle I should entirely concur; the Brahman has been always too ready to regard with melancholy indifference the innumerable fantastic forms and apparitions of the religious idea, and to observe patiently the heavy clouds of human error settling down over every glimpse of the true light that reaches the lower earth. Yet it has not been thought necessary to preach this elastic doctrine before the crowds that resort to us for spiritual direction and comforting. I fear that any religion which proclaims itself to be hypothetical and provisional, which deals in half truths and relies confidently neither on reason nor on authority, will do very little toward satisfying the needs and aspirations of average humanity.

I hope that I do not misunderstand Mr Balfour's position; I am sure that I sincerely appreciate his aims. Like all the great masters of speculation, among whom I must reckon some of our famous Hindu sages, he rejects the notion "that the universe is no more than a collection of hypostatised sense-perceptions," and he has resolved at all risks to seek higher ground. Treating, as he does, all beliefs and formulas as subject to evolution, he sees that this is incompatible with the old theologic notion of dogma as something final and immovable. "We are," he says, "like one who is perpetually engaged in altering some ancient dwelling in order to satisfy new-born needs. The ground plan is perpetually modified; we build here, we pull down there." Truly so, and in all this we are quite on his side; nor is there any scheme of religion that provides more adequately than Hinduism for the adjustment of worship and doctrine to ever-changing human conditions, whether moral or material. But to illustrate this process by the metaphor of a building that is constantly under alteration and repair, is to take the whole world into your confidence; and some people will be reminded that when a house is constantly needing repair it is usually found safer to pull it down altogether. I must confess, also, that to me this kind of analogy has an unpalatable flavour of rank naturalism. For as soon as you have vulgarised a profound truth by proclaiming that all provisional religious beliefs are subject to an inevitable evolutionary law, you are letting in the naturalistic idea, and you have admitted that religion in any shape is subject to modifications by its moral and indeed its material environment. "If (I read) the constant substitution of one explanation for another could be effected smoothly, and, as it were, in silence, without disturbing anything beyond the explanations themselves, it need cause in general neither anxiety nor regret." Well, that is exactly our Indian method, and it answers very well; but this is a very different thing from inviting public attention to the necessity of incessantly recasting established forms and beliefs, for the supply of changing intellectual demands. And how can we suppose that the common cause of theologians will not be made to suffer in the eyes of ignorant bystanders, by contrasting theology with science, and drawing not very dexterous comparisons between their respective situations? In science, it is said, "the beliefs in sense-perception provide a solid nucleus of unalterable convictions, which survive uninjured through all the mutations of intellectual fashion. . . . Theology is less happily situated. There it often happens that when a theory decays, the beliefs to which it refers are infected by a contagious weakness. The explanation and the thing explained are mutually dependent. . . . The destruction of an hypothesis may be a reason for desiring a new one, but is certainly no reason for abandoning the belief." I understand the inference to be that the true theologian ought to be able to change the explanation without disturbing the belief, precisely as alterations of your theories as to the nature of heat affect in no way the sensation itself; and that a man would be wrong to give up a dogma merely because he could not satisfy himself with any of the theories regarding it. With all this our practical reason is entirely in harmony—for in India no sacred mystery is ever allowed to fall out of repute for lack of a fresh explanation. But whether it is wise to set all this before the people, and to ask why their belief in gravitation never wavers, while they are not always unshaken about eternal punishment, is to our notions not so clear. It would have been safer to remain within the entrenchments laid out in the first portion of this book, and to repel any attempts of Science to measure herself with Theology, by reminding her that all arguments founded on fanciful resemblances and correspondences are radically baseless and unintelligible.

There is some relief, however, in perceiving that the embarrassment inseparable from explanatory formulas in theology has not been overlooked. If, it is observed, the meaning of any proposition could be exhausted in one generation, it would be false for the next; so that as a vehicle for the transmission of truth, a formula must bear "a richer and richer content as our knowledge slowly grows to a fuller harmony with the Infinite Reality." The author here shows a luminous insight into the true working principles of philosophic religion, and the passage quoted above is instinct with the central spirit of Brahmanism. So long as you abstain from giving authoritative reasons or explanations, a mysterious dogma will modify and adapt itself to varying modes of thought; and if it is pronounced inexplicable, it thereby remains unassailable; while crude attempts to simplify and rationalise are sure to inflict upon it irremediable impoverishment. In India, as in Europe, we have our phases of faith. There was a period (it was long ago) in our religious history when extreme ritualism provoked a rationalistic revolt; and conversely there have been times when unvarnished rationalism has provoked among our leading thinkers an energetic defence of the ritualistic sanctuary. I fancy that some movement of this latter character may be discernible just now in England, where in both art and religion (always so closely akin) the naturalistic school has become utterly wearisome. But as mere naturalism is the ignorant abnegation of all spirituality, so ritualistic extravagance degenerates into a lifeless formalism. The right method is to guide the devout worshipper step by step nearer to divine knowledge, while the inner light grows upon him ray by ray, until perchance he at last may attain full illumination. This is the true Brahmanic secret; we let the popular forms and beliefs work upward until by symbolical interpretation they are seen to be the rough-hewn figures of a divine idea, as the mathematical diagram is only an outward help to pure reasoning. And conversely we work allegorically, embodying in an image or myth some abstract notion of the Energy that underlies all phenomena. Only I must once more remark that in England you appear to be abandoning both symbolism and allegory, and that it is barely consistent with this book's main thesis to explain by a kind of natural evolution the recondite working of the great laws that govern the morphology of religious formulas.

"We shall more accurately conceive the true history of knowledge if we represent it under the similitude of a plastic body whose shape and size are in constant process of alteration through the operation both of external and of internal forces." Although the metaphor is perilously naturalistic, one would not quarrel with its use for denoting the incessant variations of the figures created by the popular imagination, acting under superior direction, in correspondence with the environment. But what kind of divine knowledge can this be which is subject to unending change; and what is to become, according to this train of thought, of the creeds and articles of Faith that have so long sustained Christianity? Is the development of religious ideas to be with you, as with us, a process of disillusion until you arrive at the full subjective cognition of permanent Reality? If this be intended, we shall cordially salute the author of this book as one of like mind with ourselves, who discerns the white radiance of eternity through the clouds that confine ordinary human vision. We should not, however, promulgate the doctrine in this particular form to the general congregation of devout worshippers, seeing that it is essentially explanatory. I notice with approval a remark that the decisions of your early Church regarding the mysteries were invariably "the negation of explanation"; although I have read that before dogma became fixed and formulated, the nobler minds among your sages held Christianity to be the highest knowledge of God, and philosophically provable. But it appears to me that if the evolutionary idea is once openly announced as regulating the progress of knowledge in the sphere of theology, it will not be easy to draw round the central mysteries a line within which they are to be treated and taught as inexplicable. You must be aware that Hinduism makes no such reservations, but advances fearlessly until every provisional conception is absorbed into Pure Being, absolute and unconditioned.

However, it is with great diffidence that I offer even these slight criticisms of the methods which so valuable an ally selects for use in his own country against our common enemy. We are, indeed, fortunate in receiving from a British statesman aid to resist the arrogant and insatiable empiricist who has been let loose upon us by the British Government here in India, where all creeds and beliefs are treated with such cynical impartiality that one might almost suspect in our rulers a policy of propagating the scientific bacillus. Upon an intensely spiritualistic people you have imposed a Department of Public Instruction which teaches exclusively upon an empirical basis. But what is the fundamental nature of these scientific ideas that the English are industriously disseminating? They seem quite simple "for the practical purposes of daily life, yet when they are subjected to critical investigation they appear to crumble under the process, to lose all precision of outline, to vanish like the magician in the story, leaving only an illusive mist in the grasp of those who would arrest them." And this inanity of sensational ideas must obviously react, as is pointed out, upon our proximate and practical notions of scientific certitude. Here is an admirable confirmation of the warnings so often delivered by our ancient sages against those who fancy that true knowledge is attainable through the organs of sense; and now that your countrymen and ours have been called back from the wrong road, it is time to set them on the right track, for we cannot leave them wandering in the great desert of illimitable scepticism. The ultimate scientific idea is demonstrably unthinkable; nor is it denied in this book (although we should deny it) that the theologic idea must be infected with the same weakness. Are we, therefore, to be left at the foot of a blank wall? Certainly not; and Mr Herbert Spencer is justly rebuked for allotting to science everything that is knowable; although for our own part we should make him welcome to what he calls knowledge, nor do I understand why Mr Balfour objects to his claiming that which has been proved to be worthless. Both he and Mr Spencer agree in affirming the reality that underlies all things scientifically knowable; but whereas the latter concludes this reality to be inscrutable, the former undertakes, I apprehend, to provide, if not positive information, at any rate an important theory regarding it. So we may leave Science to sort out the counters which she takes to be valuable facts, to amuse herself with the magic lantern of fleeting phenomena, and to reconstruct imaginary geologic periods which must have existed, if at all, in that Divine Mind which is ignored as a scientifically unverifiable hypothesis. The only stipulation that we need make is that she must not interrupt our meditations while we extract (to use Mr Balfour's striking expression) the certitudes of religion out of the depths of unfathomable mystery. He offers to us, as a convenient halting-place, "a theory which, though it shrinks on its speculative side from no severity of critical analysis, yet on its practical side finds the source of its constructive energy in the deepest needs of man, and thus recognises . . . the halting expression of a reality beyond our reach, the half-seen vision of transcendent truth."

With such a theory the Hindu may declare his most earnest sympathy, for he is ever in search of the beatific vision, of the illumination that discloses reality. He would willingly assent, moreover, to many of the principles upon which Mr Balfour builds up the Provisional Unification that includes a remarkable argument very finely and persuasively set out. There ought to be, we agree, no final quarrel between Science and Theology; there is no tenable distinction between Natural and Supernatural; for behind all facts and beliefs, all processes phenomenal or nominal, stands the unknown Power which in some manner informs and moulds all sensible existence. We can have no objection to the statement that ethical and scientific beliefs are both natural products, in the sense that we are thereby required to seek behind these sources, as they lie within the sphere of human exploration, "for some ultimate ground with which they shall be congruous"; and therefore we are completely in accord with the writer's rejection of materialistic Naturalism. The abiding-place of the highest Reality must indeed "be explored by methods other than those provided for us by the accepted canons of experimental research." We need take no exception to the proposition, in its widest meaning, that every addition to knowledge, whether in the individual or the community, whether scientific, ethical, or theological, is due to a co-operation between the human soul which assimilates and the Divine power which inspires; for our own philosophy rests upon Intuition, and its object is the soul's communion with Divinity. It is when we are told that as we have been moved to postulate a rational God in the interests of science, so we can scarcely decline to postulate a moral God in the interests of morality; and when the question is asked whether, and if so under what limitations, we can argue from the existence of an ethical need to the conditions under which alone it can be satisfied—that we reluctantly hesitate. The Divine Personality, possessing attributes that correspond to human desires and aspirations, the Supreme Legislator who is wise, just, and compassionate, is a magnificent ethical ideal; but we cannot bring ourselves to accept as ultimate the knowledge that is derived from perception and inference; we are compelled, like some of your ancient heretics, to look for Something beyond. These postulates will undoubtedly minister to some of our deepest intellectual needs; but they do not fully resolve our doubts or provide us with explanations. I wish from my heart that we could accept them; but if this is to be the speculative foundation of your future religion, I fear it may not altogether withstand the utmost severity of critical analysis. At any rate the incurably subtle Hindu intellect is absolutely incapable of contenting itself with a Deity whose very existence seems in a manner to depend on evanescent and mutable modes of human desire and consciousness.

III.

THE THEOLOGICAL SITUATION IN INDIA.

YOU will excuse my addressing you once again upon the subject of our theological difficulties in India. I am plagued by the inveterate habit of regarding all sublunary matters from the religious point of view. Politics I cannot help regarding as the superficial aspect of deeper problems; and for progress, that latest incarnation of European materialism, I have an incurable distrust. I am well aware that philosophers will never be kings, but I fear that rulers who despise philosophy are very apt to neglect or undervalue certain profoundly important relations between ideas and institutions; and I am very sure that a religion without any philosophy at all is no more stable than a house built on the edge of a great Indian river, which cuts away its banks or changes its course periodically.

Now, as I have said before, the point on which I desire to lay stress is that your political dominion is changing the current of our religious thought; it is inevitably threatening the ancient beliefs which form the base of our Indian society. In regard to these things your attitude is strictly neutral, but your administrative methods point towards this necessary consequence. You have organised, for the first time in Asia, an all-powerful government on avowedly non-religious principles; you are disturbing the habitual simplicity of a people whose wants have been few in a short life for which they cared little; you are stimulating their unruly affections and sharpening their appetites for civilised luxuries. And your system of public instruction is directly intended to spread abroad among all classes a middle-class European education, and thereby to materialise their habits of mind. But I do not find that the English government, which is extremely able, though intensely utilitarian, has ever troubled itself to look much below the surface of Hindu life, or to examine the present state, prospect, and tendencies of the situation which has thus been created.

Yet the ancient city in which I dwell might be regarded by a contemplative Englishman (if such persons exist) as exhibiting in its outward appearance the figures and representations of contending ideas and intellectual change. Here you may see, by the side of a sacred river, priests and ascetics, temples and shrines, mysterious doctrines, and multiform ritual—the whole apparatus of higher and lower Hinduism—side by side with schools that offer a sound English education in all elementary subjects, with a flourishing State College, with a school of medicine, and with various Christian churches. I myself have little commerce with your Department of Public Instruction; I do not admire a system of teaching which deals chiefly with phantasms and idols of the market. But I have this point of contact with the Anglo-Indian school-inspector—who is always intelligent—that he is usually discontented with the methods that he has to practise, and dissatisfied with the religion in which he has been brought up. So I consulted one of them upon the distressing platitudes contained in the ordinary missionary books, which I have been glancing through in search of some help toward my guesses at Truth: and I said that I had the most unfeigned admiration of Christianity as a moral system, but that I was looking for some deeper and wider explanation of its origin. Whereupon he placed in my hands the translated writings of a person called Renan, whom I take to be some kind of empirical philosopher; and in them I did find a subtle and imaginative treatment of the facts of religious history which is undoubtedly attractive. For the handbooks supplied to your colleges are usually mere chronicles of war and dynastic changes, of the increase of national wealth or poverty, laying much stress on Economics and Statecraft, with a varnish of utilitarian morality. They give sketches of ecclesiastical history; but in regard to the permanent relations between religion and politics they explain very little indeed.

That history may be likened to an old almanac is, I believe, an English saying. If its meaning is that the same events and modes of thought recur, though at different seasons and in a changed order, I am inclined to think that the saying is in a manner true, for in these things some recurrent similarity may in truth be occasionally perceived. And so, perhaps, one may venture to compare some features of the religious situation in India at the present day with the condition of western Asia when Christianity first took hold of it. Now Renan works like a scientific naturalist in the field of religious ideas. He stands apart, studies the interaction of religion and politics, and botanizes for specimens that illustrate the natural growth and correlation of ideas and institutions under certain environments. He observes, for example, that the religious inferiority of the Greeks and Romans was the consequence of their political and intellectual superiority. If, he says, they had had a priesthood, severe theologic creeds, and a highly organised church, they could not have created the *État laïque*, or inaugurated the conception of a national society, founded on simple human needs and convenience. On the other hand, it was an advantage, he tells us, for Christianity to have been established at a time when political life had been suppressed along the shores of the Mediterranean; because the earlier republics would have rejected a cosmopolitan faith as a danger to their civic existence. I presume that this view of the causes which favoured early Catholicism may derive some corroboration from the fact that one reason why the English threw off, in the sixteenth century, a church with cosmopolitan claims, was that it appeared to affect their national autonomy. However this may be, it seems to me that the conception which you are importing into India is that of the *État laïque;* nor, indeed, do I see how you could have founded your political supremacy upon any other system; for in the eighteenth century, when you first made good your foothold in this country, you had nothing but a rationalistic Anglicanism to import, and it is clear that your success in acquiring temporal dominion was facilitated by your indifferent attitude towards things spiritual. Herein may be detected a certain analogy between your easy success in India and the causes and circumstances that smoothed the path of Roman conquest; the loose, desultory condition of the old world's paganism, its unpractical theosophies, the weakness of petty states and semi-barbarous rulerships, compared with the tolerant, well-organised, and strictly utilitarian statesmanship of the Empire.

One great and important point in the connection between temporal and spiritual dominion has often been noticed: it is that the Roman conquest made a wide breach, which lay open for several centuries, in the immemorial barriers between Europe and Asia. A mighty gap in them had been made by the trampling of the Macedonian horsemen through Asiatic lands from the Hellespont to the Hyphasis; when Alexander, like some traveller exploring the sources of a great river, reached in India the fountain-head of all the higher and deeper religious ideas which have always flowed into Europe from the East. Nevertheless, it was not, I imagine, until Alexandria and Antioch passed under the imperial dominion of Rome, that these cities became cosmopolitan centres and marts, not only for material commerce between Asia and Europe, but also for the barter and exchange of the fine and subtly-woven tissues which clothe the Oriental conception of divinity. But while it is from Asia that Europe has drawn whatever is profound philosophical, and transcendental in your western creeds, the organisation of religion by creeds and articles, sanctioned and upheld by the union between Church and State, seems to me to have been perfected in Europe only. Without this political union no dominant faith has established itself firmly over any extensive region, or has been able to subdue the insubordinate energies of the free human intellect, that is ever rebelling against fixed ecclesiastical laws and a finite authority. It was from this strong position that Christianity, having won a great spiritual dominion, proceeded to consolidate it by issuing the decrees of her councils, making war upon heresies, breaking down the temples of polytheism, and formulating dogmas, until she finally built up in western lands the Catholic Church Universal, which survived the Roman empire and seated herself on its ruins. I am told that the process of demolition and construction lasted at least six centuries, and that during the first half of this period her serious difficulties or dangers lay not so much with the dying paganism, whose rights became gradually transformed and whose divinities were transfigured, as with the strange theosophies and cosmogonies that had poured in from Asia. So far as I can understand what I read about that confused time, the mystic doctrines, blending with the intellectualism of Greek philosophic schools, had spread abroad in western Asia a kind of restless speculative activity that long retarded the consolidation of positive dogmatic Christianity.

This, then, is the period which should be, I think, of peculiar interest to the reflective Hindu at the present time; because it illustrates the far-seeing and clear-headed polity of your Christian sages. They held fast to the great vivifying principle, unknown to the ancient world, that Theology is in the main a scheme for the moral redemption of mankind, an instrument of universal reformation. But for this purpose they had not only to inculcate upon the masses practical piety and a pure ritual; they had also to contend against a very subtle form of Rationalism, which demanded a logical explanation of existence, to be necessarily based upon some ultimate idea of the nature of the Supreme Being from whom all things proceed. Accepting the external facts of the sacred narratives, your Asiatic and Alexandrian heresiarchs sought for the inward spiritual meaning; their minds were so constituted that a religion without a metaphysical basis was unthinkable. No lower conception than that of an Absolute and Infinite Divinity could satisfy the indomitable Reason, yet how could such a Being be brought into relation with Matter? and if perfect goodness be His attribute, whence then came sin into the world? Into this labyrinth of insoluble, obstinate questionings the professors of the Divine Science plunged deep; they detached the Act of Creation from the Absolute Being, whom they could not conceive as unconditioned and yet operating upon matter; they expanded the notion of the Divine Idea hypostatised; they invented the Demiurge or secondary creative agent; they bridged over the gulf between the intelligible and the phenomenal by various logical formulas and a series of graduated abstractions. They personified the divine attributes; they allotted efficient powers to metaphysical or allegorical figures; they treated all visible appearances as symbols and shadows of the ideal; and in order to avoid Dualism by maintaining one Secondless Reality (as we call it), some of them did not shrink from declaring the whole sensible universe to be illusory. It might, indeed, be allowed to exist after a fashion, conventionally, for the transaction of ordinary business. But in certain schools of the Gnosis phenomena had no more real meaning than we Hindus assign to the theory of gravitation, as taught in the English colleges, which we take to be merely an illusory apparatus to occupy our mental ingenuity, like a problem of pure mathematics figured out on a board before school-children. All reasoning requires this kind of figuration, and it would be pedantic to haggle over the assumption that the world of sense has some degree of practical existence. But in the judgment of these mystical teachers the delusive apprehension of things apparent had gradually settled down like a dark cloud over true knowledge, until simple folk had been misled into believing the reality of their sensations; and in this manner the absolute had given birth to the relative. Nothing then remained, some said, but the vague longing after a lost truth, glimpses of veiled and forgotten secrets, which have kept alive the deeper intuitions in a few penetrative minds. They held that mankind could only be rescued out of this prison-house by the gradual recognition of the truth that material existence is a transient blot on the perfection of the Absolute, that sin is mainly nescience, and that only by slow purification and enlightenment is it possible to attain spiritual emancipation.

It is easy for a Hindu to comprehend how all this ontological speculation, flowing in from the East upon countries that were undergoing great intellectual and political changes, threatened for the time to confuse and disconcert the plain message brought by the Christian Revelation. The abstractions, personifications, and secondary powers of the heretical philosophers were the ladders which they set up in their attempts to scale the heights of the Divine Science, and which landed them among cloudy allegories. Nevertheless, the reason why orthodox Christianity triumphed is clear enough to a Hindu, who may fancy that in the state of western Asia some sixteen centuries agone he can discern the main lineaments of a picture to be seen at the present day in India, and nowhere else. On the one hand, the antique paganism was too incoherent, too immoral and irrational, to withstand a powerful movement of ethical and social reform, propelled by devout enthusiasm and directed by clear-headed leaders towards definite ends. On the other hand, the theosophies could take no hold upon the multitude, they stirred up no emotion, they encouraged doubt by provoking endless discussion, they merely represented the esoteric doctrines which in Asia always lie behind positive formulas of belief and worship. Thus far, I think, we have in outline and colour the Indian landscape; we have the paganism and we have the philosophies; but I can carry the historic parallel no further. For I can see that in the time of the Roman empire there stepped in between the subjective theorist and the objective worshipper a well-disciplined fearless Church militant, with all the momentum of a cause for which men might fight and die. For the first time in the world's annals, a great religion proclaimed itself on a distinct historical basis, on supernatural incidents attested by writings and witnesses, by signs and scripture, on sublime moral teaching, and a promise of salvation for all believers. Above all the doctrine of the Resurrection, of the after-life with pains and penalties which have in every age haunted man's imagination of the dim underworld and the soul's survival, was now at last stated plainly, confidently, as sure grounds of hope and fear. After long metaphysical controversies, the Church settled dogmatically the limits of the Divine Science, the essential objects of faith, the mysteries that are to be accepted as necessary truths, independently of human reason. But the next great epoch in the history of western Asia is marked by the inrush of Islam, the Faith incorporate with Force, which did its work so thoroughly that of all the creeds, controversies, and sublime speculations whose birthplace and seminary had been in that region, no vestiges have remained except a few obscure and persecuted sects.

But the conquest of India by the Mahomedan religion has been very partial and incomplete; while the temporal sovereignty has fallen into the hands of a civilised law-making nation from the far West. Here one may venture to take up again the historic parallel, if it be no mere hallucination for an Indian to imagine that he may now survey his own people in a religious condition not unlike that of western Asia, when it was under the supreme dominion of the Roman State, though not yet of the Catholic Church. Our whole country is within the realm of a powerful empire, governing impartially by codes which embody the customary Gentile laws, and sedulously abstaining from interference with religion, so long as religion does not meddle with politics. The masses have preserved their immemorial polytheism; they worship innumerable gods directly by prayer and sacrifice; the middle class adores the great gods of the Hindu pantheon as the signs and figures of ubiquitous divinity. The superior minds among the sacred castes and the students of orthodox Hinduism are still engaged in discussing the same problems, the same difficulties, the same metaphysical solutions, as those which were current in Antioch, Ephesus, and Alexandria some sixteen centuries ago. We are still outside the pale of Islam and Christianity; we cannot accept religion within a ring fence; we are still professors of the Divine Science, searching incessantly for the knowledge of the Supreme Being, One without a Second. We admit, provisionally, the conventional world of appearances; we quarrel with no form of worship, with no miracles, with no sacred history; we recognise the moral significance and disciplinary influence of Faith in authoritative creeds. But we are nevertheless incapable, intellectually, of understanding how such things can be conceived as imposing finality, how spirit can be brought into relation with matter, and how the persistence of evil is to be explained; and these problems are debated, not as mere subjects for academical enquiry, but as the necessary foundations of satisfactory religious conviction. How can the Unconditioned be regarded as actively creative, without entangling Him in the chain of causality; and how can any motive be imagined in such a Being that would produce the creative Purpose? I notice that in a contemporary Hindu magazine of articles devoted (of course) to metaphysical investigation, a learned Jesuit missionary presses upon us, with much ability, the well-known argument that the universe shows everywhere proof of Design. But all our polytheism is no more than a rudimentary application of that forcible argument, for the polytheist merely infers divine activity from the processes of Nature; though to him many agencies seem more probable than One, and capricious interference a more plausible induction than uniformity of plan. At best, if you press closely the analogy from human art, you have a supreme Architect; and here again you fall far short of finality, for whence came the materials? So the philosophic enquirer is driven back, like the Gnostic of old, upon the

Demiurge, the efficient without the material cause, whose own causal relation to something beyond has yet to be explained. And the visible prevalence of injustice and suffering has long since brought our earlier teachers to the expedient of attributing it to the operation of merit and demerit, an automatous evolutionary process connected with the original qualities of created souls, for which the Creator is in some way irresponsible. We all know that this is now a fundamental and powerfully operative doctrine of popular Hinduism.

But has this visible universe any reality, except as a provisional concession to the necessities of sensual existence? If it has not, the perplexities vanish; and the student may be gradually educated up to a recognition of the unqualified and unrelated being of Brahma, in whom power, wisdom, design, creative energies, are vested by the fallacious expedient of Illusory Attributism. To this gnosis, to the beatific vision, to the apprehension of absolute unity, he may attain by a long course of ascetic functions and severe concentration of thought; and although many cannot reach the clear air of these altitudes, yet very few will be found among reflective and contemplative Hindus who do not find their best consolation for the disorder and perplexities of the material world around them in a deep sense of its unsubstantiality.

I need not endeavour to lead you deeper into the tangled jungle of Hindu theosophy. The schools of Hinduism are as various as were the Gnostic heresies; the same currents of ideas still circulate in India, though their western channels have been dry for ages. I hope

I may have said enough to suggest the situation in outline—the correspondence between esoteric devotion and exoteric worship, between Pantheism, which identifies everything with God, and Polytheism, which dissipates and breaks up the same conception into a multitude of images and symbols, between the soul and the material body of our religion. A coarse and fantastic popular superstition is incessantly undergoing the refining influence of the higher intelligence; and by an inverse process a philosophic generalisation is invariably redistributed into a multiplicity of palpable forms. The more fabulous or extravagant is the myth or miracle, the greater becomes the scope for the mystic's ingenuity of interpretation. He must pretend to accept and make room for the play of fancy and credulity; but he reserves for our closer circle the hidden meaning, the spiritual light which illumines for him a map of queer rites and indecorous ceremonies. He brings metaphysics to bear on mythology; he transmutes natural deities and their history into allegories that satisfy the more inquisitive minds and the moral feeling; he promotes the divinised hero or saint into a fresh incarnation of the superior gods. Meanwhile, he inculcates upon his disciples that great principle of Reserve in the communication of divine knowledge, which has been, I think, the inner policy of all powerful priesthoods everywhere.

You may take for an example of the moralising process the doctrine universally held by all Hindus, that the human soul, the vessel which contains a particle of the divine spirit, is constantly born again and re-incarnate. The basis of all primitive religion, from the lowest to the highest, is that the vital spark in man is inextinguishable; but what awaits us beyond the gate of death? Whither depart the souls of men slain in fierce battle, of those whom we love, hate, and fear? Out of this ever-pressing mystery spring the innumerable phantoms which beset the wild folk of our woodlands by day and night, asleep or awake; a troublesome and disorderly multitude of vagrant ghosts and familiar demons. How far these re-appearances may possess actuality, it matters nothing; I myself am not concerned to differentiate them from all the other evanescent phenomena of sense. But as the people settle down into orderly habits, it becomes necessary to introduce some kind of order, regularity, and ethical significance among their incoherent beliefs. And so all these hints and dim glimpses of life after death that are given by trances, dreams, and spectral visions, this tracking of the wandering soul's passage into animals, plants, or stones—are strung together on the long line of perpetual transmigration, and interpreted as the upward striving of the soul through myriad stages towards higher existence, until it becomes purified for absorption into Infinity. To those who prove themselves fit for higher initiation something more is disclosed; they discover that all nature is the illusive wonder-play of the divine magician, that the visible world is a cipher by which those who have the key may read a secret message; that the flowing garb of appearance is but the embroidered veil which clothes ultimate Reality, the goal and resting-place of pure intellectual apperception.

Let me venture to assure you that this is in true outline the actual condition of contemporary Hinduism;

varied, of course, by many divergent schools, sects, and reformatory tendencies. It has a sublime morality of its own; and for raising our population gradually out of the depths of superstitious ignorance it is not ineffectual; but it suffers from external mutability and a certain indefinite vastness. It is nevertheless changing, like everything else (except the climate) in India, under the great moral and material transformation that we have been undergoing during this nineteenth century of your Christian era. The difficulty is to forecast the line of its organic development. Is it possible, then, to find in the theological history of your western world, in the relation between political and philosophical ideas or in the growing influence of physical science and rationalism, any precedents or illustrations that may aid us in shaping, or, at least, in conjecturing our own religious future? In Europe, as I understand, your churches have long ago closed the era of unlimited metaphysical speculation, retaining only certain mysterious dogmata that are authoritatively prescribed as facts—that are not philosophical discoveries, but are declarations of revealed truth. You have drawn up your creeds; you have settled finally all essential beliefs in future rewards and punishments, in man's redemption from sin and in resurrection, and, above all, in a Divine Personality. You have numbered and ended the list of your sacred books; you look for no fresh revelation; you have regulated by ordinances the rites and ceremonies which unite the worshippers and divide the Churches. And you send out missionaries to expound in India their ecclesiastical systems of faith and morals, which, with certain internal differences that seem to me immaterial, I admit to be of substantial ethical value and efficacy, eminently suited for man's spiritual government, for controlling his unruly affections, and expediting his civilisation. But I want you to understand that we are still wandering in the metaphysic wilderness, and that Christianity, returning at last to Asia after an interval of so many centuries, finds us still engaged on the same problems as those which occupied the schools of Antioch and Alexandria, and the secret professors of the Jewish Kabbala. We have never yet set limits, either by philosophic criticism or by ecclesiastic ordinance, to the range of free enquiry or to the thinking faculty; we cannot submit to the restrictions placed by faith upon enquiry into mysteries; we are driven by our mental constitution to overleap the bounds of sentient experience, and to construct, like your ancient heretics, some intelligible theory of the unconditioned. We are incapable of apprehending a Personality, except in the sense of something that masks or represents an incomprehensible notion; and dogmatic systems are to us no more than the formal envelopes of spiritual truth. In short, for us Salvation comes, not by righteousness, but by knowledge; not by the casting out of sin, though we long to be delivered from it, but by emerging out of ignorance. Of the two trees which stood in your Garden of Eden, we Hindus should have chosen the tree of Life, which has been mystically understood to symbolise the wisdom which apprehends reality; whereas by eating the fruit which gave discernment of good and evil, Adam fell down into the region of earthly pains and pleasures, of will and desire. Undoubtedly the multitude of his descendants in India are still in the lower state; to escape calamity and obtain benefits they make prayers and oblations; they bow down before the shrines of awful divinities. And verily they have in this visible existence the fruits of worship, but these are transient and perishable, like the hopes and fears of the worshipper. Some intimation of this inner truth is to be found in the words of one of your ancient prophets—'Sacrifice and offering thou wouldest not, but mine ears hast thou opened"; for infinite beatitude comes only to those whose faculties have been attuned to the hearing of the unspeakable word.

It may appear to Europeans astonishing that these speculations are still of intense spiritual interest to millions in India, when almost everywhere else in the civilised world they have been authoritatively discarded as incompatible with practically operative beliefs. In all civilised countries the real basis of religion is no longer metaphysical, but moral; the rules of faith have been codified; the lines of communication between earth and heaven have been laid down. But all this firm ground of belief and conduct becomes submerged in the vague, fluctuating intellectualism of the Hindus. Vainly you prove to us that the conception of an impersonal, unapproachable Being is ineffectual and ethically pernicious; we recognise the moral danger, but it does not stop us, for we are like mariners whom some magnetic attraction draws ever further beyond all havens into a boundless sea.

If, now, you rely upon western education, upon the

spread of positive information and methodical classification of facts, to control and subdue these inveterate tendencies, I think you are mistaken. The effect of such schooling, as it is universally disseminated through our society by your system of Public Instruction, is to disintegrate the immemorial paganism; it explains second causes, and diminishes the credibility of prodigies and miracles as evidence of direct supernatural intervention. The picture of a tortoise supporting the earth on its back, at which your philosophers have pointed the finger of scorn, can in this manner be rightly interpreted to be emblematic of demonstrable sustaining forces; but how the tortoise finds a footing will still remain a perplexity; nor has the ancient riddle been yet solved by those who ridicule it. And in proportion as the people become disposed to look deeper for a more reasonable religion, they will continue to find it, as they are doing already, by large recourse to the doctrines and interpretations contained in their own sacred books. The concrete images will become signs of the indwelling spirit; the words of the miraculous stories will become metaphoric; and to the spiritually-minded Hindu the substitution of scientific laws for supernatural agencies will only throw the underlying pantheism a little further back. I have noticed in some of your recent apologists the tendency to set up against the encroachments of Rationalism a kind of universal scepticism. All scientific propositions, it is maintained, are in their ultimate analysis no less incapable of verification than theological dogmas; the idea of force, for example, will be found on scrutiny to be as indistinct as the doctrine of Grace; you can only recognise its operations. The logical result of this argument is to confirm the Hindu in his conviction of the illusory nature of all phenomena, and to strengthen him in meeting the new learning with the mysticism of his ancient schools. Nor will he care to contest the authenticity, in an objective and apparitional sense, of historical religions; he will only place these things, like the Gnostics of old, in the category of secondary manifestations: he will rely upon the inward illumination for seeing through and beyond all formal beliefs and empirical philosophies.

I must say that although these habits of thought have their obvious practical drawbacks, I value them as a strong antidote against the fatal disease of materialism. Moreover, the transcendental position has other advantages. In the first place, it lies beyond the range of the erudite literary criticism which every historic religion has to face. Secondly, it avoids the immobility which is one danger of fixed creeds and articles, for it allows free scope for religious speculation among the higher intelligences; while it facilitates the gradual adaptation of the popular beliefs to changes of the moral and mental level. The contemplative Hindu, surveying the vast field of miscellaneous rites and worships presented by his country, says in his heart that these things are neither credible nor creditable; but he does not therefore proclaim a crusade against the vulgar polytheism. If any one enquires of him concerning these practices, he turns to the sacred books, or to some contemporary master of divinity, for an intelligible and spiritual explanation. Or, if the longing to see further through the outer husk of the phenomenal world overpowers and enthrals him, he may clarify the ordinary sense perceptions by ascetic exercises, which give the power of discerning subtle evolutes of matter and spirit. I have heard that certain rudimentary indications of this latent faculty, which has, of course, been known to us for centuries, have latterly attracted notice in England, where some sort of group or sect of initiates has been formed for necromantic experiments. But it is said that, in accordance with the utilitarian complexion taken by all modern research, the chief object of this sect is to communicate with the ghosts of dead kinsfolk or national celebrities. In our country the cultivation of such abnormal faculties is the stock-in-trade of wizards and other wonder-workers, whom I by no means brand as impostors; though they take a very low degree in the occult science, and the true spiritualist rather disdains their acquaintance. It is at best a naturalistic art, directed towards the extension of our bodily faculties into a new region of experimental discovery; but we are no more disposed than are the Christian Churches to find any solace within the confines of sensational experience; for to accept such conclusions would be a confession of spiritual ignorance, the dishonouring servitude out of which we are perpetually striving to escape.

On the other hand, I am very keenly conscious of the objections against a system of religious thought that has its citadel in transcendental idealism. It is administratively ineffectual; it provides no firm ground for the highest ethical injunctions; because it may regard even the moral law as a provisional ordinance devised for satisfying the finite intelligence with a semblance of

Order and Purpose in human affairs, with the illusory but indispensable notion of Free Will, and with a lofty standard of human life and labour. Your theologians will object, forcibly, that although they are ready to make use of pure reason as an ally, they will not accept it as an arbiter. They will join hands with us in holding that the essential truths of religion are inaccessible to the ordinary understanding, and can be divined only by intuition and inspiration; that the Eternal is non-apparent and unverifiable. Nevertheless they maintain, if I am not wrong, that subjective beliefs alone give no abiding-place, and that religion must stand upon definite facts to be accepted faithfully. And so they insist upon the Christian dogmas as necessary truths and fundamental axioms, from which is to be deduced the logical synthesis of orthodox Christianity. Such beliefs, they hold, are as independent of philosophic analysis as of scientific demonstration, or even of moral significance; they are facts revealed absolutely, not relatively or provisionally; they are the primary and essential objects of faith. And for the unwavering acceptance of these truths the Churches promise great rewards, far nearer and more tangible than the liberation to be attained by contemplative thought; while modern Positivism can hold out to its votaries no futurity at all.

I agree that this is a reasonable system of authoritative theology, having for its cardinal articles the sure and undoubting belief in a Personal God, in resurrection and the soul's immortality; while its instrumental mainspring is the doctrine of moral consequences. The loose, indefinite notions of divinity are seen to be administratively useless; they need to be stamped upon the human imagination as tremendous and inevitable facts, as powerful motives for conduct. And since the only universal medium for the interchange of mental conceptions is to be found in the forms of the material world, in figures which may be seen or words which are the signs of things, the Churches have therefore built up the external fabric of religion, each after its own fashion, upon rituals, rubrics, and liturgies, authoritatively prescribed and determined. All this we understand clearly, and would willingly adopt into Hinduism; but at no period in the history of India has there occurred that combination of ecclesiastical and temporal authority which enabled your Churches, after a prolonged confusion, to lay down and enforce plain rules of faith and worship. It is possible that the Buddhistic heresy, when at the climax of its extension in northern India, may have approached this degree of power and predominance; but we may guess that with the fall of the great Buddhist dynasties the whole hierarchical system was overwhelmed by a returning flood of polytheism. However this may be, we can now look for no help from a religion which intensifies the fundamental weakness of Hinduism, its incapacity to stop at any given point in the casual chain, or to be content with penultimate ideas, or to conceive any stage of being, earthly or heavenly, to be permanent. The Buddhist is not even satisfied with the soul's absorption, as a drop in the ocean, into the divine essence; he can rest only when some indefinite conception of nonentity permits him to relinquish as inconceivable any further pursuit of the soul's interminable flight, in its striving to escape beyond the possibilities of sensation.

In India, therefore, you may behold at this moment an immense and intelligent society much given to dreamy meditation over insoluble problems, and practically unanimous in rejecting any solution that stops short of Pantheism. If you offer us a definite Religion which circumscribes and controls rationalistic speculation, and includes a moral system that is admirably adapted to human needs and circumstances, we must reply that this would be invaluable if we could only accept and assimilate it intellectually. But unluckily this very quality of appropriateness raises in the Hindu mind a suspicion of anthropomorphism, of human inventiveness; while even your highest doctrines contain something that may be felt to be transient and terminable. Two cardinal ideas run through our deeper religious thought. One is the Maya, or cosmic illusion, which cuts the knot of any difficulty touching the relation between Spirit and Matter, and produces Unity, by exhibiting the visible universe as a shadow projected upon the white radiance of eternity; the other is the notion of the soul's deliverance by long travail from existence in any stage or shape. So long as these ideas are ineradicable from our intellectual beliefs, I fear that our religious anarchy will resist any attempt to organise our theology as you have organised our political government. We may agree that it is reasonable to admit the moral necessity of a supreme personal Divinity, even though such a Being cannot be demonstrated from experience or by ontological argument. If such a concept is required as the rational explanation of what we all feel and acknowledge to be duty, then one may be entitled to adopt Theism as a belief, founded on moral certainty, that is of enormous importance and benefit to mankind. I am aware that among some of my most thoughtful and high-minded fellow-countrymen there is a tendency to settle upon this conclusion, towards clothing with attributes the permanent Reality that resides, as we all acknowledge, behind appearances. Yet to the majority, who are still entangled in the Indian Gnosticism, the conception is humanistic; it resembles the demand for a settled constitution and a proper sanction for necessary legislation; it is tinged with a kind of enlightened utilitarianism.

In short, we have a religion, but no theology; we have cosmogonies and theosophies, but no dogmatic rulings upon such questions as are settled by the Christian creeds; and since we have passed no ecclesiastical laws, we cannot require any man's implicit obedience to our teachings. Above all, we have never been able so to bend and adjust our metaphysics that it might support and fit in with some far-reaching policy and practical end. I do not say that Hinduism is no more than a miscellany of speculative theories and devotional rhapsodies. In the ascetic desire to be rid of the flesh, to extinguish worldly thought, and above all, in the longing to escape illusion, change, and the pain which is the malignant curse of sensitive existence, there is a dominant strain of morality; and the doctrine of the metempsychosis may be well insisted upon as inculcating the penalties for sin and the way of ascending into salvation. But we have never succeeded, as Christianity has done, in so limiting and formulating our notions upon divine things, as to bring out of them a system of unified beliefs that are infallible rules of faith, and that can also be explained as moral ordinances. The Fathers of your Church had, like ourselves, to fight with pure rationalism on the one hand, and on the other hand with the ineradicable polytheism of the masses. They did so by settling, after desperate controversies, the Christian creeds, which determine authoritatively the metaphysical questions, and by gradually transforming the worship of many gods into a qualified monotheism, with a ritual that superseded and absorbed the pagan worships. The background of the creeds they declared to be mystery; the immoralities and indecencies of paganism were eliminated by slow purgation. The dogmatic propositions became fixed as the supernatural instruction of an infallible teacher; the State lent its aid to enforce obedience, to punish divergent opinions, and "to maintain truth." Undoubtedly, this system of religion established by law did logically produce much cruel persecution of a kind that has never stained Hinduism; but then it has also bred martyrs, who have died both for the Catholic faith and also in the cause of intellectual freedom; whereas a tolerant and even sceptical religion, undisturbed by the temporal power, neither deserves nor desires such sacrifice. Yet just as the earlier Christian martyrdoms are said to have been suffered under persecution by an intolerant State so we also should in like circumstances willingly suffer death, which has little terror for any of us.

On the whole, therefore, we may envy the strength and consistency of your organised faiths; they can insist on ultimate truths from the standpoint of dogmatic certitude; they can declare that the moral law has been positively ordained by a divine legislature, from which there is no appeal. Yet the stereotyping of your formulas has had the effect of hardening both your sacred history and your dogmas into a perilous condition of immobility, which becomes more and more disadvantageous as the intellectual atmosphere clears and widens. There is ample evidence in your creeds to indicate that they were evolved out of unlimited reasoning upon spiritual problems, at a period when the most imaginative theories and the most abstract conceptions, such as still engage our meditations, were discussed, as we still discuss them, by the acutest and most daring philosophic intelligences of the time. And I make out that the ancient Church often won by sheer force of argument. Now that you have closed the scholastic arena, the inevitable result is that you have rationalism arrayed against you. For since you allow no tampering with the facts on your sacred record by allegory or any other such process as we should use in India, they are losing credibility; and the mysteries, though originally the outcome of reason, are becoming irrational. According to the later rulings of orthodoxy a doctrine of faith is not a philosophical discovery, it is an infallible declaration of the Church; and the Scriptures give plain authentic narratives of things that were done and events that occurred. The sure consequence has been that both philosophy and physical science find themselves at issue with theology, being unable to submit to any limitation of free criticism or enquiry; while a fixed ritual brings on a revolt against formalism. I agree that this antagonism must be accepted by any Church that takes up a position and fights for it; for we know too well that an inconclusive religion is comparatively ineffectual, and that the decisive points must be drawn somewhere. A show of perfect methodical knowledge may provoke demur, but it has also, as one of your sages has said, a strong tendency to generate acquiescence; and it relieves many perplexed consciences from insecurity and indecision. Moreover, your western Christianity has the great quality of bringing the supreme Divinity into close relation with living and suffering humanity; whereas our philosophic teachers can only show us the first cause across a wide abyss, which they bridge over as they can, like the Gnostics, by the framework of arbitrary hypotheses. It has been truly observed that men will not suffer or die for an hypothesis; they will stake their lives on nothing less than unflinching certitude. And we Brahmans can thoroughly appreciate the importance of settling authoritatively and finally the rites and ceremonies which are the mystical depositories of those spiritual truths that can only be signified to the people by external observances.

I have, therefore, little doubt that the advantages of a systematic and disciplined religion probably counterbalance its drawbacks; just as the British Government of India, with its legislatures and law courts, may be on the whole preferred by a majority of peaceful and comfortable citizens to the free fighting and the uncertainty which it extinguished. Nevertheless, although your empire has given us a political settlement after the high Roman fashion, I do not yet see what aid it is likely to give us towards any kind of religious unity. It does not, indeed, profess to give any, for your government stands by religious neutrality, and attempts, as the Romans did at first, to treat the religious question with indifference.

I by no means object to that neutral attitude, for there is nothing else to be done by the rulers of a country where Hinduism is infinitely divided, and where Islam has great strength and vitality. But you will have already discovered that the pacification of a vast territory, which inevitably produces some degree of political stagnation, rather stirs up than silences religious activities, by facilitating the interchange of ideas, of correspondence, and the combination of rival sects against each other all over the country. Nor can you have failed to notice very recently in western India the bearing upon politics of Brahmanical revivalism, or to mark the sympathetic connection between increasing devotion to the god Siva, and open commemoration of the Maratha chief Sivaji, who raised the standard of Hindu revolt against a foreign domination. And it does not strike me as probable that any fresh expansion of religious zeal will develop a cordial understanding with secular education and the new learning. These are, however, matters for those who rule; and your undeniable political instinct ought to have saved you from the error of supposing that, because you are neutral in theological disputes, you are therefore entitled to be unconcerned about them.

In the religious situation of India lies my whole interest, and also my excuse for troubling you, I fear unprofitably, with our difficulties and dilemmas. You offer us your creeds; we cannot accept them with implicit faith; we are such unconvertible rationalists that we should find scope for argument in every metaphysical proposition; we should fall back again into barren dialectic. You are instructing us in your physical science with its useful discoveries and mechanical appliances, which train men to dissect the articulated organism of Nature, and to make this earth more comfortably habitable. Between your orthodox creeds and your scientific studies, the old-world pursuit of knowledge to the uttermost bounds of human reason has gone out of fashion and has become irrational. To a large number of the half-taught youths whom your colleges send out into our antique society, which they have learnt to despise, the smattering of empirical information which has been so liberally bestowed upon them is sufficient. They take their ease upon the soil out of which their bodies were formed, and among the vegetables to which they are content to belong. But to the higher minds among us physical science is entirely inconclusive, unless indeed it is read as a symbolical language shadowing forth the divine truths of our own philosophy—

> "What man that sees the ever-whirling wheel
> Of change, the which all mortal things doth sway,
> But that thereby doth find and plainly feel
> How Mutability in them doth play
> Her cruel sports to many men's decay?"

So said one of your poets, looking forward to the time "when no more change shall be, but steadfast rest of all things firmly stayed upon the pillars of Eternity." And three hundred years later one of your philosophers, whose name we curiously note to be the same as the poet's, has declared Metamorphosis to be the universal law, exemplified throughout the heavens and the earth; but for mutability he substituted the dynamic idea of Evolution. Thus the conclusions of the poet and the philosopher are, as they should be, much the same in regard to phenomenal existence, though the poet looks beyond it. The intervening mechanical processes are more accurately investigated by the philosopher, who nevertheless takes the dynamic prime mover to be neither God, nor Nature, but some unknowable power. All speculation, in whatever stage, theologic, metaphysic, or scientific, has indeed long ago reached similar conclusions, with the exception that on the vital point whether the force or forces are known or knowable, there has been very little agreement. The simple folk believe that all phenomena are, so to speak, hand-made, produced by gods and demons who preside over the machinery and fling about blessings or curses: as if a great river were worked by a hand-pump, and a disease were like vitriol malignantly thrown in your face. The superior polytheist sees that the distribution of natural forces and influences is on a loftier scale, he is so far impressed by their potency and regularity that he treats them as mighty divinities; the philosophic monotheist argues from invariable laws, moral and material, to one great Legislator. And all the highest religions have been at one in their anxiety to lift the human soul clear above the region of changes, and to bring it into some beatific state of finally unbreakable Rest.

CHAPTER II.

ON THE RELATIONS BETWEEN THE STATE AND RELIGION IN CHINA.

I

Difference between earliest and latest ideas on relations between Religion and the State—Controversies in Europe over the question —Separation between religion and civil government is becoming a recognised principle in Europe, while the contrary is still the rule in Asia—Islamitic institutions—Position of the Chinese government, and its method of dealing with the three official religions of China—Confucian, Buddhist, Taouist, all independently established as separate creeds—Public worship of the Chinese, rites performed by Emperor—The contents of the *Pekin Gazette* illustrate the attitude of the Government toward religion, and explain its influence—Posthumous honours and titles bestowed on deceased persons, their deification by order of Government—Titles and reward given to divinities for public services, instances quoted—Control exercised by the State over Buddhist incarnations, cases cited from *Gazette*—Intellectual condition of a people which sees no clear distinction between the unseen and the visible world, between gods and men—Danger of too close connection between Religion and the State.

ONE important difference between the earlier and the latest principles of government is marked by the changes which have taken place in men's ideas on the subject of the proper relations between the ruler and the priesthood, the State and the Church, the civil government and the ecclesiastical bodies. In times when all authority necessarily claimed to derive from a divine mandate, when laws were supernaturally delivered, and when crimes might be most effectively treated as sins against the gods, it was natural that the ruler should assume religious as well as civil supremacy; that he should take on himself, wherever he could, the visible headship of the external worship; and that he should employ his power to obtain command of spiritual forms and institutions. We know that the Roman Emperors long kept in their own hands the chief pontifical office, until the sacred or hierophantic functions of the sovereign vanished, in Europe, with paganism. We have read of the high paramount authority over religious affairs maintained by Constantine and his immediate successors. Then, in the Middle Ages, came the long struggle between the ecclesiastical and the civil powers; when the Papacy had concentrated and brought into focus all the independent spiritual authority of western Christendom, and declared absolute separation between the dominions of the Church and of the State. But between spiritual and temporal matters, as they affect the daily life and conduct of the people, the distinction is in practice hard to draw, and harder to maintain. The attempt to partition off such things into two provinces, and to place each province under an independent and co-ordinate authority, was inevitably followed by incessant and fervent discussion and contest over the right and recognisable border that should divide two complicated jurisdictions not easily definable.

The course and development of this conflict, which prevailed throughout Europe in various forms, have been very different in different countries: the English Reformation, which restored the Church as a national institution, is a notable instance of the manner in which some of the nations which broke away from Roman Catholicism recurred to the earlier principle of according supremacy to the State's ruler. It may perhaps be said that from the time when the Church attempted to mark off her share in the government of mankind into a separate and independent department, the controversy over the precise range and limits of that department has never ceased. And the general result, in the most civilised countries, is that while the ecclesiastical power has in these latter days been disarmed, and can no longer uphold any pretensions to concurrent authority within the domain of civil administration, on the other hand the civil power is rapidly withdrawing from its ancient claims to headship and overlordship in matters of belief or ritual. The civil government interferes very reluctantly indeed in questions of doctrine; it still maintains, under such laws as may be existing, what M. Paul Bert, the French Minister, has termed a general police of worship; but the tendency is towards repealing any laws which throw this duty upon the administration. The ruling power no longer looks to the religious bodies, as such, for support; but on the contrary is anxious rather to disown than to rely upon an alliance with any particular form of religion. The view now predominant is that which was set forth in Macaulay's essay on Mr Gladstone's book on Church and State, where the reviewer argues that a government in its public and collective capacity has no more to do with the profession of dogmatic distinctions than a railway company. In short, politics and theology, finding that they cannot work together, have agreed to stand apart, desiring to have as little to do with each other as may be possible; and upon some compromise of this kind peace is now generally concluded in the most advanced societies, except upon some debatable ground like education. There may still be found in Europe a Church party that would break in the State to the Church's harness, and a political party that would give no quarter to ecclesiasticism; but on the whole it is now becoming an established principle in western Europe, that a complete and formal separation between religion and civil rulership is essential to any rational administration either of the State or of the Church. The temporal sovereigns decline, so far as they can, interposition in spiritual affairs: the only spiritual potentate who still maintains pertinaciously his right to intervene in the temporal government of Christians has, chiefly for this very reason, been recently deprived of his own temporalities; and the main current of modern opinion sets towards disestablishment, disendowment, suppressing *budgets des cultes*, cutting the States clear of their connection with Churches, and taking up an attitude, in regard to religious institutions, of irresponsibility and more or less respectful unconcern. So that the earlier ideas on this subject are now not only rejected, but reversed; to the principle of union between the secular and spiritual authorities is succeeding the principle of divorce.

But if it is true that European ideas on the relations between Church and State are reaching this climax, this makes it very well worth while to bear in mind that in the non-Christian world the earlier notions on this subject predominate, and materially influence societies. Three out of the great Governments of

Europe—England, France, and Russia—rule over large numbers of non-Christian people, and are in constant relation with non-Christian States. And some of the many and strange difficulties besetting this position are connected with the incident that in Asia and Mahomedan Africa the temporal ruler is generally expected to do what in western Europe he is generally denounced for doing, to assume, that is, a direct and practical authority over the administration of religious affairs; while the statesman is undoubtedly expected to be a worshipping man. Moreover, these difficulties, where Islam is concerned, have not missed appreciation at Constantinople; for the Sultan has lately been disclosing some anxiety about the spiritual unity of Islam, and is showing a disposition to employ his claims to the Kaliphate as a means of taking upon himself the functions left vacant by the disabilities of a non-Mahomedan ruler in Mahomedan countries. And the mere fact that the Turkish Sultans, with no pretensions to sacred character or descent, have for some centuries been able to impose themselves as Kaliphs upon a very large part of the Mahomedan world, proves how closely the spiritual headship is bound up, outside Europe, with temporal dominion. It is, and must be, the policy of a native Asiatic ruler to secure and maintain this union of forces; since, so long as he stands outside and disconnected from the spiritualities, he is in a dangerously imperfect condition; he leaves in other hands a lever that may be used to upset him, and he is cut off from the control and direction of an active, never-resting machinery, always at work among his people. Of course, an

Asiatic sovereign may and does govern people of various creeds, as in India; and it may happen, though the case is rare, that he himself professes exclusively the creed of a minority. But in this latter case (which almost always indicates recent and incomplete conquest) the position of a native ruler is unstable; while, on the other hand, the more effectually he can combine with his secular sovereignty an acknowledged authority over and control over the religious organisation, the stronger and more solid is his dominion. The early Byzantine emperors acted upon this principle; and its most obvious and well-known illustration is to be seen in the rapid rise and the complete predominance for centuries of Mahomedanism as a ruling power throughout the greater part of Asia. For it is manifest that the early successes of Islam were due to the sudden appearance, in a part of the world divided by great schisms or petty local creeds, of a series of leaders who impersonated the full idea of a theocracy, and who united more completely and effectively than ever before or since in the world's history, the two momentous forces of military and religious enthusiasm.

But the institutions of Islam are, after all, barbarous through their very simplicity; while its intolerant monotheism is a peculiar product of western Asia. It may be more interesting to look much further eastward, and to examine the relations of the civil government to religion in a country where creeds and rituals still preserve their primitive multiformity, where they all have, nevertheless, free play, and where the ruler finds it possible and advantageous to preside over all of them.

Nowhere is this better seen than in that empire which at one time had attained, as a government, the highest level yet reached by purely Asiatic civilisation, which is the oldest of Asiatic empires, and still not unlikely to outlast all others now existing—the empire of China.

The Chinese Government is singular in Asia as representing a kind of constitutional conservatism. No other great Asiatic State ever got beyond the simplest forms of arbitrary sovereignty; whereas in China the governing class has for centuries been endeavouring to stand still at a remarkably forward stage of administrative organisation long ago attained; and this is not the immobility of mere superstition and ignorance, as in the case of the nations around, but it is apparently due to a deliberate mistrust of progress beyond the point already reached. This feeling is probably much more justifiable in Asia than in Europe; for until the incoherent groups of different races and religions which make up the population of an Asiatic empire become moulded into some sort of national conglomerate, they form a very shifty foundation for elaborate political buildings. A well-knit and long-established European nation may play fast and loose with its institutions, and amuse itself with new economical principles and experiments in governing; may allow chronic disaffection to run on in a province, on the chance of its wearing itself out, and may be indifferent to the encroachment of the legislative upon the executive power, and to the relaxing of the imperial authority. But Asiatic constitutions cannot stand such treatment, and rulers are obliged to be much more cautious in handling rough conglomerate masses of tribes and sects. Nor can it be denied that civilisation, whatever be its benefits to Asia, acts as a disintegrating force among the first principles which lie at the base of all Asiatic governments, where the corner-stone is usually the divine right of kings. However this may be, the Chinese have certainly succeeded in organising scientific methods of administration without disturbing primitive ideas; an experiment of great interest to the English, who have before them a problem not altogether dissimilar.

China has had, moreover, the good fortune of lying beyond the full sweep of the destructive waves of Mahomedan invasion, which spent their force on her extreme frontier; so she escaped the deluge which has separated all western Asia into two distinct periods, and has produced, wherever it spread, a complete interruption of political continuity. And while her religions have thus retained their natural variety, and have escaped being crushed out or overlaid by the levelling power of Islam, China has attained this superiority over India, that she succeeded centuries ago in bringing her religious doctrines and worships into practical co-operation with her secular organisation. It would seem as if the lavish fertility with which Indian soil produces religious ideas and forms has hindered them from being turned to account, and built up into any great religious system; or else that India has never had a native government large and strong enough to organise Brahmanism as a foundation and support of its authority, as the Chinese have enlisted their ancient Pantheon into the State's service;

while it does not appear that Indian religions have ever been pressed into the service of morality. The only great State religion and organised Church which ever throve in India was Buddhism; and it is precisely this religion which, after its mysterious break-up in India, found a permanent home, and an immense, though distorted, development as the greatest established religion of China. Yet Buddhism is only one among others, for the Chinese Government seems, perhaps alone among civilised States, to have solved the problem of maintaining simultaneous relations, close and sympathetic, with several established official religions. In European States, wherever uniformity of belief can no longer be preserved, the State usually finds it impossible to identify itself with several rival creeds, and very inconvenient to remain on good terms with one particular creed, whereupon it withdraws as much as possible from connection with any of them. In Mahomedan countries this difficulty is forestalled by diligently stamping out all creeds but one, wherever this is possible. But in China, so far as can be judged from written accounts, the peculiarity is not only that the State is tolerant and fairly impartial to a multiplicity of creeds and worships (for that is seen everywhere in Asia beyond the pale of Islam), but that at least three established religions are fostered and sedulously patronised by the Government according to their specialities and respective values in use for the great purposes of the orderly administration of the empire, and the upholding of the national traditions of conduct and morality. Nowhere is the principle of adapting the motive power of religion to the machinery of administration carried out so scientifically as it appears to be in China. The vast area and the immense population of the Empire afford ample room for several religions; the system of government finds employment and a congenial atmosphere for them all. The tradition of the imperial Court is to keep the emperor's person in august and majestic seclusion; the practice is to set out all their administrative proceedings and acts of State under imposing formularies and high-sounding moral ordinances, keeping the inner mechanism of the State secret and mysterious. All this system harmonises with and favours the policy of associating religion with every department of the public service, and of identifying the laws of the Government with the decrees of Heaven. The State interposes itself as much as possible between the people and their gods; the emperor claims to be the authorised *chargé d'affaires*, or chief agent and intercessor for his country with the Supreme Powers. And the Chinese Government has this advantage, that although its dynasty is to some degree foreign, it is nevertheless not so far ahead of, or apart from, the prevailing intellectual standard among its subjects that it cannot recognise or treat with religions of low or incongruous types without offending the public opinion of some influential body among its subjects. A Christian or Mahomedan Government can at most accord unwilling recognition to creeds of a totally different species. But the Chinese imperial Government seems able to work with, and to derive support from, at least three great religions of very diverse character: the Confucian system, the Buddhist Church with its Orders and the Taouist worship of innumerable magic genii and Nature gods.

All accounts of China agree generally in describing these three forms of religion as existing separately and independently, although they have influenced and coloured one another. And if this be their condition (although no one can feel sure of understanding religions who has not been among the people who practise them) it seems certainly remarkable that in China, which possesses an ancient and comparatively uninterrupted civilisation, and a highly centralised government, the various beliefs and worships should not have coalesced, in the course of many centuries, into some comprehensive national religion. Even in India, where the whole country has never fallen under complete political centralisation, and where everything has aided to prevent the regular growth of one religion, all the indigenous rituals and theologic ideas are more or less grouped under the ample canopy of Brahmanism, which has an easy pantheistic method of accommodating all comers. And in other countries some sort of general religion almost invariably develops itself according to circumstances; it selects, rejects, improves, and combines the elements of the various creeds and worships which it gradually supersedes; and the more it predominates, the faster it annexes or absorbs. There may remain formidable schisms or parties worshipping different gods, or widely at variance on points of doctrine, yet one broad band of religious affinity usually brings them all together under some primary denomination. But in China this process does not seem to have taken place; the State is uniform and highly centralised, while there are three principal religions, distinct in character and origin, all living in concord together, and in intimate association with the empire. The different religious ideas and doctrines that have from time to time sprung up in China, or have been transplanted thither, have not become assimilated, but remain apart in separate formations. The philosophic Confucianism, embodying the teachings of a great moralist and statesman, the magnificent hierarchy of Northern Buddhism, with its church, its orders, its deified abstractions, and its metaphysical doctrines; Taouism, with its adoration of stars and spirits presiding over natural phenomena, of personified attributes, divine heroes, local genii, and the whole apparatus of anthropomorphism—all these expressions of deep moral feeling, religious speculation, and superstitious wonder, jumbled together like everything in Asia without regard to inconsistencies or absurdities, seem to prevail and flourish simultaneously in China.

Mr Edkins, in his book on religion in China,* tells us that we have there these three great national systems working together in harmony. Three modes of worship, he says, and three philosophies, have for ages been interacting on each other. They are found side by side not only in the same locality, but in the belief of the same individuals, for it is a common thing that the same person should conform to all three modes of worship; and the Government willingly follows the same impartial practice. In a country of such ancient civilisation one would have expected that what has taken

* "Religion in China," by Joseph Edkins, D.D.

place in other countries during the last two thousand years would have happened to the religions of China—that they would have undergone some process of fusion, and would have been run into the mould of some general type, however loose and incoherent. Of the great historical religions that have arisen in the world, each has annexed several countries; very rarely, if ever, do we find two of them established on equal terms in the same country. It is only in China that we find two mighty religious potentates, such as Confucius and Buddha, reigning with co-ordinate authority over one nation, and their ritual mingled with the adoration of the miscellaneous primitive divinities, who have elsewhere been usually extirpated, subdued, or refined and educated up to the level of the higher and paramount religious conceptions. For, although the Chinese religions seem to have modified each other externally, and to have interchanged some colouring ideas, no kind of amalgamation into one spiritual kingdom appears to have ensued; it is at most a federation of independent faiths united under the secular empire. Whereas in other countries the chief religion is one, but the interpretations of it are many, so that the same faith is a moral system, a mysterious revelation, or a simple form of propitiating the supernatural, in China a man may go to different religions, according to his needs or feelings, for specialities of various sides or phases of belief. Confucianism gives the high intellectual morality, fortified by retrospective adoration of the great and wise teachers of mankind, and based on family affections and duties, but offering no promises to be fulfilled after death, except the hope of posthumous memorial veneration. Buddhism gives metaphysical religion of infinite depth, with its moral precepts enforced by the doctrine of reward or punishment, according to merits or demerits, acting upon the immaterial soul in its passage through numberless stages of existence. It contributes imposing ceremonial observances, the institution of monasticism, and a grand array of images and personified attributes for worship by simple folk who have immediate material needs or grievances. Buddha himself, having passed beyond the circle of sensation, is inaccessible to prayer, yet out of pity for men he has left within the universe certain disciples who, albeit qualified for Nirvana, have consented to delay for a time their vanishing into nothingness, in order that they may still advise and aid struggling humanity. Both Confucius and Buddha seem rather to have despised than denied the ordinary popular deities, and to have refrained, out of pity for weaker brethren, from open iconoclasm. Taouism has rewarded both these great teachers by apotheosis into a pantheon, which appears to be filled by every imaginable device, by personifications of everything that profits or plagues humanity, of natural phenomena, of human inventions, of war, literature, and commerce, and by the deification of dead heroes and sages, of eminent persons at large, and of every object or recollection that touches men's emotions or passes their understanding. It is worth notice that the three persons who founded these three separate and widely divergent religions appear all to have lived about the same time, in or near the sixth century B.C. And the impartial veneration accorded to them by the Chinese is shown by their being worshipped together, as the Trinity of the Sages.

Let us for a moment see by what means the Chinese Government identifies these religions with the State's administration and with the reigning dynasty. If the Government is of any one particular religion more than another, it is, we are told, Confucianist; since the literary and intellectual sympathies of the official classes are preferentially with a system of moral philosophy and practical wisdom. Nevertheless, the public worship of Taouist spirits is elaborate and carefully regulated. There are three regular State services during the year, in the spring and at the solstices, while special functions take place upon any great public event, the accession of a new emperor, and victory, or a calamitous visitation. All this is analogous to the religious customs of other countries, with the difference that in China the national prayers and sacrifices are offered up, not by chief priests or ecclesiastics, but by the emperor himself, who also performs by deputy, through his civil subordinates, similar offices throughout the kingdom. The powers of the air, the great spirits of earth and heaven, are invoked by the State's ruler to administer the elementary forces for the general benefit of the country, precisely as the meanest of his subjects implores some obscure deity to bless or save him individually. The emperor's style of address to the spirits of Earth and Heaven is lofty. To these two spirits alone he styles himself "subject"; and in making sacrifices to the Earth he offers the following prayer: "I, your subject, son of Heaven by imperial succession, dare to announce to the imperial Spirit of the Earth that the time of the summer solstice has arrived, that all things living enjoy the blessing of sustenance, and depend upon it for your efficient aid. You are ranked with imperial Heaven in the sacrifices now presented." Not less important than the oblation to spirits is the worship of ancestors (prescribed by the injunction of Confucius, but probably an immemorial usage) which the emperor celebrates with due solemnity, setting forth an example of filial piety, and at the same time claiming for the dynasty all the reverence due to the hereditary father of his people. Three of the greatest of preceding emperors are included, as a special distinction, in the sacrifices to earth and heaven; the rest are annually adored in the imperial Temple of Ancestors. "I dare (the emperor is made to say, after reciting his pure descent) to announce to my ancestors that I have with care, in this first month of spring, provided sacrificial animals as a testimony of unforgetting thoughtfulness;" and the prayer contains the titles of all the deceased sovereigns addressed. The tablets of all the deceased emperors and empresses are set out in pairs, hymns are sung, and viands and rich garments are offered. There are also minor rituals for the imperial worship of the gods of land and grain, with whom are included, as honoured guests, the deifications of two statesmen celebrated in past times for the promotion of Chinese agriculture. It is manifest that these stately official liturgies, giving elevated expression to popular superstitions, and presenting the sovereign as high steward of the mysteries, must exercise great influence over the devout multitude, and must give the State large control over the religions themselves. But here again the peculiarity is that we see the primitive ideas preserved, exalted, and utilised by a cultivated and enlightened Government; not a barbarous or backward Oriental State, but one that makes treaties with Europe, sends out ambassadors, and conducts its affairs upon equal terms with all civilised nations, according to a very distinct and serious policy of its own.

If we desire to understand how, and to what extent, the Chinese Government uses its religious position and influence, and brings what may be called its spiritual supremacy to bear upon regular administration, we cannot have better evidence than is contained in the *Peking Gazette*, which has for some years been officially translated into English. This *Gazette* is, to quote from a preface to the volume for 1874, "the daily record of Imperial decrees and rescripts, and of reports or memorials to the throne, together with a brief notice of Imperial and official movements, to which the name of *Peking Gazette* is given by Europeans"; it has an official status, and is circulated to all provincial administrations. If such an institution as a Gazette were found in any other Asiatic country one could hardly be wrong in taking it to be a very recent importation from Europe; but the Chinese, we are told, were publishing their *Gazette* many centuries ago. It is said to have been first issued in the year 911 of the Christian era, and has been regularly published since 1351 A.D., and is at the present time edited by a committee of six members of the Academy of Han Lin. Not only is it by far the oldest newspaper in the world, but it also is infinitely more instructive and interesting than all other existing official *Gazettes* taken together. To the student of Oriental statecraft in particular the yellow volumes in which these *Gazettes*, translated into English, are bound up and issued annually, should be of remarkable value. For here, in the formal record of all the important ordinances, ceremonies, proceedings, judgments, opinions, and transactions of the Chinese Government, we can see partially unfolded the working constitution of the greatest native Asiatic empire and the oldest empire in the world; we can follow the movement of the administrative wheels, and obtain a glimpse of the system upon which the machinery is constructed. It becomes thus possible to form some trustworthy conception of the principles that underlie this vast organisation—unquestioned authority; lofty ostentation of public morality; the affectation of profound reverence for churches, rituals, and all things pertaining to divinity; deep respect for tradition and ancestral usage coupled with steady encouragement of classic learning; entire religious toleration conjoined with the peremptory assertion of civil supremacy; provincial home rule controlled, at least in form, by a despotic central executive; in short, the continuous experience of many ages applied to the management by a foreign dynasty of miscellaneous tribes and races, and an immense mixed population. We are shown, of course, only the external aspect of things; we probably see no more than an astute and carefully calculating Government thinks expedient to disclose. And we may assume that nowhere are the *arcana imperii* more strictly withheld, so that the reality may be safely guessed to be very different from the outward published aspect of affairs. Nevertheless, in this ample chronicle of current events and transactions, in the notifications and orders, in their style and their substance, we can recognise a Leviathan government in full play and power, dealing in a masterful and apparently successful fashion with at least one problem that has long troubled the world, and still occasionally perplexes even European statesmen.

The *Peking Gazette* announces all acts of State, regulations, decrees, orders on important cases, and ceremonial proceedings of the imperial Government; and it is certainly unique among *Moniteurs* and official publications of that kind in its incessant and impressive illustration of the relations of the Chinese State with the established religions. The grand functions of imperial worship are of course all formally ordained and reported for general information by edicts, and by orders of the Board of Sacrifices; and the *Gazette* contains many orders allotting to the princes and other high officials the different temples at which they are to do duty. But the strange and interesting phenomenon is to find, in such a modern-sounding publication as a Government *Gazette* and "Court Circular" the deities figuring, not occasionally but very frequently, in every department of official business, and treated much as if they were highly respectable functionaries of a superior order, promoted to some kind of upper house, whose abilities and influence were nevertheless still at the service of the State. Those who hold the first rank, with very extensive departments specially connected with the general administration, are recognised as State gods—such gods as those of war, literature, or instruction having pre-eminent position. There is also, it is understood, a distinction between the gods who are occupied with the material or physical concerns of the country, and those who preside over intellectual and moral needs. But beside and below these chief office-bearing deities there are evidently very numerous gods of the counties and boroughs, to whom the imperial edicts secure regular and proper worship, whereby their influence is enlisted upon the side of Government; while the provincial officers are expected regularly to visit all those registered as State gods, much after the fashion in which European prefects are supposed to pay attention to persons of local influence. All these deities seem to be rewarded, decorated, promoted, or publicly thanked by the supreme Government according to their works, with due gravity and impartiality. The God of War, whose department may have increased in importance in these days of great armaments, was judiciously raised, by a decree of the last Emperor but one, to the same rank with Confucius, who had before occupied the first place in the State Pantheon. Constant reference is made in the *Gazettes* to the performances of the minor deities, and they seem to be all co-operating with the prefects or the magistracy in grappling with administrative difficulties, insomuch that local government appears to consist of a coalition between local deities and provincial officers, who divide the responsibility, and share praise or blame. Whatever may be the position of the more privileged and aristocratic class of governing divinities, the minor Chinese deity is not allowed to sit with his hands folded, like Buddha, or to indulge, like the gods of later Hinduism, in grotesque amusements or disreputable caprices, or to decline responsibility for storms and earthquakes, on the plea that such casualties are part of some plan beyond man's present understanding, which will all come right in the end. On the contrary, the condition on which the Chinese Government patronises the Pantheon is evidently that it shall make for morality, support the cause of order, and assist, promptly and efficaciously, in preventing or combating such calamities as floods, famine, or pestilence. And since in China the State deities, at any rate those who represent outlying places and provinces, are not sent to the Pantheon by popular election, as elsewhere throughout Asia, but are appointed by the Government, it is obvious that they must be in some degree under ministerial influence. A remarkable personage, whether he be eminent for bravery, virtue, public charity, or any other notable characteristic, may be honoured after death by deification at the hands of the Imperial Court; whereby the State rewards a distinguished public servant or private benefactor, and at the same time retains his interest and goodwill in "another place," and in a higher and broader sphere of usefulness.

To begin with the ordinary and numerous decrees acknowledging the good services of deities. "The Governor-General of the Yellow River," says the *Gazette* of November, 1878, "requests that a tablet may be put up in honour of the river god. He states that during the transmission of relief rice to Honan, whenever difficulties were encountered through shallows, wind, or rain, the river god interposed in the most unmistakable manner, so that the transport of grain went on without hindrance. Order: Let the proper office prepare a tablet for the temple of the river god."

"A memorial board is granted," says the *Gazette* of April, 1880, "to two temples in honour of the god of locusts. On the last appearance of locusts in that province last summer, prayers were offered to this deity with marked success."

February, 1880. A decree ordering the Imperial College of Inscriptions to prepare a tablet to be reverently suspended in the temple of the Sea Dragon at Hoyang which has manifested its divine interposition in a marked manner in response to prayers for rain. In another *Gazette* the Director-General of Grain Transports prays that a distinction be granted to the god of winds, who protected the dykes of the Grand Canal; whereupon the Board of Rites is called upon for a report. Also the river god is recommended for protecting a fleet carrying tribute rice; and the god of water gets a new temple by special rescript. In fact, decrees of this kind, which merely convey public recognition of services rendered by the State gods, appear in almost every issue of the *Gazette*.

The following decrees refer to the process of qualification for divine rank:—

"The Governor of Anwhei forwards (November, 1878) a petition from the gentry of Ying Chow, praying that sacrifices may be offered to the late Famine Commissioner in Honan, in the temple already erected to the memory of his father. The father had been Superintendent of the Grain Transport, and had greatly distinguished himself in operations against some rebels. The son had also done excellent service, and the local gentry had heard of his death with great grief. They earnestly pray that sacrifices may be offered to him as well as to his father. Granted."

"A decree issued (May, 1878) sanctioning the recommendation that a temple to Fuh Tsung, a statesman of the Ming dynasty, may be placed on the list of those at which the officials are to offer periodical libations. The spirit of the deceased statesman has manifested itself effectively on several occasions, when rebels have threatened the district town, and has more than once interposed when prayers have been offered for rain."

The *Gazette* of June, 1880, expresses the Imperial regrets at the death of the Commander-in-Chief in Chihli, and gives him an obituary notice:—

"He was indeed a brave, loyal, and distinguished officer. During the time he served as Commander-in-Chief he displayed a high capacity for military re-organisation. We have heard the news of his death with profound commiseration; and we command that the posthumous honours assigned by law to a Commander-in-Chief be bestowed on him; that a posthumous title be given him, and that the history of his career be recorded in the State Historiographer's office. We sanction the erection of temples in his honour, at his home in Hunan, and at the scenes of his exploits."

"October 27th. A decree sanctioning the erection of a special temple to a late Commandant of the Forces, who was killed at Tarbajatai."

These last-quoted decrees, selected out of many similar ones, throw much light upon the process of the evolution of deities under State supervision in China. We know that in other countries, notably in India, the army of deities is constantly recruited by the canonisation and apotheosis of great and notorious men; but in other parts of Asia this is usually done by the priests or the people. In China a paternal bureaucracy superintends and manages the distribution of posthumous honours, beginning with honours of much the same kind as those given in Europe to celebrities, and gradually rising through the scale of ancestral worship, sacrifices, temples, and celebration by the public liturgies, to the full honours of recognised and successful divinity. It is easy to perceive how the formal bestowal of posthumous honours, in their first stage not unlike our State funerals and monuments, with memorial tablets, mausolea, and titular distinctions of a sacred character, must attract the religious feelings of the multitude, and stimulate the world-wide propensity towards adoration of the dead. The Government has therefore no difficulty in promoting the spirits of deceased notables to the superior grades of divinity, whenever this may seem expedient; and has only to anticipate and direct public opinion by a judicious selection of qualified personages. In this way the emperor, himself a sacred and semi-divine personage, seems to have gradually acquired something like a monopoly of deification, which he uses as a constitutional prerogative, like the right of creating peers. And the special value in China of posthumous honours is, that they have a natural tendency to qualify the recipients for this higher promotion to the grade of divinity.

The system of posthumous distinctions is not confined to the recognition of eminent services rendered officially, or in a private capacity, to the public. The state in China occupies itself directly with morality as well as with religion; and any person whose conduct has been meritorious or exemplary may be reported, after death, to the proper board or college, which decrees appropriate marks of approbation. Cases of filial and conjugal devotion are constantly reported by the provincial authorities, also instances of devoted widowhood. There is one example of reward sanctioned to a young lady who died of grief at the death of her betrothed; and another *fiancée* who starved herself to death for the same reason gets posthumous approbation. In all these instances the virtuous deeds of the persons mentioned are solemnly rehearsed by the *Gazettes;* while, on the other hand, the neglect of filial duties is properly stigmatised. In April, 1878, the Censor reports an individual who, besides wearing a button to which he was not entitled, "continued to perform his official duties after his mother's death, and wore no mourning for her."

A distinguished spirit may often obtain further advancement by diligent wonder-working. A decree of 1878 deals with a petition that a girl who died many years earlier may now be formerly deified upon the ground that whenever rain has failed, prayers offered up at the shrine of the girl angel have usually been successful. Whereupon an official enquiry is made into the earthly history of this lady; and the report shows that "during her childhood she lived an exemplary life, was guiltless of a smile or any kind of levity, but on the contrary spent the livelong day in doing her duty," refused to marry, and addicted herself to religious exercises. On her death the people built her a temple, and found her very efficacious in seasons of drought. The memorial urges that she has now earned a fair claim to be included in the calendar, and to enjoy the spring and autumn sacrifices. And the Board of Ceremonies, after due deliberation, records this official status.

But the Government not only bestows on deceased persons its marks of posthumous approbation and rank in the State Heaven; it also decorates them with titles. The *Gazette* of May, 1878, contains:—

"A decree conferring a great title upon the Dragon Spirit of Han Tan Hien, in whose temple is the well in which the iron tablet is deposited. This spirit has from time to time manifested itself in answer to prayer, and has been repeatedly invested with titles of honour. In consequence of this year's drought . . . prayers were again offered up, and the provinces (mentioned) have been visited with sufficient rain. Our gratitude is indeed profound, and we ordain that the Dragon Spirit shall be invested with the additional title of 'the Dragon Spirit of the Sacred Well.'"

Another spirit had already obtained the title of "Moisture - diffusing, beneficial-aid-affording, universal-support-vouchsafing Prince," and receives additional titles in a *Gazette* of 1877. And a decree of an earlier date refers to a request submitted by a provincial governor, recommending that, in consequence of aid given in maintaining certain river embankments by the canonised spirit of a former Governor-General, he be included for worship in the temple of the Four Great Golden Dragon Princes, and that a title of honour be conferred by the Emperor upon this divinity. Apparently the Board of Ceremonies, carefully hoarding its resources for the encouragement of divinities, had admitted the Governor-General's spirit to the Dragon Temple, but had reserved the title "pending further manifestations of divine response." The spirit, thus put on his mettle, acquitted himself so well during the next flood time, that his case was again laid before the Emperor in a fresh report, which gave in detail repeated proofs of the spirit's interposition when the banks were in peril. The case is referred to the Board of Ceremonies "for consideration," December 7th, 1874.

It may be worth while to repeat that in all this system the remarkable feature is not that notoriety in life-time should lead to posthumous worship and divination, or that a deity should continue to increase in reputation in proportion as prayers to his temple are successful. The point is, that the Government should have thus successfully laid hands on, and systematised, the immense power which is given by the direction and control of that deep-rooted sentiment towards the dead which leads to their adoration, a power that has elsewhere almost invariably passed from the earliest mystery men to the superior priesthoods, and which the priesthood has usually been able to make its own. If, as Mr Edkins tells us, the common people believe that the Emperor has the power to appoint the souls of the dead to posts of authority in the invisible world, just as he does in the visible empire, it is manifest that such a prerogative confers illimitable range upon the imperial authority. Thus the system of posthumous honours and appointments not only harmonises with and satisfies the deepest feelings of the people, but it gives to the Government a hold upon them through their beliefs not altogether unlike the influence which the doctrine of purgatory may have given the Church in the darkest of the Middle Ages. Moreover, the system has this advantage over the European custom of giving peerages and distinctions during life, that it is more prudent and economical. In Europe we honour and reward the posterity of an eminent person; in China they not only honour the man himself after death, but it is well known that they also honour his ancestors, who require no hereditary pensions, and can never discredit their posterity. In December, 1878, we find a provincial governor proposing that, in recognition of the conspicuous charity during a famine displayed by Brigadier-General Chen Ling, he and his ancestors for two generations may have the first rank bestowed on them. Also that memorial arches may be put up to two old ladies, the mothers of high military officers, who have been generous in a similar way. "Granted by rescript. Let the Board take note."

We can understand how it may have been comparatively easy for the State to manipulate and utilise in this way the simple and common superstitions of popular Taouism, giving the humble deities the benefits of official patronage, and honouring the higher deities according to their rank and prestige in the country. Whether seriously or cynically, the Government evidently thinks fit to fall in with and humour the anthropomorphic fancies of its subjects; and the policy is probably a very good one for keeping the gods in hand, and for preventing their concentration into some too powerful a divinity by fostering diversities of worship. The system of civil administration in China is very broadly based upon the principle that the honours and emoluments of the governing body are open to all classes of the people according to merit; and the same principle of *la carrière ouverte aux talents* seems to be applied to the honours obtainable after death. To adapt and utilise for State purposes the worship of ancestors, and the deification of famous men which developed out of this commemoration of ancestral spirits, was no arduous task for a government of literati and philosophers, ruling over a people to whom the difference between life and death, between the phenomenal and the spiritual existence, is far less clear and striking than to modern minds, and is in fact merely shaded off as in the foreground and background of a picture.* But it might have been expected that Buddhism, one of the three organised religions of the world, with set doctrines and traditions, with its monastic orders and successive embodiments of spiritual chiefs, would have held even the Chinese Government at arm's length. Against the vagrant and inorganic natural religion the Buddhist Church stands out in strong relief as an organised sacerdotalism, with canonical scripture, monastic orders, an imposing ceremonial, and a good tradition; yet over this Church the State maintains outwardly a strict and imperious superintendence. Buddhism undoubtedly enjoys much independence in China; in Mongolia the Lamas have great political influence; in Tibet itself the Imperial Government allows the Grand Lama to do much as he likes, and the provincial administration is in his hands. It is well known that Tibet, the chief seat and sanctuary of northern Buddhism, is a province governed by the Lamas in political subordination to the Chinese Empire; and the reality of the home rule vested in their priests has been proved by the war which they recently began and waged against British India quite independently of the Pekin Foreign Office. There are many instances in the *Gazettes* of the sedulous care taken by the central Government at Pekin that its political residents at Lhassa shall pay due reverence to Lamaism—that is, to the priesthood representing the dogma of emanations from Buddha, which become incarnate by spiritual succession in the Dalai Lama and other chiefs of the Buddhist hierarchy.

* "The sleeping and the dead
Are but as pictures."—*Macbeth.*

Every succession to the chief offices in this hierarchy is in form simple, the transmigration of a soul; nevertheless every appointment of this nature requires confirmation by the Chinese sovereign. The Dalai Lama, who is co-regent of Tibet, is chosen, as is commonly known, upon each vacancy by the process of discovering the mortal body in whom the spirit of his immediate predecessor, when evicted by death from his former tenement, has taken up its abode. Two or three very young children are produced, whose birth had been accompanied by marvellous sights and sounds, and in whom have been observed signs of preternatural wisdom, and an air of strange unearthly dignity. The records of prodigies and miraculous indications are compared and duly verified by the imperial Commissioners; the divine intention is also ascertained by casting lots and finally a report is submitted not unlike the "Relatio" of miracles drawn up by the Roman theologians when a Papal Bull is to issue for the canonisation of a saint.

Then comes, in the *Gazette*, the order for installation.

> "Memorial from the Imperial Resident at Lhassa announces that a day has been fixed for the enthronement of the incarnation, and that the High Treasurer has respectfully solicited that the re-embodiment of the thirteenth generation of the Dalai Lama, having now attained the age of four years, and being possessed of extraordinary spirituality and intelligence, the spirits have now been reverently appealed to, and Buddha has been solemnly invoked by genuine and earnest divination. The result has shown that the only superlatively auspicious date is the 31st of July; and on this day it is proposed to go forth to meet the re-embodiment, and bring him to Mount Potala for enthronement."

A decree follows, sanctioning the enthronement and the presentation of the usual gifts; whereupon the Resident reports that the imperial gifts have been placed under a yellow canopy in a certain temple, "where they will be received by the Re-embodiment, kneeling on his knees, and prostrating himself with his face to the Palace in thanks for the Heavenly Bounty."

A *Gazette* of 1874 publishes a despatch from an Imperial Resident in Tibet, reporting his arrangements for proceeding in person, with guard of honour and escorts, to escort the primate of Mongolian Buddhism, who has recently succeeded to his office by embodiment, from Lhassa, where he had appeared in the flesh, to his post at Urga near the Russian frontier, a great distance. And it might well be supposed that an established and richly endowed hierarchy, under a sacred chief who has also large governing powers in his own province, would decline to submit its spiritual operations to the revision and censorship of the State. Yet we have seen that in the matter of the incarnations, the central mystery and essential dogma of northern Buddhism, which furnishes the process by which all successions to the chief spiritual offices are managed, the Government interferes authoritatively, calls for reports, and issues the most peremptory orders. The *Gazettes* of 1876 contain three decrees illustrating the attitude of the State towards the lords spiritual of Lamaism, who, it should be understood, are also very powerful officials. The published papers begin with abstracts of an official letter from the Resident, or political *chargé d'affaires* on the part of the empire at Lhassa, the capital of the province which enjoys, as has been said, home rule under the hierarchic administration of the Grand Lama. A report had been received by the Tibetan Council that the Dharma Raja, or chief of religious law, had reappeared by metempsychosis in a certain person at a place in Mongolia, where he had been discovered and identified in due form—this being the accepted method by which the priests make their selections for such offices, and maintain the spiritual succession by transmigration of souls. The Tibetan Council reports, after proper enquiry, that this new birth turns out to be the reappearance of a religious chief who had in a former life behaved very badly indeed, and had been degraded for scandalous misconduct. Nevertheless, the Council certifies that the present embodiment is perfectly authentic, and they earnestly implore the Emperor to sanction it, one of the reasons being that in his penultimate life—that is, in the existence preceding the life which he had led so badly—this very person had done good service to the State. They promise that he shall henceforward confine himself to religious practices, and shall not again meddle with worldly affairs.

For the State to deal with such metaphysical processes as these would seem to European administrators a somewhat formidable assumption of authority over things spiritual, involving delicate and somewhat mysterious problems of government. However, on the Tibetan petition there is only a brief order: "Let the Department consider and report to Us." The second decree sets out the report of the Mongolian superintendency, stating that the re-embodiment is perfectly authentic, but showing cause why, for this very reason, it should not be allowed; and repeating that the person who has ventured to come to life again is no other than one Awang, who was degraded and punished for a heinous offence in the year 1845, banished from Tibet, subjected to rigorous surveillance, and placed on the official list of those "from whom the privilege of successive births into the world is withdrawn for ever." His conduct, it appears, had been so intolerably disgraceful that it was ordered that "on his decease, whether this should occur at his place of banishment or at home, he should be for ever forbidden to reappear on earth in human form, as a warning to those who bring disgrace upon the Yellow Church"; and in 1854 he died while under surveillance. Lastly, we have the final orders on the case pronounced by Imperial rescript, upholding the previous sentence, and deciding authoritatively that the re-embodiment is not to be permitted. Obviously the Government has no notion of allowing an offender of this degree to elude surveillance by a temporary retirement into incorporeal existence, or to whitewash himself by the simple subterfuge of a fresh birth. The case seems to have been important, and the decision must have caused some excitement in Lhassa, for vague rumours of trouble caused by an unauthorised incarnation spread as far as India, through the Buddhist monasteries on the Indian slopes of the Himalayan range separating Tibet from Bengal. At a later date, however, the sentence of perpetual exclusion appears to have been commuted on political grounds, for a subsequent decree pronounces that

"We have now received a memorial from the Military Governor of Ili stating that the Tibetan Lamas, with the chiefs of the tribes (who are willing to provide 1000 horse for the public service), begged that we would allow Awang to become a Lama. We grant him permission to join the priesthood and return to Tibet, there to study the sacred writings, but the request that he shall be recognised as the embodiment of the Nomën Han is refused."

Ili is that province in the far north-west of Mongolia which the Russians for some time occupied, but afterwards restored to China, and this semi-condonation of the spirit's iniquities in a preceding existence is evidently given upon political considerations. The case affords some measure of the vast territorial range of these pretensions to spiritual autocracy, and of their use in strengthening the imperial influence among the distant border tribes. Not the faintest hesitation on the point of authority can be traced in these decrees: the temporal sovereign deals absolutely with the ghostly chiefs; the embodiments are treated formally as sacred mysteries, and practically as conventional fictions, that are useful under due control; while the publication of all these proceedings in the *Gazette* keeps this aspect of the relations between Church and State well before the people, by whom it is probably appreciated and in form, at least, accepted.

It seems, indeed, that prohibition to reappear is not an uncommon exercise of control by the Government over disorderly Lamas; for, in another case, where a spiritual dignitary had been dismissed, and transmigration interdicted, a lenient view is taken, and the sentence is rescinded on petition of appeal, after the appellant's death (be it noted), at Pekin. "We decree that, as is besought of us, search may be made to discover the child in whose body the soul of the deceased Hucheng has been reborn, and that he be allowed to resume the government of his proper Lamasery." All these proceedings afford evidence of the apparent rigour with which the imperial Government asserts its supremacy over all matters spiritual; and they are curious as illustrating the little deference paid to religious susceptibilities whenever the public service, or the police of the Empire, or morality generally, is concerned. The Chinese Government surrounds itself with fictions and formulas; it seems to encourage every possible development of superstition, and to let the people be priest-ridden and spirit-ridden to any extent, on the understanding that the State is always master, whether of priests, spirits, or deities. There is nothing unnatural in a despotic ruler wishing to hold this attitude, although it is very rare that he succeeds in doing so; nor is it strange that, as seems to be the case in China, the people, and even the priests, acquiesce thoroughly in the arrangement. All these things are to be explained by the peculiar religious atmosphere of Asia (as once of the whole primitive world), in which forms and fictions are real and yet unreal, familiar and yet mysterious, and where the gods are mixed up with actual everyday life, not separated off from the world of humanity by vast distances of space, or known through traditions of what happened long ago. Where infinite and various supernatural agencies are incessantly abroad upon earth, and at work, it becomes obvious to the practical sense of mankind that unless they submit to some kind of regulation, society can hardly go on; and thus the civil ruler, who is after all immediately responsible for keeping things in order, is allowed some reasonable and reverent latitude in dealing with the national divinities. Some compromise, or concordat, is almost always discovered, whereby a *modus vivendi* is arranged between the spiritual and temporal powers; although, as has been said already, in China it is very striking that the predominance should be so much on the temporal side. But in order to appreciate properly the patronising or (if necessary) unceremonious ways of the Chinese Government towards spiritual or divine manifestations, we have to recollect that a belief or doctrine such as that of transmigration does not usually harden into the consistency of a mysterious dogma, or become the exclusive property of theology until it has passed far beyond the range of everyday popular experience. So long as these ideas about the gods, or about the re-embodiment of souls, are being actually applied to account for, or to conceal, events and actions that go on all round us, they are subject to the wear and tear of practical life; and they can be, and are, constantly modified to suit varying circumstances and emergencies. While they are in this loose, flexible stage, a strong and shrewd Government can seize the occasion of shaping them to its own purposes. It is clear, indeed, that unless some such control were insisted upon, a Government would be exposed to all kinds of trickery and imposture, such as probably underlies the system of Lamaist embodiments; and could be met at every turn by pretensions to immunity from administrative discipline, based on claims to divine or sacred character. To deny such a character, or to uncover and prosecute the impostors, would shake the whole edifice, and might drag the civil power into controversy between the police and the priests as to the identity of a reappearance, wherein the police would lose all *locus standi*, being manifestly incompetent to distinguish between true or false divinity, while the position of the priest would be impregnable. So the Chinese prefer to act as if the spiritual or divine character of a *mauvais sujet* should make no difference to the authorities; and the people would probably think much less of a ruler who should take a religion of this kind too seriously, when they themselves are by no means blind to its practical working. Various reverential fictions are occasionally invented to save the reputation of deities or spiritual personages whenever their privileges are being pushed so far, that to yield implicit deference to supernatural manifestations would be clean against plain reason and common sense. Of course any considerable *coup d'état* against factious or obstructive divinities must be a stroke needing great resolution and an eye for the situation, but it can be done, as the Chinese example shows, by a consistently devout and religious Government, when necessary for the preservation of order and the proper conduct of public business.

To modern habits of thought, which conceive a great gulf set, or a blank wall standing, between life and death, between the body and the spirit, the human and the divine, this grotesque intermixture of religion with municipal government, of miracles with police regulations, must appear strange and bewildering. The epigram that was supposed to have been written up over the place in Paris where the convulsionist miracles were suppressed by royal ordinance—

> "De par le roi, défense à Dieu
> De faire miracle en ce lieu—"

reads in European history as a profane jest; but apparently, it might be accepted in earnest, as emanating from proper and uncontested authority, if it were issued on a similar occasion by the Board of Worship or of Ceremonies in China. The fact seems to be that the mass of the Chinese are still in that intellectual period when, in regard to the conditions of their existence, and to the nature of the agencies and influences which surround them, men's ideas are altogether hazy and indefinite. The Emperor lives far away at Pekin, shrouded in semi-divine mystery, making himself heard at intervals by his majestic ordinances, or seen occasionally at high altars in the performance of some stately ceremonial. Between him and his ministers on the one hand, and the gods of heaven and earth on the other hand, there can be to the multitude little or no difference of kind, and not much of degree. Such doctrines as those of transmigration and re-embodiment obviously tend to deepen the cloudy confusion which hangs over the frontier separating the phenomenal from the unseen world. That world is not a bourne whence no traveller returns, but only a stage in the circle of existence, a place where you change forms as costumes are changed behind scenes, and whence you may come forward again to play a different part in a different character or mode of being, or in a subsequent act of the same drama. And beneath all this stage play of the natural imagination there probably lies the Pantheistic feeling that perceives the substantial identity of divinity with every act and phase of nature with men and spirits indifferently. One can comprehend how a highly-organised State could take firm grasp of all these shifting and anarchic ideas, and retain command over them as a natural incident of supreme rulership, without giving offence to its subjects, indeed with their full approbation. It may be supposed that this position must add immensely to the moral authority of the reigning dynasty; and that, for example, the strange power of veto exercised over re-embodiments must be very useful in a country where ambitious and turbulent characters set up as revivals of precedent gods, or heroes, or prophets. In different forms, indeed, the practice is universal throughout Asia; in Mahomedan countries it constantly shows itself in the expectation of coming prophets or Imams; in India there are continually circulating papers which proclaim the advent of some miraculous personage, with a mission to revive some creed by forming a new and purified government. Nor indeed would any ordinary revolt or disturbance go far unless its leader assumed a religious character, mission, or motive. Even in British India a new embodiment can still give some little trouble, as we have seen not long ago from a newspaper account of an attack made by a new sect upon the Jugunnâth temple. In India the matter was simply one for the police, and the Courts will have kept carefully clear of any opinion as to the spiritual status or antecedents of the sect's leader. Whereas in China the authorities would probably have pronounced the embodiment not false or counterfeit, but simply contraband, and they would have ordered him out of the world back into antenatal gloom, as if he had been a convict returned from beyond seas without proper permission.

Whether the Chinese nation is naturally, or by reason of the teachings of Confucius and the higher Buddhism, more inclined to connect religion with morals than elsewhere in eastern Asia, or whether the Chinese Government, which has undoubtedly realised the enormous value of outward morality to an administration, has really succeeded by persistent supervision in maintaining in all external worships a general show of morality and propriety, it is hardly safe to conjecture. But all observers appear to agree that in China the public practices and the acknowledged principles of religion are decent and ethically tolerable, which is more than can be said for all rites and doctrines in adjacent countries. And it is not difficult to see how the Buddhist dogma of promotion by merit through various stages of existence must have worked in with the system of open competition for official employ, which in China binds up all classes of the people so closely with the State's administration. So also the systems of re-embodiment and deification serve to keep up the prestige and dignity of the Great Pure dynasty, for the Emperors of previous dynasties are not only worshipped as gods, but they may reappear and reign again, occasionally, in the person of later sovereigns, thus attesting the divine right and the true succession of the present family. On the other hand, all these devices for identifying the Government with the prevailing religion have one weak side: a religion may fall, and by its fall may drag down the dynasty. How dangerous to the empire may be a religious uprising founded on a principle that escapes from or rejects the traditional State control, was proved some forty years ago by the Taiping insurrection, which is stated by all accounts to have derived its religious character and fervour from the misunderstood teachings of Christian missionaries. The enthusiasm of the new sect at once took a political form, and the leader credited himself with a divine mission to seize temporal dominion, according to the invariable law of such movements in Asia, whereby the conqueror always claims religious authority, and the religious enthusiast declares himself ordained for political conquest. The whole atmosphere became rapidly charged with fanatic energy of a type more characteristic of western than of eastern Asia. Tai Ping, the leader, denounced idolatry, condemned the Taouist and Buddhist superstition, and proclaimed fire and sword not only against the creeds, but against the dynasties that encouraged them. Probably nothing is more perilous to a Government that has incorporated the elder and milder religions into its system, and has soothed them and lulled them into tame and subordinate officialism, than an assault upon those very religions by a wild and ardent faith suddenly blazing up in the midst of them. The fabric of conservative government is threatened at its base; the more it has leant upon the old creeds the greater its risk of falling; and this is evidently the vulnerable point of the whole principle of using religion as bulwarks to the State. A great ruler, like Constantine, may have the address and foresight to save his government by going over to the winning side in time, but this has been rare in all ages and countries; while in Asia strong religious upheavals still shatter dynasties and subvert empires.

II.

Spiritual and temporal jurisdiction—In China both exercised by State—Examples from *Gazette*—Official superintendence of divine affairs—Contraband wonder-working—Fabrication of legends—Emperor's spiritual prerogative confers canonisation, sanctions apotheosis, controls both existences—Migration of souls—Trances, temporary disembodiment—Relations of State with polytheistic religion—Definition of Piety—Propitiation—General administration of popular worship—Concluding remarks.

In Europe the relations of a State to religion have been usually determined only after much conflict over the issues involved; the balance of power has taken many centuries to adjust. We have seen that in western Asia, the position was fixed by Islam, that is, by intolerant uniformity; and that in India political anarchy and a wondrous confusion in things divine were prevailing, when the English came in to solve the question by cutting off all connection with spiritualities. We have also shown that in China the civil power still holds a third and very different course; it not only tolerates all religions equally, but has placed them all under its own direct jurisdiction; the emperor is supreme Pontiff as well as supreme Governor. Here we may see verified the saying of Hobbes, that the religion of the Gentiles is a part of their polity, and nowhere have his principles found stronger illustration than in the practice of the Chinese Government. "Temporal and spiritual," said Hobbes, "are but two words brought into the world to make men see double and to mistake their lawful sovereign;" an error that would be very speedily corrected by the Board of Worship at Pekin. Taking for its constitutional theory the political philosophy of the Leviathan, the natural subordination, as by God's law, of the ghostly powers to the visible sovereignty, profound contempt for the popular superstitions disguised under an imposing display of external respect for all forms of religion, we can arrive at some conception of the attitude of the Chinese Government towards the complex problem of according an equally reverent recognition to a variety of discordant beliefs and worships.

It has been observed that the gradual differentiation between spiritual and temporal jurisdictions has usually been accompanied by a corresponding growth of the notions of a distinction between matters of religion and worldly affairs, and of the belief in a future existence entirely apart from this present life. But in polytheistic societies, no such clear divisions are found to prevail; the deities are present everywhere, interfere upon all important occasions of everyday life, are concerned in the success or failure of all human exertion, and the tour of man through phenomenal existence is personally conducted by divine agency. All notions regarding the origin and meaning of spiritual things are fluid and arbitrary; there are no fixed creeds or exclusive articles of belief which may be set against, and may claim to supersede, the commands of an earthly ruler. A politic Government may evidently find its advantage in upholding this state of things, which prevents the establishment of a jurisdiction over which the priests, rather than the prefects, can assert their claim; and, accordingly, the Chinese governing class, whose members are usually philosophic Confucians, appear much concerned to preserve undiminished the close connection between the nature, actions, and motives of gods and men which is a characteristic of early religion.

The official *Gazette* deals indifferently with science and theology, with public instruction and superstitious usages, with the latest European inventions and the most primitive forms of worship. Rules for competitive examinations and the conferment of educational degrees alternate in the regulations for sacrifice and orders for the deification of local worthies; high civil and military officers are promoted and decorated with equal gravity in life or after death; the establishment of free schools, the launching of steamships, irrigation works, post roads, legal decisions, the appointment of imperial concubines, appear in company with orders touching the propitiation of ghosts, the worship of spirits, the canonisation of notables, and the promotion of efficacious divinities. We find decrees awarding incense sticks to river gods, tablets and titles to wonder-working shrines, prescribing the ritual for allegorical and heroic deities, and for those who preside over State departments, natural forces, or human duties, over War, Wind, or Patriotism. The frequent references to ancestor worship and the offerings to the dead, show the universality of these aboriginal customs; the decrees regulating the incarnation of the Buddhist Lamas recognise officially the great mystery of the transmigration of souls. From the commixture of human with divine duties and actions, works and ways, reflected by these miscellaneous notifications, we may plainly discern the ways of a Government which draws no fine metaphysical distinctions, and which takes the important superintendence and authoritative direction of all beliefs and worships, the humblest as well as the highest, to be an important department of imperial administration. Nor need we go back to a classical dictionary, or collect from all parts of the outlying world, the grotesque fancies and practices of savage tribes, as evidence and examples of the connection between primitive and posterior forms of natural religion. We have here the chief stages and steps in religious evolution officially recorded and authenticated: we see the civil power dispassionately patronising the whole series of beliefs and institutions, on the sole condition of retaining supreme authority over all of them.

In making, from this point of view, the selection of a few out of many notifications in the *Gazettes* of later years, we may begin with a report that illustrates the widespread notion, which lies at the root of all ghost worship, that the spirits of those who, after death, are left without the proper obsequies must be laid at rest by propitiation. This belief may be supposed to be as old as the time when men first began to bury, burn, or otherwise dispose of their dead kinsfolk or companions; and in China, where the wandering ghosts and hungry demons are innumerable, it is probably one of the original ideas out of which has been developed the paramount importance attached to the rites of sepulture. The present example is furnished by an incident of the French war against China in 1884.

The Military High Commissioner at Canton writes, that in the recent campaign on the Tonquin frontier, a terrible pestilence broke out among the troops, who were obliged to live in holes dug in the ground in order to avoid the large shells that burst over them. From ten to twenty thousand men died, and were "laid in flocks like sheep" in great pits.

"The memorialist would venture to remark that the soldiers in question, who were doing their duty in the ranks of battle, and went forth on distant service with their lances on their shoulders, were the victims of a malignant poison, and died one after another, phantom fires playing over their lonely graves in a distant land into which their bones were thrown. The officers and men returning from Tonquin, as they passed through Kuangsi, were unanimous in asserting that the cries of the ghosts of their dead men could be heard in the still watches of a cloudy night. Although their case may differ from that of soldiers killed in battle, they nevertheless 'gave their lives for their country, and are therefore certain of a place in his Majesty's compassionate heart.'"

In these circumstances it is proposed to require the regimental commanding officers to send up a list of all those who perished in this way, so that they may share in the compassionate distinction already accorded to the soldiers who were killed in action. It is added that their omission has caused a feeling of disappointment in the army generally; and possibly the report may be substantially little more than a recommendation in favour of commemorating those who died on service with those who were killed in action; but the reason stated is the necessity of appeasing unhonoured ghosts. A subsequent *Gazette* announces that the Commander-in-Chief in Hunan has allotted the rent of lands towards defraying the cost of periodical rites performed to the memory of men who fought and died under his command. He himself has never allowed the anniversary to pass without sacrificing to the spirits of his departed companions-in-arms.

In this context may perhaps be placed, as relating to military hygiene, a decree exhibiting the imperial concern for the health as well as for the spirits of the Chinese army. The decree reviews and commends a report of measures taken to chastise certain rebels in Hainan, confers upon the general, as a special decoration, a white jade thumb-ring and a dagger hilted with jade, and concludes thus :—

"In view of the pestilential character of the country, as described by the Governor-General, in which operations are being carried on, her Majesty the Empress has been pleased to order that ten boxes of the pills known as *p'ing an tan*, or the pill of peace and tranquillity, which have been prepared for Imperial use, be bestowed on the officers and men of the force. These pills will be distributed by General Feng Tzutai, who will proclaim the Imperial will to the army under his command."

But since ten pill-boxes would scarcely go far against epidemic sickness among troops serving in unhealthy districts, it may be conjectured that her Majesty relied principally upon the honorific or possibly miraculous effects to be anticipated from this benevolent issue of medicine from her private dispensary.

If demon worship develops out of the fear of malignant ghosts, the following extract carries us a little further along the connecting line of superstitious usages. A memorial from the Governor of Formosa describes an outburst of pestilence in the island, where the savage tribes, who suffered severely from the disease, "endeavoured, according to their ordinary custom, to avert it by putting people to death." The victims were Chinese; their heads were exposed in front of the houses of the murderers; and these outrages became so frequent in parts of the island as to be suppressed only after a petty war. Here we have one of the earliest forms of sacrifice and expiation representing the belief, which seems to be indigenous among all primitive societies, that some virulent plague, like the small-pox in India, is the literal embodiment of the wrath of an offended demon, who goes about like a wild beast seeking what he may devour, and whose hunger must be satiated by victims. In a later stage of the same belief we have the formal human sacrifice, when the victim is offered up according to settled ritual or custom. But the simple random killing of the first comer seems in the beginning to be sufficient; for in certain parts of India a mysterious and apparently aimless murder may be occasionally explained as the fulfilment of a secret vow to one of the fiercer divinities. From the expiatory assassinations of the Formosa savages, and from the universal Chinese practice of leaving out food to appease a ghost's hunger, up to the annual offerings and libations made by the Chinese emperors, the sacrificial feasting and commemorative sharing of food, one may venture to trace, in long succession, the genealogy and gradual refinement of a natural religious idea. That the plain unvarnished worship of ghosts, demons, and animals may be traced upward to the higher forms of anthropomorphic religion is a well-known and well-evidenced theory, supported by the survival in the latest stages of some incongruous habit or function obviously belonging to the earlier conceptions. A curious article in the *Gazette* seems to indicate that in China, as elsewhere, a man may be duly divinised according to advanced spiritual notions, while he retains a denominative or symbolic name that probably points backward to some anterior adoration of him under an animal form.

The Governor-General at Foochow reports receipt of a

petition with regard to a temple erected to the honour of one Kô Chang Kêng, canonised as the "White Divine One," whose Taouist synonym is the White Jade Toad.

"This individual was born in the Sung dynasty, and was skilled in literature and the art of medicine. In 1881 he was found responsive to prayer, and on application to his Majesty he was invested by imperial decree with the title of Divine Aider. Last year a long drought prevailed in the province, but after gatherings for prayer had taken place at his temple a bountiful rain was vouchsafed. The petitioners crave from his Majesty the bestowal of a votive tablet upon this saint, together with an additional title, and the enrolment of his name on the list of worthies to whose manes sacrifice is offered."

The prayer is granted by decree; and thus, if any conjecture may be hazarded upon the indications afforded by such passages in the *Gazette*, the White Jade Toad of Taouism mounts higher in the order of divinities, becoming identified with a saint, assuming new titles and attributes that tend to disguise a humble or merely symbolic origin, and gradually dissolving connection with an obscure and somewhat ill-favoured animal. The toad is understood to owe his early honours to his reputed power of living for centuries, and to the miraculous qualities which he thereby acquires. The Frog god of China is known to be the symbolical impersonation, by an easy association of ideas, of Rain. It is clear that divine animals often become entangled in many accidental and arbitrary ways with legendary men; and since the fancies and queer incidents out of which fables shoot up among primitive folk are endless, any single explanation of animal worship must be utterly inadequate. One can only say that it is characteristic of the primitive races of man to feel an instinctive affinity with the creatures around them; their strong belief in the interchangeability of shape and habits between man and other animals may almost be thought to come from a kind of reminiscence of a common origin and cousinhood. Their minds accept no sheer division between monkeys and men, or between the manners of a bear and of some rude hunter clothed in a bearskin; nor, in fact, is there anything in the savage mode of living that denotes unquestionably the superiority of man over the higher beasts in strength or sagacity. And as the absence of a clear dividing line between men and gods favoured the myths of divine ancestry (which indeed mean in China only that the ancestor has been duly divinised), so this sense of kinship with other creatures, of being a part of all that one beholds, has probably engendered most of the vague traditions of animal descent. Any accident or apparition would convert this floating impression into the realisation of the presence of a familiar spirit in some animals; while the very common belief that the souls of living as well as dead persons transfer themselves frequently into animal bodies, may account for many of the complex worships and some of the mythical descents. But in China the various shapes and significations of popular religion appear to be singularly complicated and interfused. The intelligent Chinese layman is understood to define his ordinary attitude towards the religions of his country by explaining that, not being a priest, he belongs personally to none of them, so that he may consult impartially any saint or god, shrine or temple, whose response may be expected to remedy his grievance or fulfil his desire. Nor do the divine persons or emblems remain attached to a single liturgy; they are occasionally found crossing over into another rite, when they take higher or lower attributes and metamorphoses according to the particular cult or conception implied, representing different religious constituencies according to their positions. For idolatry is only the hieroglyphic writ large, in popular character; it came because unlettered man carves in sticks and stones his rude and simple imagination of a god; and this manner of expressing the notion by handiwork continues among even highly intellectual societies, until at last the idea becomes too subtle and sublime to be rendered by any medium except the written or spoken word.

It is obvious, however, that at a period when the productive forces of natural religion are in full vigour, a Government which tolerates and even encourages a fantastic polytheism—undertaking only to regulate its practical operation, to run the spiritual electricity along manageable wires—must maintain strict watch over the manufacture and circulation of marvels, and upon pretenders to supernatural energy. The *Gazette* furnishes frequent examples of very vigorous dealing with unauthorised religious movements, such as are apt to breed tumults and sedition in all times and countries, particularly where the deities take an active part in all human enterprise. A bureaucracy which identifies the supernatural element so closely with administration must be prepared to find supernaturalism meddling with politics, and cannot afford to overlook the efflorescence of disorderly enthusiasm. According to Hobbes, the "feare of power invisible, feigned by the mind or imagined from tales publiquely allowed, is Religion; not allowed, Superstition." And "he that presumes to break the Law upon his own or another's dream or pretended Vision, or upon other fancy of the power of Invisible Spirits than is permitted by the Commonwealth, leaveth the Law of Nature, which is a certain offence, and followeth the imagery of his own or another private man's brain." These somewhat cynical maxims of the Leviathan have assuredly been adopted as guiding principles by the philosophic rulers at Pekin, where short and summary ways are taken against the disturbers, upon any such pretext, of public order.

"A memorial from the Governor of Kneichow reports the capture in that province, of the chief of a seditious gang, and his execution. He was by trade a carpenter, who picked up in a ruined temple a mutilated book of incantations, and set up as a healer of diseases by the recitation of charms. He placed in his room a bowl of pure water, before which he engaged in worship, morning and evening, and further took to himself twelve disciples, who used to join him in daily worship. Having imbued these disciples with a number of theories, and told them false stories which they took to be true, he ordered them each to take to themselves twelve other disciples, that these might again augment their numbers, and raise a large following. Eventually it was decided to organise a rising, but before the movement could be well matured it came to the notice of the authorities"—

who executed the unfortunate carpenter on the spot, leaving it doubtful whether the story of the intended rising was not invented as an excuse for getting rid of an enthusiast.

But in 1887 a religious impostor succeeded in stirring up an actual outbreak, which was put down by troops after a fight in which the leader of the insurgents was taken and immediately decapitated. From the subsequent examination of some prisoners before the judicial commissioners it appeared

> "that Chao, the Ogre, as he styled himself, had persuaded his followers that he was gifted with supernatural powers, and was in affinity with the spirit of a certain mountain. He told them that he could make fighting men and horses out of paper, and that he possessed a charm which, if eaten, would enable the partaker to do without food."

The enquiry closed with the decapitation of the witnesses as soon as their statements had been recorded; and although the imperial decree commends highly the promptitude of the local authorities, yet to those versed in the methods of Oriental officialism this remarkable alacrity in taking off heads suggests an uneasy suspicion that some tangible grievance, or maladministration, lay at the bottom of the commotion.

> "The Governor-General of Chihli reports that, in obedience to imperial edict, he has succeeded in capturing certain members of a heterodox sect, who have been in the habit of worshipping an imaginary being, and unsettling the public mind by other superstitious observances. The ringleaders of the sect, when examined, stated that their society was divided into four branches, named after the four cardinal points, and met together four times a year for worship. Nothing beyond this could be established against the sect. . . . The two ringleaders have been sentenced, according to the law on subject, to be sent to Urumtsi as slaves to the soldiery, the rest to punishments less severe."

In this condition of the public mind, when the unbounded credulity of a vast population has to be humoured and yet to be controlled, a prudent Government will look closely to the promulgation of the laws against contraband wonder-working. The *Gazette* publishes a memorial from a member of the Court of Censors, referring to the laws enacted by the present imperial dynasty in severe prohibition of supernatural stories intended to delude the masses, and interdicting "the fabrication of heterodox and strange wonders by a vicious priesthood for the bewilderment of simple folk." His Majesty's attention is then drawn to a great assemblage of men and women that is held at a certain temple, where it is given out that the genii gather together, and where women sit at night in the corners of the building in order to see fairies. All this, the memorialist declares, is clean against faith and morals; and he asks "how, in the centre of enlightenment and civilisation, can such doings be tolerated?" Upon this a decree issues, condemning and prohibiting them.

"The fabrication of legends by the Buddhist and Taouist priesthood for the beguilement of the multitude, as well as the admission of women into the temple for the purpose of burning incense, are alike prohibited by law."

Returning to the orthodox views and practices, we may observe that the general aim and tendency of the *Gazette* notices is toward enlisting the divine influences on the side of public utility and public morals. If plagues and earthquakes occur, they are part of Heaven's design, to be interpreted by reference to human sins and shortcomings. The Censor of the Fakien circuit, reporting on the casualties caused by a recent earthquake, shapes his conclusions upon the system of a *savant* of the Han dynasty, who, in explaining the operations of the five elements, traced all physical calamities to the actions of men. The Censor adopts this theory as reasonable and probable seeing that ever since the Taiping rebellion frequent calamities have visited the empire, and, in spite of the constant imperial exhortations, few of his Majesty's servants honestly do their duty. Of late years there has been so much especial laxity in the province recently afflicted, that the reporter cannot avoid suggesting this remissness of the executive as a probable cause of the disaster. One might have supposed that of all sublunary ills an earthquake would be most difficult to bring home to the account of a government, unless it should be taken to indicate defective grasp of the situation, and a certain degree of ministerial vacillation. Yet the Chinese *Gazette* finds in this incident an excellent occasion for reading the people a moral lesson against disaffection; so that between the caprice of the gods, and the iniquities of men in this and previous existences, the share of responsibility for national misfortunes to be eventually accepted by the temporal ruler may be considerably reduced.

What, then, is the system upon which this immense structure of supreme authority in all departments has been built up and is maintained? In the Chinese Government the temporal and spiritual powers, instead of leaning toward different centres, meet and support each other like an arch, of which the emperor's civil and sacred prerogative is the keystone. The emperor is himself the Son of Heaven; he performs the highest sacrifices as Pontiff for the nation; and official hierarchy includes the chief Buddhist and Taouist ecclesiastics, graduated according to spiritual rank and attributes. The head of the Taouist priesthood is the Heavenly Master, in whose person the spirit of one of the earliest Tao mystics has its official residence. According to M. de Groot, this High Priest from time to time revises the list of urban and municipal deities, striking out those whom he thinks fit to remove, and usually filling up the vacancies by the promotion of mandarins recently deceased. But these changes are all submitted for precedent sanction to the Board of Worship.

"Tous les ans le pape communique au ministère la liste des mutations qu'il se propose de faire dans le personnel divin ; et ce n'est qu'après avoir été nanti de la confirmation ministérielle de ses décisions qu'il porte celles-ci à la connaissance des autorités provinciales."

These urban gods are, it should be explained neither more nor less than divinised men; they represent the post-mortem promotion of distinguished officials to the rank of tutelary deities; they are clothed in official dress, and are all in a manner subordinate to the spiritual Lord Mayor at Pekin. They are consulted by the local judges, who pass the night in their temple for meditation over a peculiarly difficult case; and the importance of these functionaries is in no wise diminished by their death, for the urban god acts as agent, or *chargé d'affaires,* within his municipality for the God of Hell, to whom all misdeeds are by him regularly reported. It is also his duty to arrest and despatch guilty souls to their appointed place of punishment below. A similar organisation presides over the village community, where one of the more venerated elders is first revered as an ancestor, and imperceptibly takes rank on the spiritual Board of Guardians. And just as these powerful local divinities virtually hold office at the State's pleasure, so also the Lamaist representatives of Buddhism depend for recognition of their successive embodiments upon the imperial mandate, or *congé d'élire.*

We can now understand how this unexampled position of the imperial Government enables it to exercise such formal and deliberate control, through the Board of Censors, over disorderly spiritualism, and all undesirable manifestations of superstitious reverence for the dead. A decree, passed upon a protest by the Censors against certain sacrificial honours that had been unduly paid to a deceased magistrate, points out that these honours necessarily imply official recognition of public merit, and directs that no application for them be transmitted until the claims of the dead man shall have been carefully verified. And another decree publishes a long report in which the Board of Ceremonies make their recommendations as to the limitations to be placed upon the canonisation of deceased officials. They find, after consulting the dynastic institutions, that the erection of special temples in honour of defunct worthies is the peculiar prerogative of the throne, and that the privilege of doing worship to provincial officers within their own (late) jurisdiction was extended to the provinces by a recent order in council, having formerly been confined to the metropolis. Various suggestions follow regarding the class and kind of distinction to be conferred in ordinary cases, with special rules as to persons killed in battle, or in resisting seditious revolts; so that one almost begins to doubt whether, after all, the Chinese system of posthumous honours differs greatly, except in outward form and treatment, from the pantheons, mausolea, epitaphs, and statuary memorials so common in Europe. But in the

Western world these things have now become purely commemorative; nor—

> "Can honour's voice provoke the silent dust
> Or flattery soothe the dull cold ear of death;"

whereas, in China, the images, the tablets, the annual offerings of flowers, the *Gazette* notifications, are actually intended, according to their popular meaning, for the gratification of illustrious spirits, and to conciliate them by compliments. But as worship and wonder-working react upon and stimulate each other, the promotion of a notable spirit to be a demi-god, and thence to the full rank of a divinity in charge of some great human interest, is found to be a simple matter of notoriety, popular credit, and court favour.

The meritorious official appears, indeed, in the *Gazette* nearly as often after death as before, with little change of duty or even of character; since the fact of titles and decorations being still showered upon him indicates that even by putting off this mortal body one does not always become perfectly incorruptible. The special commissioner for the survey of the Yellow River writes that "the deceased high officers who have been canonised as saints of the river have appeared in different shapes on the water's surface at times of imminent danger from its rise." While one particular breach was under repair, a deceased worthy, named Pai Ma Chiang, was constantly present; and at a critical moment, when the embankment was giving way, he calmed down the flood by a most timely apparition, whereby he has justly merited an additional title, "in recognition of his services to mankind." Another memorial claims honorary titles for a spirit who guarded the fields from a swarm of locusts; while a famous virgin, who served in the army, like Joan of Arc, and died in great honour, is reported for decoration, on the ground of having twice (since her death), saved a fort that was besieged by rebels. There is also a decree conferring honours on the original discoverer of a salt spring, who had for centuries become the tutelary deities of the locality, and who are now officially recognised. And we have numerous edicts prescribing ritual, and insisting on the decorous and exact performance of the periodical sacrifices.

> "En Chine, donc, un dieu est l'âme d'un mort, qui au lieu de ne recevoir les hommages que des descendants du défunt, reçoit des honneurs et des offrandes de la nation entiere ou d'une partie considérable de la nation, avec la sanction du grand prêtre de l'empire." *

This is no place for the theory adopted by Euhemerus, which was also positively affirmed by the Christian apologists who stood face to face with heathendom, that all the gods of polytheism were divinised men. The sources of superstitious phantasy are innumerable, fortuitous, and in the highest degree variable; nevertheless the Euhemeristic hypothesis does seem to gain ground into the extension of accurate enquiry. In India it is largely supported by direct observation, while in China it is not only corroborated by ample evidence, but is officially attested. We find there the earliest and latest stages of deification joined in a connected series; we have at the bottom the universal worship of ghosts, partly ancestral

* De Groot, ii. 657.

and commemorative, and in part propitiatory, while at the top we have the full-blown adoration of some of the loftiest deities who preside over the operations of nature or the interests of man. No one contests the authentic descent, either of the ghost or of the god, from the common stock of humanity. The biographies of the ancient personages who have now become the God of War and the Goddess of the Seas, two deities of the first rank in the Chinese Pantheon, are said to be on record in the public archives; there appears to be no more doubt as to their human antecedents than as to the identity of the mandarin who died last year with the urban deity in whom his spirit now resides. The deities generally are no less historical than the saints of a European calendar, than St Denis, St Dunstan, or St Thomas of Canterbury; and their earthly origin seems in no way to affect their popular reputation.

But since in China the right of canonisation and the conferment of all celestial honours are retained by the State in its own hands, neither sanctity nor even deification appears to have acquired for its possessors any political independence. And the foregoing extracts from the *Gazette*, which might easily be multiplied, show the vigilant solicitude with which the imperial Government upholds its prerogative of supremacy and strict superintendence over polytheism in all its branches. This system stands out in strong contrast against the modern Occidental principle, which we have imported into India, of complete dissociation between the Government and the religion of its subjects. For a thorough-going philosophical exposition of the Chinese theory of government we must go back to the Leviathan, where the position is that all power rests ultimately in the sovereign, who decides in all disputes, and must be obeyed by his subjects in every conceivable case. "The points of doctrine concerning the kingdom of God have no great influence in the kingdom of Man, are not to be determined but by them that under God have the sovereign power." Where this is accepted universally, a State need not trouble itself to enforce religious uniformity, because no difference of opinion or multiplicity of worship under public sanction can put the country's peace into jeopardy, while in the multitude of divinities there is safety. And according to Chinese statecraft, the proper way of maintaining this supreme appellate power is not by ignoring impartially all creeds, but by impartially professing them all; whereby those difficulties are avoided which have been much felt among European governments in countries that still possess a single Established Church. Between the view that a government has no concern with any particular form of religion, and the Chinese principle, that a government should belong to all religions in order to rule them all, the two opposite poles of theory on the subject are well staked out; and both theories are the fruit of intellectual indifference. Whatever may be said against deliberate official encouragement of popular superstitions, it has been asserted by those who know the country's history that the religious policy of China has at least been successful in preventing religious wars, intolerant outbreaks, and any virulent conflict of sectarian animosities, so long as it has had to deal only with the tolerant natural religions. But wherever it has been confronted by an energetic proselytising Faith, like Christianity or Islam, this conciliatory policy has inevitably failed. The Christian missions have brought China into continual trouble with European Powers; while in south-western China the Panthay Mahomedans, and in the north-west the Turkestani tribes, have raised violent revolts that were only quelled by merciless severity.

There can be little doubt that this system of bringing both the living and the dead, men, ghosts, and gods, equally within the imperial prerogative must help to confirm and perpetuate that fusion and intermixture of human and divine affairs, the indistinctness of the dividing line between the two spheres of existence, to which reference has already been made. A recent English writer has ingeniously twisted certain Scriptural expressions and metaphors into a chain of evidence to support a hypothesis of natural law in the spiritual world, which would square very well, in many respects, with the popular Chinese notion of the subjection of spirits to human statute. For it is also a Chinese notion that the law of visible nature extends to the world of spirits, and if the imperial ordinances do not actually run in the realms below, they have, at any rate, to be obeyed by all who desire to revisit the upper regions. And one obvious consequence of being incessantly under such a dispensation, in such an environment, is, that many of the Chinese myths and fables bear an administrative character, and are founded on the fancy, serious or sarcastic, of a Plutonic bureaucracy and a well-organised official system in Hades. Some years ago Mr H. Giles brought out, under the title of "Strange Stories from a Chinese Studio," a translation of the most popular story-book in China. It opens with a tale headed "Examination for the Post of Guardian Angel," relating how a graduate having been mysteriously summoned before a board of examining deities, apparently presided over by the God of War, was appointed Guardian Angel in Hunan. As this was equivalent to promotion into the next world, because the qualification for angelship is Death, he pleaded hard for a respite, and was allowed to adjourn joining his post for nine years; whereupon he awoke as out of a trance, tarried nine years longer in life, and passed away quietly at the appointed time. There is also an odd tale of a man whose degree was gained for him by a ghost; and another of certain *literati* who were sent for by Yen Lo, the ruler of Hades, to compose an inscription for a tower that he had erected there, and who showed no alacrity in obeying this euphemistic summons to depart hence. From another story it appears that although devils are ordinarily commissioned by the Chinese Pluto to convey messages from below, yet since they are unable, like fish out of water, to endure beyond a short time the light and air of the earth's surface, the authorities of Hell and Purgatory are often obliged to press the souls of living men into temporary employ. It is also necessary to disembody a soul whenever some one is wanted to do an errand from earth to Hades, because the devils do not take orders from an earthly official; and while a diabolic messenger can only communicate with mortals by assuming some phenomenal human form, so the soul cannot make its journey to the shades below except by leaving its body behind in a cataleptic condition, awaiting return. We have thus a constant interchange of states through the facility of disembodiment, and the incessant reappearance of spirits and wandering ghosts in various shapes and *rôles*, making personal identity uncertain, mingling apparitions and *revenants* with the palpable human crowd, and familiarising the mind with the sense of frequent passage to and fro, as if the gates of Life and Death stood always open.*

Mr T'aing Ping, "who took the highest degree in the year 1661," had the misfortune to lose his soul, which escaped one day like smoke from a chimney, and was unable to find its way back to its mortal tenement. The lost spirit found a Buddhist priest sitting by the road-side, who recommended him, as a scholar, to apply to Confucius and the God of Literature, by whom the case seems to have been specially laid before Buddha himself, who at last gave him a guide to show him where his body still lay. The story is noticed here because it introduces the representatives of three religions as consulted in the matter, although the last and highest place is allotted to Sakya Muni, the Buddha. But perhaps none of these

* The obvious necessity that a spirit who appears must be embodied, seems to be the origin of that Docetism, or philosophy of illusive Appearance, which has played so large a part in the religious imagination of Eastern races, and still causes them great perplexity. It is often impossible to determine whether a familiar form may be a friend or kinsman, or a spectral deception cloaking a mere ghost or demon. This question may arise when some one re-appears after long absence and reported death, declaring that he has not died, and claiming marital or other rights. He may be a dangerous vampire or wandering spirit, who has assumed the dead man's body. Plutarch ("Roman Questions") enquires the reason for the custom of re-admitting such a person into the house, not by the door, but by a hole in the roof. And the difficulty becomes more complicated if his funeral rites had been performed on receiving false news of his death.

fables bear more instructively upon the point for which they are now quoted than the anecdote (in a note) of the Emperor T'ai Tung, whose soul visited the infernal regions, and promised to send Yen Lo (Pluto) a melon.

"When his Majesty recovered from the trance into which he had been plunged, he gave orders that his promise was to be fulfilled. Just then a man named Lin Chu'an observed a priest with a hairpin belonging to his wife, and, misconstruing the manner in which possession of it had been obtained, abused his wife so severely that she committed suicide. Lin Chu'an himself then determined to follow her example, and to convey the melon to Yen Lo, for which act he was subsequently deified."

Nor is this the only instance of deification for personal service to an emperor. It is related elsewhere that an emperor of the Ming dynasty, to whom shaving was most painful, was one day attended upon by a person who shaved him with such miraculous ease that a large reward was at once offered to the operator, who then revealed himself as an ancient sage canonised, and demanded admission to the higher order of State divinities. His claims to official apotheosis as the God of Letters were admitted, and the foregoing legend explains why he is also the patron saint of Chinese barbers.

Two distinct, yet closely allied, conceptions may be traced in these stories, which are mentioned here because they may be taken to represent the rudimentary forms of imaginative belief that expand later into the grand processes of deification registered in the *Gazette*. The first is, that a person who falls into a swoon, or deep sleep, has been possibly placed on some incorporeal duty, or is visiting that extra-mundane region which can only be reached by putting off this mortal vesture of humanity. It is the notion of the adventures of a soul in dreamland being real. The second conception carries us from the domain of Sleep to that of Death, his twin-brother and co-regent, from a temporary excursion to an absence that may be permanent, though return is possible if a new habitation can be found. And we may remember that death is to a race no more than sleep is to the individual; there are incessant interruptions of consciousness as the generations pass, but the body corporate survives and is strengthened, while the ideas, feelings, and habits are transmitted unbroken. According to this latter conception, messages may be sent to Hades by men who shall have been specially despatched there by death, or who shall have departed this life on some particular duty in that quarter. We all know that these are two very ancient, almost ubiquitous, ideas, that have ramified widely into various modes and expressions of primitive superstition, and have had a long development in the history of religions.

> "From this ignorance of how to distinguish Dreams and other strong fancies from Vision and Sense did arise the greatest part of the Religion of the Gentiles in times past."

The quotation is again from Hobbes, who says that in the conscript of primitive mankind, "the soule of man was of the same substance with that which appeareth in a dream to one that sleepeth, or in a looking-glasse to one that is awake." In another passage he places "Opinion of Ghosts" among the "foure things in which consisteth the natural seed of Religion," and has thus anticipated, in his Leviathan, some of the latest conclusions of modern anthropologic research. The notion that the soul leaves the body during a trance or lethargy lies, according to Mr Herbert Spencer, at the root of conceptions of a second life after death; a soul may go and return, until to the body it finally returns no more, but it nevertheless exists, and can be communicated with, in an invisible region beyond. To that region, whenever a message is to be sent, the second idea naturally follows among those with whom human life is of no more account than spilt water, of liberating some unlucky soul from its body, with orders to be carried into the next world. It is upon authentic record that human beings were formerly slain in China at the obsequies of great persons, though the practice, which was evidently the survival of earlier tribal customs, softened down into the milder form of voluntary self-sacrifice, usually by self-inhumation with the deceased. It then entered the symbolic and fictitious stage, when the custom of interring with a corpse images of wood or of straw became universal, until it now seems to have dwindled down into the burning of paper dolls at a funeral. And thus, from the bloody immolation of victims at the funeral of a savage warrior, up to the tranquil self-sacrifice of the Chinaman, who agrees in remorseful expiation to accommodate his sovereign by delivering a present in Hades, one may trace the upward modification in form and sentiment of this antique custom which, in the present writer's opinion, indicates one of the principal and earliest motives of human sacrifice. In a ruder society poor Lin Chu'an would have been violently despatched to the infernal gods, while, under the civilised

Chinese *régime*, it is at least assumed decorously that he happened to be going that way on his own affairs, and might do the Emperor's bidding without personal inconvenience. Among savages the "other self" is occupied, during a swoon, in some congenial manner—usually brutal or absurd; among the Chinese it is passing an examination, discharging municipal functions, or engaged in some other business that accords with the day-dreams of a highly-educated and much-governed people.

It is easy to perceive how all this vivid realisation of two existences, with similar environment and occupations, may fall in with and support the cardinal political theory of the subordination, for all administrative purposes, of things spiritual to the temporal authority. For if the two states of being so much resemble each other, if intercourse between the two worlds is not much rarer than between two strange countries, and if the spirits who haunt the visible world are merely disembodied men whose previous history is perfectly well known, and who are open, now as formerly, to official manipulation—this leaves little room for pretension on sacerdotal or supernatural grounds to independence of the sovereign power. Hades itself can be treated like Tibet, as an outlying province of the empire, under a mysterious kind of hieratic home rule; and, within the Emperor's terrestrial dominions at any rate, any tendency of spiritual persons, disembodied or divinised, to insubordination or local disaffection would be inconsistent with their accepted position under his government. As politicians who can command success do not always trouble themselves to deserve it, so a potentate who bestows distinctions upon divinities need not be at the pains of securing their approbation or mitigating their anger by any such self-humiliation as has been practised by priest-ridden kings. A simple tribal chief may prostrate himself before the god of his family or his mountain; but a mighty emperor, though he shows all decent reverence to established images and worships, has, in fact, more dignified ways of dealing with a great multitude of deities, among whom it is obviously necessary to uphold the authoritative principle that order is Heaven's first law. Here again, it may be said, we may follow a primitive idea through the process of gradual refinement; beginning with the grotesque supplications of a savage to wandering ghosts or capricious sprites, and rising gradually to the high regulative ceremonial of the Chinese government. We see the gods improve steadily in form and function; the rites are organised and subjected to proper control; in short, we see religion, politics, and society keeping step, and marching abreast, as they submit to discipline and go through their evolutions. The cardinal fact of the religious system, the line that strings together all these formal changes, is the apotheosis of man; "the great idol of the pagans is deified humanity."

The religious polity of the Chinese is thus a powerful pagan realisation of Hobbism; and though it seems to have been carried further in China than among the empires of antiquity, we may conjecture that the principle has prevailed more or less in all governments that have had to deal with polytheism, especially with the complex and commixture of gods, under an extensive territorial dominion. The State has always endeavoured to control and organise the religion of the people. Something of the kind may even be observed in the philosophic statesmanship of Plato, who, while insisting in the "Laius"* upon the moral and spiritual essence of religious service, lays stress also on the necessity of maintaining by law the prescribed ritual, of honouring the Olympian gods, the gods of the State, the gods below, and, next to the gods, the demons, spirits, heroes, and ancestral Manes. And although the strange doctrine of certain philosophers, "that the gods exist neither by nature, nor by art, but are such as the laws ordain," is condemned as inadequate and harmful, taken by itself, this is mainly because a wise legislator should use persuasion, as far as he can, to induce men to accept the established religion. So long, indeed, as the temporal power is more enlightened, and consequently higher in the moral scale, than the hierarchies, it must be the constant endeavour and aim of the rulers to regulate and confine, within rational limits, all their loose and disorderly spiritual manifestations. And thus, in China, we can still survey the spectacle of a great civilised government face to face, not only with an organised church claiming direct succession and inspiration from the founder, but also with religion in its inorganic state—in fact, with natural religion, as it grows up out of the free exuberance of man's fears and fancies. This is the more interesting and instructive because it reflects a survival from the time before creeds and churches began in Asia (and they have begun nowhere else), when all religions upon earth were in a similar condition. Since that time Islam has conquered western Asia, and in eastern Asia Buddhism has a vast

* The references to Plato are taken entirely from Jowett's translation, not from the original.

predominance; they represent the two opposite principles of war and peace, of action and meditation; while India lies interposed between these two first-class religious sovereignties, having expelled Buddha and only partially submitted to Mahomet.

In western Europe, where we have been for centuries accustomed to treat religion metaphysically, it may appear surprising that even towards polytheism a Government should be able to assume so dictatorial and cynical an attitude. But we have to remember, in the first place, that polytheism has, in fact, never been treated seriously by statesmen or philosophers, except possibly by the English in India; and secondly, that this practical way of handling it is warranted, and partly explained, by a right appreciation of the ideas which, from the times of classic paganism, underlie the popular worship. It is not so much a moral or metaphysical system, as a method of propitiation. Look at the dialogue in Plato's "Euthyphro," where Socrates tries to extract from a learned Athenian divine and soothsayer some definition of "this attention to the gods which is called piety."

Euthyphro. "Let me simply say that piety or holiness is learning how to please the gods in word or deed, by prayers and sacrifices."

Socrates. "Do you mean that piety is a sort of science of praying and sacrificing?"

Euthyphro. "Yes, I do."

Socrates. "And sacrificing is giving to the gods and piety is asking of the gods?"

Euthyphro. "Yes, Socrates."

Socrates. "Upon this view, then, piety is a science of asking and giving?"

Euthyphro. "You understand me capitally, Socrates."

. . . .

Socrates. "Then piety, Euthyphro, is an art which gods and men have of doing business with one another?"

Euthyphro. "That is an expression which you may use if you like."

Here we have the foundation of natural religion briefly and plainly defined; it is the aboriginal application of the principle of *Do ut des*, the simple feeling underlying the multiplicity of expression; and the most ingenious researches into the evolution of primitive ideas will hardly take us beyond or behind it. The difficulty which Socrates puts to his diviner, as to what benefit can possibly accrue to the gods from the service or gifts of man, seems intended to drive him into the dilemma of admitting either that the gods are merely magnified men with human tastes, or that prayer and sacrifice are wholly superficial customs, being unconnected with justice and holiness, which the true gods really love. But such a difficulty would give little trouble to the Pekin Board of Worship, which openly does business with the gods on behalf of the various departments of government for the judicious maintenance of useful popular illusions. In the *Pekin Gazette*, as in the Platonic dialogue, we find the ritual and worships of polytheism treated as the Art of dealing with the unintelligible influences and incalculable forces by which the unlearned multitude finds itself to be surrounded. So long as these invisible forces are believed to be more or less under the influence of the invisible beings who rise to distinction in the domain of ghosts and spirits, this art consists mainly of propitiation by prayers, gifts, and honours; and when wider experience, and more accurate observation of consequences, prove this method to be at least uncertain, religion tends naturally to withdraw within the sphere of metaphysics and morality. For morality, being a generalised experience of the right way of living, may, in this sense, be regarded as a wise and far-seeing appreciation of the conditions of the struggle for existence. To say, as is often said, that it is opposed to this struggle, or ignored in it, is an error; for the moralist utilises these forces reasonably instead of battling against them; they are made conducive to human welfare, like a river that is drawn off to turn a water-mill. In the same manner the Chinese government, conscious of its inability to dam up or disregard the floods of superstition which saturate the Chinese people, endeavours to treat this kind of religion as a natural phenomenon, like the rains or the shifting rivers, and makes the best of it by taking the matter under executive control, in order to direct the inundations into fixed channels.

There has of late been much speculation, in books and lectures, regarding the origin and evolution of natural religion; and the outlying corners of the earth have been searched for any myth, legend, custom, or fanciful delusion that may be supposed to throw light upon the connection between the earliest and later superstitions. If it were possible for any one to make a comparative study, within the countries themselves, of the popular religion now existing in India and China respectively, the results would be probably far more instructive to the scientific enquirer than collections of dubious folk-lore, or the idiotic stories told by Digger Indians and Esquimaux. Here, in eastern Asia, we may see two societies of first-class magnitude resting upon high antiquity and continuous traditions, in one of which natural religion has for centuries been under the moulding hands of a powerful priestly caste, by whom polytheism is fostered and humoured as the embroidered veil of certain profound inner truths and doctrines that lie behind it. In the other country the State, not the priesthood, has assumed the supreme direction of divine things, and the deep metaphysical background is necessarily wanting. In both countries the polytheism seems to have this common characteristic, that it has come down to the present day from time immemorial without essential change; that it has grown up, and still flourishes freely and naturally, as it was in the Juventus Mundi. The primordial ideas as to the nature of the gods, and their ways with men, survive side by side with the loftiest liturgies, with philosophy, with rationalism; the simplest rites are practised more or less by all classes, indiscriminately and good-humouredly; it is like a religious fair open to all who cater for the amusement, the astonishment, or the credulity of the crowd. To the Chinese man of letters, or the Hindu transcendentalist, as formerly to the cultivated Roman of the empire, the inconsistency and multiplicity of beliefs and worships present no administrative or intellectual difficulty. One explanation is found in the confluence of races and deities under a single great territorial dominion; for trade and conquest, military or commercial expeditions, the opening out of new communications, the annexing of new provinces, all tend to cross, complicate, and multiply the myths and forms of worship, so long as the world practises free trade in religious things. We all know how the influx of strange gods and foreign rites produced the confused polytheism of the Roman empire, where, however, it fell so far below the intellectual level of civil society that it was easily swept away by Christianity. Then came a reverse process, when religion attained its highest elevation, and civil society relapsed into barbarism. From the period when Christianity and Islam made a partition of the provinces of the dismembered Roman empire, these two great militant and missionary faiths have for centuries been treating all other worships in a manner unknown, it may be said, to the præ-Christian world—stamping out obscure rites and indigenous deities, extirpating them utterly by fire and sword. Remembering that the destruction of paganism, and the tremendous conflicts of rival religions, are facts of capital importance in the history of the nations from Ireland to the Indus, we may well regard with attentive curiosity the spiritual condition of a country like China, in which no such events seem ever to have happened on any great scale before the Taiping rebellion of our own era. And now that England has added to her Indian sovereignty a great Indo-Chinese kingdom, peopled by Buddhists, it may be worth her while, for reasons which concern our administrators, to remember that the modern State policy of leaving a religion to shift for itself has not been universally applicable or appropriate.

CHAPTER III.

"THE GOLDEN BOUGH: A STUDY IN COMPARATIVE RELIGION" *

Story of the Arician priest—Its origin and meaning—System of interpretation—Kings as priests—Kings deified—Incarnation of Tree Spirits—Perils of the Soul—Taboo—Examples and conjectures—The Flamen Dialis—Criticism of the theory proposed—King-killing, god-killing—Allegories from decay and revival of vegetation—Doubtful generalisations—Other possible interpretations—St Denis and Dionysus—Harvest customs, rural games, and primitive ritual—Animal worship—Connection of these things—The misletoe—Totemism—Concluding remarks.

THE origin of human ideas and institutions, their causes and their development, their genealogy and interconnexion, have latterly been explored and examined to a degree that has profoundly influenced contemporary habits of thought. In every branch of investigation our opinions have been greatly affected by the enormous expansion of the field of enquiry and collection; by the gradual unfolding of the scattered, torn, and disfigured pages of the prehistoric record; and by observation of the various phases of primitive society still surviving in those corners of the earth that have not yet been swept out by the besom of civilisation. Out of this vast accumulation of

---

*** J. G. Frazer, M.A., "The Golden Bough: A Study in Comparative Religion."**

material, out of this opening of fresh sources of knowledge, has grown up the comparative method, the most important arm of precision that has yet been invented by the science of research. Men have discovered, as they suppose, that the ideas of the world can be treated like its flora, can be gathered together, classified, and used for philosophic demonstration of some comprehensive theory of their general characteristics and growth; can be traced down to the primordial root, and upwards to their highest form of expansion and refinement. And nowhere has the doctrine of evolutionary development produced a more remarkable change than in the point of view from which recent writers have approached the study of primitive ritual and beliefs.

Mr Frazer, in his book of "The Golden Bough," uses the comparative method as his instrument in a peculiarly abstruse and complicated operation. He undertakes to explain a very ancient custom, extinct many centuries ago, and known only through a few fragmentary descriptions and allusions preserved from classical antiquity, that have been here put together in order to give what is known of the legend and the rite. It is the story of the priest of Aricia, who dwelt by the Arician lake in a grove sacred to Diana Nemorensis, wherein was a tree of which no branch might be broken. According to the rule of this shrine, as it can be gathered from the passages to which the reader is referred, the priest held office until some runaway slave could first break a bough from the tree and then slay the priest in single combat. Not before he had broken the bough could he fight the duel; and not until he had killed the priest could he succeed to the office of *Rex Nemorensis*, which he held until a stronger than he should overcome him. "Tradition averred that the fateful branch was that 'Golden Bough' which, at the Sibyl's bidding, Æneas plucked before he essayed the perilous journey to the world of the dead;" and this accounts for the title given by Mr Frazer to his work, although the words subjoined, "A Study in Comparative Religion," give a better indication of its true aim and character.

What is the meaning, he asks, of this strange rule, which has no parallel in the records of ancient Greece or Rome? One might reply that upon such scanty and ill-verified data it would be impossible to build any hypothesis; or we might observe that any hypothesis could be made to accord with a vague and mysterious tradition. The rationalising Euhemeristic interpreter would probably conclude that the story contained a nucleus of real incident, magnified into a rite, and perpetuated by popular imagination. He would surmise that the priest for the time being may have been once, or more than once, murdered by runaway slaves who had established themselves in his place, and who might have succeeded in convincing the people that they acted by divine command, so that the ungodly custom hardened into an essential rite that would, nevertheless, be only acted upon occasionally. It is clear, at any rate, that the peculiarly savage nature of this rite can be accounted for by its foreign origin. The temple in the grove was dedicated to the Taurian Artemis, who had been a barbarous female divinity, worshipped with bloody rites and human sacrifice at Tauris, whence the Asiatic Greeks, identifying her with their own goddess, imported her into Europe. Strabo himself calls the custom barbarous and Scythian; and the shrine is thus very likely to have had an ill reputation. The priest might have been seen, according to Strabo, prowling round the grove with an air of wary suspicion and a drawn sword; but this kind of outward parade and dramatic representation of a traditional custom often survives as a fiction when the reality has long fallen into disuse. Under another process of interpretation, the whole story would dissolve into a solar or lunar myth, produced by a misunderstanding of the metaphors used by primitive men to describe the operations of Nature. Mr Frazer, whose reputation as a collector and analyst of folklore stands deservedly high, proposes to attain his solution of the problem by a much wider method of investigation. According to his view, the Arician rite belongs to, reflects, and illustrates certain primitive customs that have their place in all early societies; and these customs he traces back to their origin and motive in some very primary mental conceptions, some ultimate religious ideas, out of which many savage customs and barbarous institutions have been evolved, and which still survive among the rustic sports and ceremonies of European nations. So that the Arician legend chiefly serves, in this book, as a text for dissertations upon the folklore, the mythology, and the ritual of many lands and ages; upon their forms and significance, and particularly upon the connection, transmission, and modification of different species.

Mr Frazer's quest takes, indeed, so broad a range and

his excursions into remote times and countries lead him so far, that he is sometimes embarrassed by the necessity of keeping up communication with his starting-point, and of making all his lines of enquiry converge upon the central issue. He has gathered together and collated a vast quantity of myths, legends, rituals, worships, queer ceremonies, crazy superstitions, and all the grotesque fables and fancies weaved in the brains of barbarous folk; he has arranged and combined all this heterogeneous matter with great ingenuity; he has pressed it into recognisable shape and tolerable coherency; and with this conglomerate he has built up some very curious, interesting, and suggestive theories. If we are obliged to confess some doubt as to the solidity of some parts of his edifice, it is because we question whether any skill or industry can bind together or solidify such stuff as dreams are made of; or can fill up the gaps inevitably left in such a long-winding, many-sided, and intricate demonstration.

"Why had the priest to slay his predecessor?" and, secondly, why, before slaying him, had he to pluck the Golden Bough? Mr Frazer begins his answer to these questions with a section headed "Primitive Man and the Supernatural," which launches him at once into the open sea of speculation and research. In the first place, why was the priest called by Suetonius King of the Wood? One would not have thought this appellation very remarkable, seeing that kingly and priestly functions and titles were constantly combined in ancient days, that at Rome the priest who performed public sacrifices was called "*Rex Sacrorum*"; and that everywhere a chief usually had some sacerdotal character, while a priest often had temporal jurisdiction within his domain or sanctuary. This is, indeed, the upshot of the explanation reached after a long and somewhat circuitous, though picturesque, excursion through diverse regions of thought and realms of superstitious phantasy. We all know that the kings of old heathen times were commonly priests and often gods; in both capacities they were expected to control the wind and the rain, to bring pressure to bear upon the barometer, and to manage the seasons; they were, in short, made as indirectly responsible as any modern ministry for everything that happened to the community under their charge. All this is in familiar accordance with the reasoning of primitive societies, who seek only to find where power resides, and with whom a powerful chief's authority, visible or invisible, is just what he chooses to assert. The deification or pontificate of the temporal lord soon became a principle of administrative expediency, which has had a long history under various fictions and disguises. Mr Frazer refers, in passing, to this general conception of divinity in rulership as one way by which the idea of a man-god is reached; upon which we will only observe that the conception and the idea, as understood by very primitive minds, are indistinguishable. But there is another way of reaching the same idea—

"Side by side with the view of the world as pervaded by spiritual forces, primitive man has another conception in which we may detect a germ of the modern notion of natural law, or the view of nature as a series of events occurring in an invariable order without the intervention of personal agency."

This germ is, we learn, the conception of sympathetic magic, the producing an effect by imitating it, as when a man is killed by making and destroying his image, "which is, in fact, the modern conception of physical causation"; and a man-god is only an individual endowed with extraordinary magical powers over Nature. Wonder-working persons and wonder-working processes abound all over the world; the vein of illustration in this department is inexhaustible. Nor can it be doubted that magic is founded on some dim notion of cause and effect which is the necessary basis of all human reasoning from experience. Mr Frazer distinguishes between two types of man-god, the embodiment of divinity and the magical operator; but the primitive witch is usually no god at all, he is the aboriginal scientist. We are told, however, of rain-gods, weather-kings; of making sunshine and making wind, of charms, tricks, and incantations; and so we are led on through the ideas of incantation, inspiration, the deification of men, possession, and all the countless varieties of demoniac or divine embodiment, up to the Dalai Lamas of Tibet, the Incas of Peru, the Chinese Emperor, and the Arsacidæ. Whence it appears that the same union of sacred functions with a royal title which meets us in the King of the Wood at Nemi, is a common feature of societies at all stages from barbarism to civilisation. The phenomenon is, as we have said, perfectly well known; and, indeed, of the two ways by which the idea of a man-god is attained, the second may be thought to be little more than the reproduction, on a large scale, and with the stages marked out, of the first; since it is indubitable that kings become gods, as gods become kings, by reason of certain super-natural powers or privileges assumed and admitted to reside in them. A suggestion is thrown out that the Nemi king might have had a political origin, that his predecessors might have been a line of kings whom a republican revolution stripped of their political power, leaving them only their religious functions. But the hypothesis [which may be found in Plutarch,]* is too rationalistic, and it is dismissed in favour of the much more pregnant conception of the Nemi priest as a king of Nature, having the wood for his special department.

Now Kings of the Rain, of Water, and of Fire, have been discovered in various outlying corners of barbarism, among the African tribes, and in the backwoods of Cambodia; though, from the description of them in the Golden Bough, they appear to be mostly no more than ordinary conjurers, or great medicine-men, who are knocked on the head if their spells fail. We are in search, however, of a King of the Wood to match the Arician priest; and in order to hit off the clue we are taken back to the extensive subject of tree worship. Here we are at once upon wide, well-trodden, and very familiar ground; we can wander at will in a jungle of primitive beliefs, for plants, trees, groves, and forests have played numberless parts on the different stages of religious evolution. Beginning with the primary and universal animism which invested motion with conscious life, we pass easily and obviously to plants and trees with mysterious attributes, to haunted woods, to trees with souls and spirits immanent, to wood nymphs, sylvan deities, and the higher notions which impersonate the

* "Roman Questions."

vivifying powers of Nature, to Diana and Dionysus. In this class of myth and ritual the connection between ancient and modern practices is very attractive; we may be indulgent to those who see in maypoles, green bushes, Whitsuntide queens, harvest homes, Christmas trees, in the games and ceremonies of the vintage or the reaping, nothing but a survival of the quaint poetically symbolic rites by which the earliest races of men figured the spring, ripening, or decay of vegetation. Mr Frazer conjectures that Zeus and Hera at the Bœotian festivals were the Greek equivalent of the lord and lady of the May, and "the story of Hera's quarrel with Zeus, and her sullen retirement, may perhaps, without straining, be interpreted as a mythical expression for a bad season and a failure of the crops." In the vernal pastimes of French and Russian villagers, the boys and girls sometimes dress up in leaves and flowers, and one of them goes to sleep, to be awoke by the rest, or acts the part of a forsaken bride or bridegroom. "Is the sleeper," asks Mr Frazer, "the leafless forest or the bare earth in winter? Is the girl who wakens him the fresh verdure or the genial sunshine of spring?" The evidence, he thinks, is hardly adequate, and one may decidedly agree with him; for here, as throughout his book, he seems to lean overmuch toward the poetic and allegorical interpretation of customs and manners that derive easily enough from the incidents and circumstances of everyday life. This inclination takes also an additional bias from the turn that is necessarily given to all his materials in order to join in and fit them neatly into the general plan upon which he is working. After this fashion, and by various similar analogies and examples the inference is drawn that the cult of the Arician grove was that of a tree spirit. Now we know that the priest of this cult was King of the Wood; and that his life was in some sense bound up with the tree. For this and other reasons drawn from comparative folklore, it is provisionally assumed that the King of the Wood was a king incarnation of the tree-spirit; in fact, that the priest was the god himself.

To this conclusion, which is reached at the end of his first chapter, it would be illiberal to demur *in limine.* For whether the Arician priest and rite were the product of long religious evolution, the mysterious emblem of Nature worship, or whether he may have been the fortuitous outcome of some such violent deed or marvellous incident as has so commonly made famous a shrine or a deity, is unknowable and really unimportant. The story is here used as a starting-point for a series of discussions upon the ways and thoughts of man in a state of barbarism, ignorance, or rusticity. Mr Frazer has made a large collection of quaint, outlandish specimens of folklore, archaic ritual, and vagrant superstitious fancies; all of which he desires to arrange so as to bring out the main lines of their development and decadence, and the connection between earlier and later forms. He wishes to do something in religious palæontology, to reconstruct the mouldering skeletons of extinct worships, and to prove the pedigrees and remote yet unbroken descent of village games or goblins from sylvan deities and their ritual, and from the impression produced on man by the circling seasons. The study is so fascinating that much must be forgiven to him who ardently pursues it; and we can understand the pleasure of leading us onward, like an Oriental story-teller who ends each tale with an event or allusion that requires another one to explain it. But it must be confessed to follow him from branch to branch of his enchanting subject requires some mental agility; one has to take occasional leaps at the nearest analogy, to make clutches at slender arguments, and generally to risk what the French would call *conjectures de casse-cou*.

For instance—The first chapter takes us to the point that the Nemi priest was once a tree-spirit incarnate; a conclusion of much novelty and enterprise, with which some people might rest contented. But the next chapter opens with the Perils of the Soul; and we are immediately introduced to an old acquaintance, the Mikado, as the type of those mysterious and sacred beings who are strictly guarded and secluded, because upon their purity and preservation is supposed to depend the order of Nature. This brings us to the custom of Taboo; and thence by the ever-widening stream of associated ideas we drift out into the illimitable sea of fancies, fictions, and fables regarding the soul, if by that word we may designate the principle of life or consciousness which is parted from the body temporarily in sleep and trances, permanently in death. Whither goes the soul after quitting its mortal tenement, and how does it fare? can it be lost, stolen, or strayed? does it wander about the earth until it finds another habitation in stock or stone, in beast or man? is it carried up to some heaven, or down to some

Hades? does it become god or demon? can it expiate offences, be comforted by offerings, or avenge its wrongs? —all such questions mankind has been asking from time immemorial, and has caught at every sign or shadow of an answer.

> "Animula vagula blandula,
> Hospes comesque corporis,
> Quæ nunc abibis in loca?"

Bodily death is the giving up of the ghost, which thenceforward haunts primitive man; and in man's supposed relations with the innumerable phantoms that surround him for his plague or protection lies the mainspring of endless superstitions and the germ of far-reaching beliefs. Mr Frazer has no difficulty in selecting from all parts of the world abundant examples showing that the soul, being the personal self, and identified with the visible breath, with the shadow, or the reflection on water, is to the savage mind a thing incessantly surrounded by physical changes and easily damaged. Out of the precautions necessary for the safety of important souls arise, he says, the customs of royal and sacerdotal Taboo, which he further explains, very simply and sensibly, to be after all no more than a set of rules for safeguarding the lives of kings or priests. Nor, indeed, need we dive very far into the depths of primeval animism to grope for and emerge with the plain observation that a chief who has to manage wild and credulous people must very soon hit upon the device of declaring himself too holy to be touched or even approached with impunity. Almost all forms and Court ceremonies were originally intended to keep intruders at arm's length; and the essence of caste rules is in the avoidance of strange, untrustworthy company, especially with regard to food, drink, or social contact. Mr Frazer follows out this very intelligible principle into various minute and curious particulars, exhibiting the connection between unlucky omens and portents, magic charms to avert dangers, taboo customs, caste prejudice, sanctity, divinity, and Court etiquette. The whole subject has been examined at length in Mr Herbert Spencer's chapters on Ceremonial Institutions, where the common origin of all these observances —religious, political, and social—is very sufficiently expounded. Mr Frazer contributes some anecdotes that are at least amusing. When Dr Bastian attempted to touch the skull of a Siamese prince, "in order to illustrate some medical remarks," he was warned by a threatening murmur that he was committing a breach of etiquette; and among North American Indians a young brave while under taboo is so strictly prohibited from touching his own head, that he must scratch it with a stick. Such anecdotes may illuminate an abstruse law of mental evolution, or they may be the natural outcome of circumstance, or they may be little more than random answers to satisfy curiosity. Dr Bastian's behaviour could scarcely have passed current among civilised royalties; and if one asks an Indian why he scratches his head with a stick, he will give the first answer that occurs to him. The wild man pleads custom for everything; and a very little pressure will make him add that it is awful, ancient, and invariable. As he lives in constant terror of death, so anything odd, unaccountable, or unusual, impresses him with fear and suspicion;

he invents every kind of magical prophylactic, antidote, and prohibition in order to keep off or neutralise malignant influences. Thus is formed a code of regulations which may, perhaps, be conveniently described as the practice of Taboo, being for the most part, as Mr Frazer remarks, nothing but maxims of common prudence, under the mask of mysterious laws sanctioned supernaturally. He would probably agree with us that no more recondite explanation of all these ideas and customs, taken as a class, is required; but he desires to show how they grew and were generated one from another; he wishes to lay out and assort a large and miscellaneous repertory of folklore upon the lines of his hypothesis. Why was the Flamen Dialis not allowed, according to Plutarch, to walk under a trellised vine? The answer suggested is

> "that plants are considered as animate beings which bleed when cut, the red juice which exudes from some plants being regarded as the blood of the plant. The juice of the grape is therefore conceived as the blood of the vine, and since, as we have seen, the soul is often believed to be in the blood, the juice of the grape is regarded as the soul . . . of the vine. Wine is considered as a spirit, or containing a spirit, first, because it is identified as a red juice, with the blood of the plant; and second, because it intoxicates or inspires. Therefore, if the Flamen Dialis had walked under a trellised vine, the spirit of the vine, embodied in the clusters of grapes, would have been immediately over his head, and might have touched it, which, for a person like him in a state of permanent taboo, would have been highly dangerous."

I have quoted this elaborate exposition as exemplifying what I venture to regard as the defects of Mr Frazer's method. He is not content with proving the main steps required by his general theory, such as that the early animism of tree-worship concentrated into the notion of special divinity immanent in certain particularly valuable trees, and latterly into the conception of abstract deities presiding over the vineyard or orchard. He subjects stray traditions and customs to minute analysis, yielding results that may or may not be futile. It does not seem to me probable, or even possible, that the utmost ingenuity and learning can hope to succeed in unravelling an ancient interdict of this trivial kind, by stringing together a few conceptions that are so general and natural as to be applicable to almost any special case. The vine may easily have always been a sacred tree; the rare qualities and intoxicating effect of its fruit are very ample reasons not only for investing it with divinity, but also for placing any one who should touch it under a curse or ban. This is the view of Plutarch,* who believes that the interdict laid on the Flamen meant that holy persons should beware of wine. And he gives the same explanation of the rule that a Flamen must not touch ivy; it is because the vinous Bacchanals wore ivy wreaths. In fact, the numerous prohibitions laid upon the Flamen are all interpreted by Plutarch as symbolic rules of discipline. This interpretation is fairly reasonable, being in accordance with sacerdotal ordinance generally, and to go farther is to strain the very slender thread of hints and imperfect indications that have come down to us. It would be easy to parody the interpretations in "The Golden Bough" by arguing that the most commonplace prejudices and presages of ill-luck contain the elements of savage demonolatry, or are tinged with

* "Roman Questions."

elementary nature-worship. Whereas most of them are distorted generalisations from some actual experience, as when a man who has come to harm or peril after seeing or doing some noticeable thing, thenceforward marks off all such coincidences as uncanny and mysteriously dangerous; or else they are mere scarecrows and bugbears set up to frighten off trespassers by diabolical menace.

The second chapter of this book ends with a passage that is earnest and sympathetic in tone, although it accepts a view of savage life that is, perhaps, too ideal and symmetrical for what is actually a very confused, unintelligent, and haphazard state of existence.

"To students of the past the life of the old kings and priests thus teems with instruction. In it was summed up all that passed for wisdom when the world was young. It was the perfect pattern after which every man strove to shape his life; a faultless model constructed with rigorous accuracy upon the lines laid down by a barbarous philosophy. Crude and false as that philosophy may seem to us, it would be unjust to deny it the merit of logical consistency. Starting from a conception of the vital principle as a tiny soul or being existing in, but distinct and separable from, the living being, it deduces for the practical guidance of life a system of rules which, in general, hangs well together, and forms a fairly complete and harmonious whole. . . .

"Contempt and ridicule, or abhorrence and denunciation, are too often the only recognition vouchsafed to the savage. Yet of the benefactors we are bound thankfully to commemorate many, perhaps most, were savages . . . and what we have in common with the savage, and deliberately retain as true and useful, we owe to our savage forefathers, who slowly acquired by experience, and transmitted to us by inheritance, those seemingly fundamental ideas which we are apt to regard as original and intuitive."

These words are imbued with a spirit of generosity, of

fellow-feeling with forgotten times and vanished races, that touches the imagination and corrects the too common tendency of those who enjoy the full light and security of civilisation, to ridicule and despise the struggles and blunders of primitive man. Nevertheless, the tone of this passage corroborates the general impression conveyed by Mr Frazer's book, that he discovers coherence, consistency, and orderly sequence in a confused medley of savage ways and notions, which can be sorted out into large groups according to a certain order of intellectual development, but cannot, we think, be particularly affiliated or attached, lineally or laterally, in any certain relation to each other. Natural religion and natural society follow certain well-known grooves and shapes drawn by the instinct of self-preservation and moulded by the environment; but within a very wide and elastic range of thought, and of pressure by material circumstances, these lines and forms are constantly changing, and the individual fancies of ignorant men are blown to and fro, like thistledown, with every wind of terror and delusion. There is no perfect order or unbroken affinity; there is no rigorous accuracy or logical consistency; these terms have no meaning or place in application to the irrational ideas, the random guesses, the incessantly shifting practices, of superstitious barbarians. What are, in sober truth, the true and useful ideas on such subjects as are dealt with in "The Golden Bough," that we are apt to regard as original and intuitive yet owe in reality to our savage forefathers—"the nameless and forgotten toilers whose patient thought and active exertions have largely made us what we are"? They are somewhat difficult to specify; and, even if one now and then finds among rude tribes some glimmering of a deep philosophic truth, it is not easy to decide whether it is theirs by origin. The note of the primitive mind is amazing inaccuracy, coupled with wonderful receptivity; the savage will adopt any new fable or ritual that strikes his fancy; he will represent a custom picked up last year as a rite of hoar antiquity; he will produce impromptu a legend or sacred ordinance to satisfy an enquirer about the origin of worship or caste rules; he borrows readily from the latest, as well as the lowest, faith or liturgy. He will transmit through generations some distorted version of early missionary teaching. Who shall decide what we owe to the savage, or how much the modern savage (of whom alone we know anything accurately) owes to the reflex action of the loftiest upon the lowest religious ideas, wherever there is possibility of commixture? We are told that "Buddhist animism is not a philosophical theory; it is *simply* a common savage dogma incorporated in the system of a historical religion. To suppose with Benfey and others that the theories of animism and transmigration current among rude peoples of Asia are derived from Buddhism is to reverse the facts. Buddhism in this respect borrowed from savagery, not savagery from Buddhism." It is unsafe to treat as simple and demonstrable a point which is complicated and exceedingly debatable; for savagery may have borrowed much from Buddhism. Is it to be supposed that the powerfully organised religions which have spead over Asia during the last 2000 years have not influenced enormously the petty superstitions within their range, or that the savage who dreams about losing his soul is necessarily the direct intellectual ancestor of the Buddhistic teacher? This may be true in the sense of saying that the inventor of the steam locomotive is the scientific descendant of the first savage who lighted a fire; but such a genealogy is hardly worth formal announcement. In all times and countries there is constant degradation as well as evolution; the upper and nether ideas throw out fresh shoots and intertwine; they become inextricably twisted up and interfused, like the trees, brambles, and creepers of a primeval forest. The highly cultivated faith of an original religious thinker will run wild; a rough and rudimentary idea will strike root and spread, until the two become mixed and intermarried. We all know that the belief in souls, ghosts, and spirits has been universal, and has undergone transformation in various stages of physical and metaphysical speculation, and we can see that the rudimentary notion is earlier than the refined dogma, as barbarism existed before civilisation. But any attempt to lay out distinct lines of transmission, or to determine the necessary connection of higher and lower customs and superstitions in any particular case, is, so far as I may venture to judge, a very hazardous and unprofitable undertaking.

Among very rude and wild tribes there prevails the intelligibly utilitarian institution of putting to death persons that have become decrepit or sickly. When a chief is old and weak, he is killed in order to make room for a vigorous successor; and since a chief or king is often, as we have seen, also a divine incarnation, this may be equivalent to slaying a man-god. Mr Frazer considers that in many parts of the world the principal object was not so much to slay an impotent ruler as to get rid of a debilitated divinity, that the god was systematically killed with the object of causing the divine power or spirit to pass into another receptacle before it could be affected by decay or disease.

> "The divine life, incarnate in a material and mortal body, is liable to be tainted and corrupted by the weakness of the frail medium in which it is for a time enshrined; and if it is to be saved from the increasing enfeeblement which it must necessarily share with its human incarnation it must be detached from him as soon as he exhibits signs of decay, in order to be transferred to a vigorous successor. . . . The killing of the god is, therefore, only a necessary step to his revival or resurrection in a better form."

The analogy upon which this argument rests is bold, for the conjecture that the god was killed as a god lacks the support of evidence; but the deductions made by its author are so important and curious that the hypothesis may stand provisionally. His view is that as manners became softer, and bodily vigour grew less essential to rulership, the custom of king-killing and god-killing passed slowly through the usual fictitious stages into desuetude; a mock king was sacrificed, or some unlucky slave, or child, or prisoner suffered vicariously, and thus arose gradually the custom of human and animal immolation. At a Babylonian festival a prisoner was dressed in royal robes, and treated for five days as a prince, being even allowed to enjoy the king's concubines before his execution; a fact which Mr Frazer takes to be decisive against the commonplace supposition that this was merely a brutal jest or pageant. I suspect that a few unfortunate concubines would have been of no account at all for the due performance of a popular Babylonian masquerade, which might just as well mimic earthly kingship as symbolise divine mysteries. However this may be, the view here is that kings were formerly sacrificed as gods, that they contrived to substitute other victims — their sons, or the sons of others, or a fictitious king—and that from this barbarous rite came the custom of sacrificing the first-born, and the wholesale immolation of children practised at Carthage, with other ulterior ramifications of the sacrificial idea that are followed up later in the book.

But how does this hypothesis bear upon the killing of the Arician priest in particular? The reply is that he was King of the Wood, an incarnation of the spirit of vegetation, who must have been powerful over fruit and crops, whose precious life was probably hedged in by an elaborate system of Taboo, and whose spirit or soul it was essential to transfer in unabated vigour to each human successor. He was accordingly subjected to a chronic struggle for existence; so long as he could beat off his assailants, his vigour proved itself; if he were killed he was losing strength, and it was time for a new god-man to take office. It is somewhat hard to reconcile the idea of Taboo with a custom which left the sacred personage exposed to the perilous necessity of fighting for his life against all comers; and one may also take leave to doubt whether the most stupid savage would fail to perceive that, since the fiercest warrior may be taken unawares and slain by a very puny enemy, the custom of Nemi would by no means fulfil the purpose here suggested of securing a continuous supply of robust incarnations. But Mr Frazer goes on to guess that the wood-king was formerly put to death at the expiry of a set term, and as he proposes to confirm this conjecture by evidence taken from the rural festivals of the peasantry, we perceive that he has skilfully operated an agile transition to a fresh department of folklore. Then follow a great number of very curious and amusing descriptions of picturesque rustic ceremonies and games surviving among the outlying country folk, which are undoubtedly excellent evidence that the antique pagan superstitions hold ground tenaciously in remote districts, and which also prove abundantly that the religion of primitive man is founded on an imitation and imagery of the course of Nature. Now the supreme fact in Nature is the eternal succession of birth and death, of verdure and decay, of reaping and sowing, of destruction for the purpose of reproduction. In these phenomena are found the roots of all natural religion; and even the gods are only respected as agencies for the control of the blind natural forces against which man is constantly striving. No wonder, then, if we find running through so many agricultural feasts and rough dramatic ceremonies a strain of alternate rejoicing and lamenting, of worshipping the god in effigy and then dooming him to death, of adoring queer emblematic figures which are afterwards led out to mimic execution, sacrificed, buried, and mourned over. The allegory is clear enough; it pervades all the philosophy and poetry of the earliest races; the course and constitution of Nature lie at the base of some of the loftiest religions, whose summits are lost in metaphysics. But it may be asked—Why kill the personages who in these pageants symbolise the outburst of flower or leaf? The answer given is that here we may discover the germ of the custom of god-killing; for as in Nature all things must die in order to spring up again, so the spirit of plants or trees is killed in imitation of Nature's law, and eventually the animal or human being that personates or embodies the spirit comes to be periodically slain, in order that the divine element may revive and flourish in a fresh incarnation.

What are we to say in regard to this exceedingly interesting and clever speculation, which spreads out before us a new and still more extensive field of folk custom, allegory, myth, and mystery plays? Is the mock trial and execution of Jack-in-the-Green really a relic of the symbolic slaying of a tree-spirit, and are all the innumerable commemorative funerals, lamentations, burials in effigy, and other forms of mortuary rite, the wailing for dead heroes or demigods, to be counted as variously modified traditions of the idea of killing the Nature gods in order to revive them? The notion of representing the harvest and the fall of the leaf under the figure of human death and interment, is easily intelligible as one of the sources of these customs; but, setting theories aside, why should these funeral ceremonies be generally allegorical, and why insist on a remote figurative interpretation of a whole class of usages that reflect the deepest feelings of ordinary humanity? In a large number of the customs mentioned by Mr Frazer, the images, or mythic figures, which undergo death or resurrection, manifestly represent the seasons; but the great historic examples of periodical obsequies in memory of famous personages, of the hero or demigod, may be claimed as belonging to a different category. Nothing in human feeling is stronger than the passion, in all ages and countries, for commemorating the mighty dead, or those who have been loved and are lost. It is, at any rate, probable that these legends and traditions are of a very complex origin, have become mixed up and entangled with a variety of dimly remembered facts and diverse superstitions, born of universal natural emotions.

Under the names of Osiris, Adonis, Thammuz, Attis, and Dionysus, various nations of antiquity represented, we are told, the decay and revival of vegetation. One need not quarrel with a moderate use of this interpretation; but it has no more right to a monopoly of the sources of mythology than other equally ambitious theories; and one may decline to admit, with Mr Frazer, that all these ceremonies have grown up exclusively out of a single idea or allegory. The five personages mentioned are all supposed by tradition to be mourned on account of violent or untimely death; and it is quite certain that men who have so died have been deified, worshipped, or canonised throughout many centuries all over the world. There are very few allegories that have taken possession of man's imagination which have not either gathered round some human personality, or been stiffened by the introduction of some historical substance; while, on the other hand, the biographies of genuine heroes and saints are constantly found overgrown and interlaced with obvious Nature myths. That a divine hero, Adonis or Attis, may have originally been a vegetable spirit is, of course, possible; it is equally possible that his legend may have derived from some locally famous person, whose life and death struck the popular imagination, and whose story has now become entirely wrapped up in parasitical superstitions. In investigating such questions as these it would be useful to lay down some rules as to the admissibility of evidence, and as to the application of analogy. In all forms of adoration and ceremonial, plants and flowers, leaves and garlands, occupy a prominent place; they are scattered in a stream to the river god, they are used to crown a fetish, to adorn a temple or an altar, they are strewn in churches and cemeteries. From time immemorial the fruits of the field, the vineyard, and the garden have been worshipped, personified, allegorised, or offered to the invisible giver and protector of them. It is open to us to conclude broadly that these are signs and expressions of a natural and reasonable impulse or taste, blending the wish to please or propitiate with some faint reminiscence of the transitory bloom of all nature, which has taken various shapes at different stages of the religious evolution. Or else, finding a mere generalisation insufficient, we may condescend to particulars. We may undertake to string together in one connected series all these manifestations of the same idea or ceremony, asserting that, because they have a certain resemblance, therefore they are actually in the relation of ancestors and descendants, that the latest customs are lineally connected with the eldest. The following citation from "The Golden Bough" shows how this latter doctrine may be handled so as to sweep within the circle of common affinity all customs that have any outward visible similitude :—

"At the approach of Easter, Sicilian women sow wheat, lentils, and canary seed in plates, which are kept in the dark and watered every two days. The plants soon shoot up; the stalks are tied together with red ribbons; and the plates containing them are placed on the sepulchres, which, with the effigies of the dead Christ, are made up in Roman Catholic and Greek churches on Good Friday, just as the gardens of Adonis were placed on the grave of the dead Adonis. *The whole custom—sepulchres as well as sprouting grain—is probably nothing but a continuation, under a different name, of the Adonis worship.*"

The sentence that we have italicised strikes the keynote of the method of harmonising interpretation to which, in this book, I think exception must be taken on the ground that it is unsupported by proof. If the author can find customs that resemble each other by any note of similarity, or outward accordance, he infers that they are, so to speak, blood relations; he presses into the service of the spiritual or imaginative order of association the analogy of natural propagation and the family tree, so that all usages having some common feature or chance likeness are grouped together as allied species. But since certain very simple and obviously appropriate practices, like the use of flowers, or of water, or of decorated images, characterise every phase of religious worship, the sources out of which one may draw similitudes, survivals, and variants of the same idea or usage are quite inexhaustible; they may be picked out of the heap and adapted to fit into any theory whatever. Mr Frazer perceives this clearly enough when he is combating rival hypotheses, such as the opinion of Renouf that Isis was the dawn; and such as Tiele's view that Osiris is the sun, because he is said in a hymn to glitter on the horizon and send out rays of light, and for other reasons which Mr Frazer justly calls bad. But Mr Frazer's reasons for holding both Isis and Osiris to have been corn spirits are of much the same texture. Manetho tells us that the Egyptians used to burn red-haired men and scatter their ashes with winnowing fans; whence it is conjectured that these sacrifices were intended to promote the growth of crops, and the red-haired victims "were perhaps selected as best fitted to represent the spirit of the golden grain." Again, if Osiris is sometimes depicted on the monuments as black, and still more commonly as green, we are to remember that a corn god may be conceived as black while the seed is under ground, and green after it has sprouted. An adversary might observe that it is scarcely possible to spin out a finer web of not impossibly associated ideas, or to colour an argument with a lighter tincture of superficial resemblance. I do not press these instances as fair samples of the proofs on which the writer mainly relies, so much as illustrating his somewhat arbitrary habit of forcing into the ranks of his own army a great multitude of petty details which might just as well have served any other theory whatever. If a god or hero is to be reduced to an incarnate vegetable, or corn spirit, on such evidence, there is but little security for the most highly placed and substantial personalities.

With Demeter and Dionysus our author's work is easy. They are the impersonated creations of the divine myth, and dissolve readily into spirits of the cornfield and the vineyard. That Dionysus was also worshipped in the form of a bull and of a goat, that these animals were also sacrificed to him; that a bull was torn to pieces before him because the god had been slain by a bull, and that the goat was sacrificed because it injured the vine—these are all facts to which Mr Frazer rightly points as indicating a confusion of ideas and legends, and of which he gives some very subtle and adroit interpretations. The plants and animals were, he believes, first killed as the embodiments of deities or spirits whose death was necessary, as has been already shown, for vigorous resurrection; and latterly they became propitiatory offerings to the anthropomorphic god; so, when the earlier goat divinity is sacrificed to the full-fledged Bacchus, the god is thus slain on his own altar, and is sacramentally devoured by his worshippers. This view seems to me novel, remarkable, and well worked out in the particular case of Dionysus; although I hesitate to follow Mr Frazer upon the wider ground of his conjecture that "whenever a god is described as the eater of a particular animal, the animal in question is nothing but the god himself," and that human sacrifice arose out of the same complication of ideas. According to this view the human victim merely suffered vicariously for the incarnate divinity, being killed on the altar in commemoration and imitation of the god's annual death, which, in its turn, is a ceremony traceable, through the rites, in mimicry of corn-reaping, down to the birth and death of vegetation, the alternation of spring and summer, and the universal analogy of all-producing and all-wasting Nature. And so we find strung together, on a somewhat fantastic and loosely-weaved pattern or woof, such distant and differing customs as the song of Linus (a lamentation for the dead corn spirit), the mysteries of Osiris, the bloody human sacrifices of Mexico and the Indian Khonds, the killing of old men, old kings, old gods, in various parts of the world, the harvest-home of Devonshire reapers, the crying of the Neck, and a chance medley of fables, plays, and pastimes still surviving among the country-folk in France, Germany, or Russia. They have all their appointed places in the serial development and radiation of one comprehensive idea; they signify and preserve the universal impression made on the primitive imagination by the endless iteration of birth and death, the perishing and resurrection of all animate things.

Upon this theme Mr Frazer enlarges throughout his second volume, showing how the spirit of vegetation passes into the bodies of animals and of men; how beasts and human beings are slain as gods, adored as divinities, become burnt-offerings, scapegoats, ancestral totems, demons, divine kings and pontiffs, accursed men like Jonah, devils incarnate, and beneficent deities. In short, his book supplies us with an almost complete hypothetical sketch of the natural philosophy of religion, and explains its morphology by reference to the persistence under incessant transformation of one or two primordial conceptions. The scheme is elaborated with much skill and labour; the whole work is ornamented with picturesque detail; and it is easy to understand the attraction of a scheme which takes in every side of this immense subject, and enables the writer to range over heaven and earth for myths, legends, rites, customs, and supernaturalism, in every phase or shape, to support his arguments. He has but to cast his net into the waters of folklore, it is sure to bring him a miraculous draught of mingled fact and fiction, none of which is so intractable but that some part of it can be joined into the composition of so elastic a theory. It is no wonder if, under these circumstances, a writer should have yielded to the temptation that seems to beset all comparative mythologists, and should have been seduced by the numerical strength and embarrassing wealth of, his materials into the errors of over-running more territory than he can possibly hold, of undertaking to build up his vast hypothesis on a somewhat extravagant scale.

The profusion of information in the matter of the multitudinous superstitions of mankind, past and present, which is in these days accessible to the diligent reader, offers an irresistible enticement to the modern spirit of inquisitive research and scientific classification. A religious naturalist feels uneasy until he has assorted and catalogued all this jumble of disparate notions and customs; until he has brought it into some kind of order similar to that which now rules in the departments of physical research; and human fancy is so prolific, so mutable, and so boundless, that its products can be made to assume numberless shapes, and every kind of meaning can be extracted from them. When you have selected the specimens wanted for your religious mosaic, when you have put together a map of the spiritual world after your own notion of such geography, no one can positively verify any mistake, or prove that either your premiss or your processes are demonstrably wrong. No one can demonstrate fatal flaws in systems purporting to explain the obscure and haphazard correlations of these mental phenomena, or to exhibit the connection between funeral wreaths and the worship of a flower sprite. No one can positively deny, on evolutionary principles, that the *Kurioktonia* of our loftiest theology may be allied in some circuitous manner with the harvest ceremonies that from remote antiquity have symbolised the death of the cornstalks and the bleeding of the grape. But to many of those who have been accustomed to examine the generation and growth of divine things, and who have compared what can be seen with what can be read, the enterprise of linking together in a chain of necessary causative or biological series the forms and species of religious beliefs separated by vast intervals of space and time, must appear to need great hardihood of imagination. Without doubt their morphology can be described in broad outline, a task that has already been accomplished by such writers as Mr Herbert Spencer and Mr E. B. Tylor, whose profound yet moderate generalisations divide and subdivide the field of speculation into manageable areas, lay bare its main stratification, and distinguish the stages to which the chief ideas and practices belong. The connection between savage animism, the worship of trees, animals, ghosts, and gods, has long been observed; the main fountains and currents of evolutionary symbolism and allegory, which are fed from manifold tributaries, have long been searched out; the secrets of mythology have been unlocked with many keys, and have been fully deciphered by none. Mr Frazer has amassed much valuable evidence bearing in different ways on these general conclusions; he has used it to throw some light on certain recondite and mysterious corners of superstition, and he has hit off one or two promising clues that lead some way into the labyrinth. But I submit that he presses his points too far; he makes too much play with uncertain resemblances, and he builds too much upon stuff that dreams are made of, upon temerarious inference and guesswork. Many of his conjectures are remarkably suggestive and fairly credible; but they often proceed out of facts which might be as well adapted to rival hypotheses, or which are susceptible of plainer or more direct explanations. A sleeping girl in a pastoral play may typify the winter, and her awakening may signify the spring, but she might, with little less probability, be found to symbolise the sunset and the dawn; for in fact the tracing of all myths and rituals to the seasons is merely a varied repetition of the solar and lunar theories, of systems that deduce all myths from the primordial observation and worship of the cardinal phenomena which regulate heat, cold, and the divisions of time.

But the standard difficulty in the way of any extensively uniform interpretation of religious customs as direct modifications of universal nature-worship, is that it leaves no room for the realities of human life, for the chapter of strange accidents and remarkable events, for the prehistoric record of great men and their deeds. Myth and ritual, custom and ceremony, usually wear the appearance of a reminiscence of some memorable event or personage, of a representation of some scene or story. Much of this is undoubtedly pure symbolism, allegory, and distorted nature-worship; but no one can say how much of it may come out of the universal habit, among primitive folk, of dramatic commemoration of real incidents and characters.

One main objection to the plan of interpretation which this book unfolds is, that it sets aside, or takes no notice of, this incontestable fact, that prehistoric tradition survives in the religious myth. This consideration, indeed, would appear to have been excluded, if we are to accept in their entirety certain axioms that are laid down in regard to the relation of myth to custom. "No people," he writes, "ever observed a custom because a mythical being was said to have acted in a certain way. But, on the contrary, all peoples have invented myths to explain why they observed certain customs." It is unsafe for the most industrious mythologist to frame rules which pre-suppose universal knowledge and unerring intuition upon such a question as the myths of all nations; and on such paths documentary evidence, not tested by actual observation or experience, is almost sure to lead him astray. As a matter of fact, if this means that a story or event upon which a custom is traditionally founded is invariably an invention to explain that custom in a popular way, the contention is not historically maintainable. On the contrary, whenever we examine the development of any religion or sect whose origin is more or less authentically known, we find that the ritual, liturgy, and tradition undoubtedly rest upon at least a nucleus of genuine incident; insomuch that hardly a single rite or religious custom purporting to celebrate important events or memorable scenes can be shown to be founded entirely on myth; the fasts, festivals, and essential ceremonies almost invariably run back to something real, whatever may have been the subsequent distortion or disguise. The passion plays still existing among Christians and Mahomedans, the memorial services, the annual shows or processions, can all be traced back to a discoverable origin; they have their roots in some remarkable occurrence, in some great political or religious triumph or catastrophe; the mythical being is a travesty of some historical personage. Mysterious meanings, allegorical readings, and miraculous indications, are commonly superadded; but so far as we can analyse with certainty the elements out of which religious traditions are composed, an element of truth and reality can always be extracted. Why, then, should all the legends and ancient stories of gods and heroes, which Mr Frazer would melt down into pure nature-worship and instinctive superstition, be no more than pure fables invented to account for the custom of propitiating a corn spirit, of slaying and adoring the divine embodiments of vegetation, of representing dramatically the flowering and the falling of the leaf or the fruit? And is not our author committing an error, too common among comparative mythologists, when he spoils an interesting theory by straining it? when he provokes criticism by endeavouring to establish a monopoly of inspiration on the subject of the right meaning of myths, and tries to explain so many of them by a method that is at most good for a part? It is impossible not to feel some distrust of a system that might be easily applied, for example, to reduce to a nature myth the annual chairing of Guy Fawkes; or to show that the lamentations of the Shiah Musulmáns for Hasan and Hosein are, like the weeping for Thammuz, mere anthropomorphic dramatising of our sorrow for nature's decay. These and many other such ceremonies are only saved from annexation to mythologic cloudland by lying within the region of accepted history; while all that are found beyond that pale seem to be treated as fair prize by victorious analysis;

and a fierce war goes on over legends and customs that occupy the debateable border-ground between fact and fiction, romance and reality.

Mr Frazer examines the heroic myth of Balder, the Norse hero, who was killed by a mistletoe branch; and he decides that the circumstantiality of the story suggests that it belongs to the extensive class of myths which are invented to explain ritual. His reason is that "a myth is never so graphic and precise in its details as when it is a simple transcript of a ceremony which the author of the myth witnessed with his eyes"; though upon what evidence he makes this positive assertion we cannot imagine, since it implies a large personal acquaintance with the authors of myth. It is equivalent, moreover, to declaring that a story is false in proportion as it pretends to circumstantiality; whereas the true view is that myths, divine and heroic, are often bred in great and manifold luxuriance out of the feats or fortunes of some real personage. However, since the Balder legend has for its two main features the pulling of the mistletoe and the burning of the dead hero, the whole story is here dissolved into a transfiguration of the customs of bonfires and mistletoe worship, which again are merely symbolic, in different ways, of the life and death of the nature gods. The objection to this uncompromising method of simplification is that it runs counter to so much that we actually know regarding the formation of stories whose gradual growth and accretion can be fairly tested. Wherever a legend can be decomposed, it is almost always found to consist of truth and error, things credible and incredible, rudimentary and recent ideas, inextricably mixed and pounded together; it is a complex, not a simple organism.

Let us take a legend which, if it had belonged to prehistoric times, would undoubtedly have lent itself to the process employed in the Golden Bough for the precipitation of primeval nature worship out of the vaporous figures and fantastic cloud scenery of a divine myth. It is the story of the martyrdom of St Denis, as it has been analysed by M. Jean Réville in an essay upon the complexity of myths. The official martyrology records no more than the ordinary account of his decapitation; the popular legend adds that the martyred saint walked down the hill of Montmartre carrying his head in his hand, and was ultimately buried in a field which thenceforward became marvellously fertile. Gregory of Tours tells us that Bishop Dionysus, sent from Rome to evangelise the Parisians, was put to death by the Roman officers nearly three centuries before the date at which he wrote. But the name Dionysus at once starts us on the scent of a nature myth, since Dionysus was incontestably the god of vintages, and Mr Frazer has triumphantly proved him to have been a vegetable deity, whose violent death typified the harvest, and whose blood was merely the spirit of wine. And when we learn that the Emperor Probus revived the culture of the vine in central Gaul about the time of the saint's martyrdom, the scent becomes much stronger, until our myth is run finally to ground and unearthed by the remarkable coincidence that St Denis suffered on 7th October, the very day, according to M. Réville, on which the vintage festival was celebrated by the pagan Parisian. After this we hardly care to be told that a head without a body is often found among the emblems on the sacrificial vessels used in the cult of Dionysus; for the case is already as clear as any of those cited in the Golden Bough, and there can be no doubt whatever that St Denis is a tree-spirit canonised. He is crusted over with miracles and anachronism; he is identified with Denys the Areopagite, whom Paul converted at Athens: he bears the marks of various phases of belief and ritual, pagan and Christian; the only certain thing, according to our author's method, would be that he never existed. He is a myth, first invented to substantiate a natural allegory, then to justify a curious rite; and latterly he passed from the condition of an abstract, pagan, departmental nature god to the character of a wonder-working saint. The process of transition can be pursued and demonstrated by showing that similar ideas and customs, the worship of the vine, the shedding of blood, the decapitation of plants, the apotheosis of the grape deity, the conversion of heathen feasts into Christian holidays, are known to have prevailed commonly throughout Europe and elsewhere, and can be arranged in the order of their affiliation.

Notwithstanding this convincing demonstration, we do not feel sure that Mr Frazer would sacrifice St Denis to his theory; for the solid reason that continuous tradition and strong probability weigh heavily in favour of a real martyrdom having taken place. But why, then, must we ask, does he throw such weight, in constructing his scheme of interpretation, upon similar coincidences and analogies that he detects in other legends and customary observances, merely because in these cases the real *origines sacræ* can never be verified? The truth is that the difficulty, in the greater number of customs and sacred narratives, of distinguishing germs of fact among masses of mere imaginary tale-telling and random fables, founded upon natural phenomena, is insuperable. Where we find in existence an unmeaning, irrational usage, it has most probably arisen out of the universal instinct which impels men to adore the hidden powers that bring to life or to death; but to what extent this element is interspersed in any particular legend or myth, god or ritual, is too uncertain for the establishment upon any such basis of a connected system of evolution.

The Golden Bough contains so much that is of high interest and instruction, it has so many suggestive ideas, that I am reluctant to press adverse criticism too closely; but I must again sound a warning against incautious and unverifiable generalisations. Among the marks of a primitive religion these are particularly noted:

"(1) No special class of persons is set apart for the performance of the rites; in other words, there are no priests. The rites may be performed by any one, as occasion demands.

"(2) No special places are set apart for the performance of the rites; in other words, there are no temples. The rites may be performed anywhere, as occasion demands.

"(3) Spirits, not gods, are recognised."

Now it is certain that man in a state of very rude savagery has neither priesthood nor temple; neither, indeed, has he any settled institutions whatever; but it is equally certain that the two first marks would serve to denote the latest as well as the earliest forms of worship, such as Quakerism, Mormonism, and some of the most refined spiritualisms of Asia and America. The recognition of spirits instead of gods is also a characteristic both of modern and of primitive psychology, for savages draw no such fine distinctions, if, indeed, there is a difference. One might even argue that it is in the highest mind more than in the lowest scale of intellectual belief that we must look for the feeling which dispenses with Levites, holy places, and prefers unsubstantial or impersonal conceptions of divinity. But, without laying stress on this application, which may be thought an abuse, of his definitions, let us see how their author employs them—

> "Judged by these tests, the spring and harvest customs of our European peasantry deserve to rank as primitive. For no special class of persons and no special places are set apart exclusively for their performance; they may be performed by any one, master or man, mistress or maid, boy or girl; they are practised, not in temples or churches, but in the woods and meadows, beside brooks, in barns, or harvest field and cottage floors. The supernatural beings whose existence is taken for granted in them are spirits rather than deities...."

Other characteristic features that assimilate harvest customs to primitive ritual are enumerated; nor can it be doubted that Mr Frazer has successfully proved these customs to belong, in the main, to one and the same habit of thought, arising out of similar occupations, interests, and environment. Nevertheless I must point out the somewhat extravagant disregard of the theologic principle of economy, involved in framing definitions which identify a maypole dance with primeval nature worship through the absence in both cases of temple, priest, or god; and which use this same test for discovering the same origin and final cause of country games, harvest merry-making, Christmas revels, village play-acting, and of all the endless varieties of mystery, and mummery. The genealogy of all these things is specifically traced backward to fetichism, animism, the divinisation of plants and beasts, sacrifice, god-killing, and the whole apparatus of primitive thanksgiving or propitiation.

My own view is that no such circuitous route need be followed for the discovery of the relics of primeval superstition, which lie scattered among these queer games and outlandish usages. In early societies all games, dances, feasts, and plays have a religious pretext; in later days the pretext drops off as the forms of religion change; the national custom or amusement remains. But mythology and pagan ritual preserved a great deal more than fanciful superstitions; they reflected and recorded everything that fixed itself deeply on the popular memory and imagination. Every striking story or surprising occurrence, terrible or pathetic adventures, the deeds of heroes or wizards, the realities of a wild and perilous existence—all these things become raw material for myth, allegory, and tradition, they are worked up into marvellous tales and divine legends, they are dramatically acted and depicted with incessant change of name, place, and signification, in the festivals and folklore of the ancient or barbarous world. I apprehend that it is not possible to range into classes and orderly succession of types a miscellany of fanciful tales and usages, ancient and modern, raked together from among Polynesian savages and English harvesters; or to distinguish the products of aboriginal nature worship from the other ingredients, real or fabulous, by which the whole mass of superstitious observances has been formed and leavened.

Nevertheless, Mr Frazer who, after all, does not ask his readers to accept more than probabilities, has contributed some shrewd and valuable suggestions to the science of mythology. His account of the passage of the invisible corn spirit, the soul of the ripe and waving wheat crop, into animal forms, and of its detection in the shape of some creature that lurks in the last standing patch at reaping time, is excellent—

"Reapers and others often stand round the last patch of corn armed with sticks and guns, with which they kill the animals as they dart out of their last refuge. Now primitive man, to whom magical changes of shape seem perfectly credible, finds it most natural that the spirit of the corn, driven from his home among the corn, should make his escape in the form of the animal which is seen to rush out of the last patch of corn as it falls under the scythe of the reaper.... The sudden appearance of an animal issuing from the cut corn is enough to identify it with the corn spirit escaping from his ruined home."

The propensity to locate a dying soul or fleeting spirit in any thing or creature that appears or flies off at the moment of death or at a funeral, is still so common all over the world that it must have powerfully influenced early ideas and customs. It seems to be the original form of that incapacity or desperate refusal to believe in the finality of death, which is the cardinal principle of all religions. The soul, which is the same in men and animals, is never extinguished, but migrates incessantly. Mr Frazer illustrates the persistency of this conception by some fresh and picturesque examples drawn from his very copious repertory of folk custom, and he proceeds to enquire: "May not this fact (that in peasant lore the corn spirit is very commonly conceived and represented in animal form) explain the relation in which certain animals stood to the ancient deities of vegetation, Dionysus, Demeter, Adonis, Attis, and Osiris?"

Upon this text Mr Frazer enlarges with much skill and sympathetic appreciation of primitive modes of thought. He is occasionally at unnecessary pains to warn us that the early pagan mind was not troubled with inconsistencies, and so that a god of vegetation may, when promoted to be a goat, feed upon the vegetation he personified, the truth being that consistency is a thing totally unknown to such people. And some of his examples belong rather to well-known classes of religious phenomena than to the particular hypothesis which he employs them to support. The immense storehouse of superstitious usages and fables current in heathendom or among the peasantry will provide hints and conjectures in abundance for any theory; they are shaped according to the natural mental conformation of the people; like ready-made shoes in a warehouse, which are made to fit any foot tolerably, but none precisely.

But Mr Frazer is probably aware that he is surrounded by these difficulties; and I think that in spite of them he has done good work in marking out one of the many lines of transformation which may connect by an ascending gradient the celebration of seasonal changes, through the worship of fruits and plants, with zoolatry and the anthropomorphic divinities. He shows the likelihood that sacred animals were sometimes, among agricultural folk, the embodiments of corn spirits, that the animal may have become confounded with an anthropomorphic god, and that sacrifice may have grown first out of the custom of killing your god as you cut your corn, and latterly out of sacramental feasts and the sharing of food between the god and his worshippers. All these apparently discordant ideas very possibly became general and blended in the ever-burning furnace of human credulity and imagination; they melted into different combinations according to needs and circumstances; so that some germ of the highest religious mystery may perhaps be latent in the lowest fetichism, and cannibalism may have a remote connection with a metaphysical dogma. But wary enquirers need hardly be cautioned against the natural attractiveness of far-ranging adventurous analogy, or against the fallacy of assuming, because all religious ideas and practices have had similar motives and some generic resemblance, therefore they are genealogically akin.

The necessity of bringing in the Arician rite at certain stages of the discussion imposes occasionally somewhat of a strain upon the general line of argument that is followed in the Golden Bough. There is a tradition that Virbius, first King of the Wood, was killed by horses, which were consequently excluded from the sacred precincts. Now spirits of vegetation are sometimes represented (we are told) in the form of horses, as, for instance, when the Hertfordshire peasant "cries the mare" at the end of the reaping; although in this context one may be reminded of the etymology of the word nightmare. And since the animal that killed the god was often the original god himself, "we may conjecture that the horses by which Virbius was said to have been slain were really embodiments of him as a deity of vegetation;" the myth that Virbius had been killed by horses being probably invented to explain the custom of their exclusion from the grove. We are further cautioned against drawing the rash inference that because horses were excluded therefore they could not be sacred animals; but, on the contrary, we are invited to make the conjectural inference that they may have been sacrificed annually at Aricia, because it is known that the goat was excluded from the Athenian Acropolis, except when driven in once a year to be immolated. This reasoning upon doubtful parallels is hardly compact enough to produce conviction, nor is it in Mr Frazer's best manner; but it is not given as a fair specimen of his contributions to the science of comparative mythology.

In attempting to elucidate an obscure and manifestly difficult passage in the mythologic scroll, one may often be driven to far-fetched conjectural restorations of the text. But in the present case a simple reading would suffice; for if any one should prefer to believe that some ancient Virbius was really killed by horses, this view of custom's origin would be in no way discordant with what we actually know by observation of the generation of myths and customs from some authentic incident. Mr Frazer would, I am aware, discard this rationalistic interpretation; he would treat the Virbius myth as devised to explain a custom, and the customs as embodying some phase of a primary religious idea. I will only say that the possibility of the story being founded on fact might be established by comparative illustrations quite as numerous and forcible as those arrayed to throw light upon the much more profound and abstruse speculation pursued in this book. However this may be, our author prefers to regard the horse of Virbius as an amalgamation of the fructifying spirits of the tree and the corn, and the Arician priest's death as the sacramental killing; while he is convinced that the harvest suppers "of our European peasants have furnished unmistakable examples of the sacramental eating of animals as representatives of the corn spirit." And thus the dissertation broadens out again in the second volume into such ample fields as the prevalence of animal worship and totemism, pastoral sacrifices, whether of first fruits or animals, and all the contradictory and circular trains of savage reasoning which led men to adore what they have killed and kill what they have adored. It is in these tangled by-paths that Mr Frazer delights to follow the wandering savage mind, though occasionally he does not disdain the straight and more prosaic high road which directly connects a custom or worship with the nearest motive of expediency. To the savage a fierce animal is unquestionably a demoniac being, probably possessed by some malignant ghost; the bear, for example, is worshipped and honoured, yet he is hunted and killed for his flesh and skin; but the crocodile, on the other hand, is worshipped and not killed, seeing that he is not worth eating. All this is easily reconcilable with commonplace notions of utility, which is a prolific mother of religious rite and usage, and Mr Frazer by no means excludes her influence, in a modified shape and a secondary degree:

"On the principles of his rude philosophy the savage who slays an animal believes himself exposed to the vengeance of either its disembodied spirit or of all the other animals of the same species, whom he considers as knit together, like men, by the ties of kin and the obligations of the blood feud, and therefore as bound to resent the injury done to one of their number. Accordingly the savage makes it a rule to spare the life of those animals which he has no pressing motive for killing. Crocodiles are animals of this sort. They are only found in hot countries where, as a rule, food is abundant, and primitive man has therefore no reason to kill them for their tough and unpalatable flesh."

They are only killed, it is explained, in retaliation for the slaughter of men by crocodiles; and the same *lex talionis* governs the relations of certain tribes with tigers and rattle-snakes, which are merely killed by men in self-defence or in revenge. Here we are on a very intelligible and practical ground; we might, indeed, extend the deduction to include the habits of civilised folk, who kill uneatable animals only when they are noxious or troublesome, and whose practice in this respect might be described as the perpetuation of a blood feud, and shown to descend lineally from the figments of their remotest ancestors.

Let us take another quotation in the same vein of refreshing utilitarianism :—

"Thus the primitive worship of animals assumes two forms, which are in some respects the converse of each other. On the one hand animals are respected, and are therefore neither killed nor eaten. Totemism is a form of this worship, if worship it can be called; but it is not the only form, for we have seen that dangerous and useless animals, like the crocodile, are commonly revered and spared by men who do not regard the animal as their totem. *In both forms of worship the animal is revered on account of some benefit, positive or negative, which the savage hopes to receive from it.* In the former worship the benefit comes either in the positive form of protection, advice, and help which the animal affords the man, or in the negative one of abstinence from injuries which it is in the power of the animal to inflict. In the latter worship the benefit takes the material form of the animal's flesh and skin."

Here, then, we have in a nutshell the philosophy of natural religion, the general motive underlying both the propitiation and the destruction of useful and terrible animals; and some might be disposed to rest content with this fundamental explanation of the universal practice of zoolatry. We have before our eyes, in the beliefs and usages of all savage and semi-barbarous races, and in the superstitions running among the higher nations, abundant illustrations of this sentiment in every stage of vagrant metamorphosis; the animistic feeling, which invests everything with a soul, the dread of queer appearances and invisible forces, are ever present and operative; nor is it difficult to connect the leading expressions of instinctive hopes and fears in an ascending series of causation and development. In a superstitious atmosphere, with this all-pervading habit of deification, any incident, apparition, or unintelligible movement will be assimilated into and accounted for by these paramount formative tendencies of the savage imagination, directed by inclination or aversion, and moulded by the pressure of surrounding circumstance.

But is it possible to get beyond these broad conclusions upon the general conditions and tendencies of primitive beliefs, and to treat the swarming brood of superstitious folly, the vague delusions, as one treats the fauna and flora of the material world, arranging them in species and genera? In this direction I think that Mr Frazer attempts too much, that he relies too confidently on shades of resemblance, which may or may not be quite superficial. If I understand him correctly, he would trace all sacramental offerings and the religious sharing of food to the practice of god-killing; and this signification is ascribed to what is termed the form of communion with the sacred snake, as observed by a tribe in the Punjab. A basin of curds is reverentially offered at the tomb of a counterfeit snake; after which the rest is divided among children; but may not this be a specimen of the half-serious mummery that any child might have invented? Mr Frazer finds that ceremonies closely analogous to this Indian worship of the snake have survived in Europe; the best known example being the hunting of the wren, where the wren is hunted, killed, and solemnly paraded about from door to door, as the mock snake is carried about in India; while another example is drawn from St Kilda, where the cowherds go about with one of them wrapped in a cowhide, distributing bits of the hide, as the wren's feathers are given out in the Isle of Man.

"In the hunting of the wren, and the procession with the man clad in a cow-skin, there is nothing to show that the customs in question have any relation to agriculture. So far as appears, they may date from the pre-agricultural era, when animals were revered as divine in themselves, not merely as divine because they embodied the corn spirit; and the analogy of the Gilyah procession of the bear, and the Indian procession of the snake, is in favour of assigning the corresponding European customs to this very early date. On the other hand, there are certain European processions of animals, or of men disguised as animals, which may possibly be purely agricultural in their origin, in other words, the animals may have been from the first nothing but representatives of the corn spirit in animal shape. But it is at least equally possible that these processions originated in the pre-agricultural era, and have only received an agricultural tinge from the environment in which they survived. But the question is an obscure and difficult one, and cannot be here discussed."

There seems to be room here for wholesome scepticism,

and for the objection that our author is dealing too seriously and systematically with what may be little more than the ordinary rustic propensity for horseplay, hunting, and dressing up in the spoils or symbols of animals. Whether ideas of deeper significance and divine import underlie and inspire this propensity, is a question which it is but fair to leave for final determination by readers of the book itself, since neither the evidence nor the argument could be briefly summarised to the author's satisfaction.

We are invited to survey another aspect of human sacrifice viewed as the development of god-killing. The belief that human suffering and misfortune, pain and plagues, hail and tempest, can be averted or stopped by shifting the burden upon some other person or thing, has prevailed everywhere; the idea that ills and divine anger are transferable may be hunted all over the world and unearthed, not only in the remotest corners of savagery, but in the profound recesses of higher tradition. The devices for passing on an epidemic or any mysterious affliction, for expelling its cause by symbolically driving it out in some visible shape, are obviously represented in exorcism, witchcraft, devil-dancing, charms, disease-boats, scapegoats, Jonahs, and a legion of superstitious practices. Sin-eating at a funeral prevailed not long ago in Herefordshire; the sin-eater took upon himself, for a consideration, all the dead man's sins, in order to lay his ghost. When ill luck sticks to a community an offender is in the midst of them. A Buddhistic story tells how five hundred fishermen could catch no fish; they divided and subdivided until the ill luck was brought home to one boat, of which the owner was promptly expelled. Among barbarous nations the very natural desire to kill rather than be killed, to revenge evil upon its supposed author, and to propitiate angry divinities, has led to human sacrifice, mysterious assassinations, sorcery and witch-torture, bloody African massacres, and every variety of attempt at atonement and vicarious immolation. It can therefore be understood that so indefatigable a collector as Mr Frazer has easily brought together an abundant miscellany of customs appertaining to this category; and he employs this material in a manner that is undoubtedly interesting, although it exhibits the defects inherent, to my mind, in his general method. The sacrifices for the expulsion of evil were often annual, and corresponded with seasonal changes; the victims were frequently divine animals, divine men, or, what is the same thing, gods.

> "If we ask why a dying god should be selected to take upon himself and carry away the sins and sorrows of the people, it may be suggested that in the practice of using the divinity as a scapegoat we have a combination of two customs, which were at one time distinct and independent. On the one hand we have seen that it has been customary to kill the human or animal god in order to save his divine life from being weakened by the inroads of age; on the other, that it has been customary to have a general expulsion of evils and sin once a year. Now, if it occurred to people to combine these two customs, the result would be the employment of the dying god as a scapegoat."

Moreover, it appears that in Greece certain outcasts and deformed persons were maintained at the public expense for sacrifice on extraordinary occasions of public calamity, and that before death they were sometimes beaten with branches of wild trees in such a manner as to convince

Mr Frazer that the object was to release the divine victim's reproductive energies from any magical restraint or spell; while in Athens the annual sacrifice was at a harvest festival. The human scapegoat is therefore recognised as a representative of the creative and fertilising god of vegetation—

"annually slain for the purpose . . . of maintaining the divine life in perpetual vigour, untainted by the weakness of age, and before he was put to death it was not unnatural to stimulate his reproductive powers, in order that these might be transmitted in full activity to his successor, the new god or new embodiment of the old god, who was doubtless supposed immediately to take the place of the one slain."

Two ideas, according to this theory, became blended and confused in the custom of human sacrifice—the idea of slaying the embodied divinity, with certain invigorating processes, in the shape of a substitute, and the notion of sacrificing one person who should bear the sufferings or sins of an afflicted community. So far as both these ideas belong to the general conception of vicarious propitiation as one main source of sacrificial rites, Mr Frazer's interpretation is within the limits of fair conjecture, and is by no means to be dismissed without consideration, if only on the score of its originality. We shall be much more inclined to object to the undue stress which seems to us to have been laid upon minor details and accessories, such as the scourging of the Greek victims with certain plants (which is compared with the modern Russian practice of beating truant children with palm branches on Palm Sunday), for the purpose of hooking together all customs in which trees, beating, and sacrifice have any kind of share, and grouping them in aggregate illustration of the theory regarding the Arician cult. According to that theory, it will be remembered, the Nemi priest was slain as a representative of the wood spirit; and in the absence of any evidence that the custom of killing embodied deities was known among the Latin or Greek races, we are brought back to the conjecture that the human scapegoat, who was occasionally honoured and sometimes whipped with particular twigs before sacrifice, may have been regarded by the nations of classic antiquity as an incarnate deity, originally a god of vegetation. At all events, if in Italy the man-god was not slain, in Mexico he was unquestionably sacrificed, "by a people whose level of culture was probably not inferior, if not distinctly superior, to that occupied by the Italian races at the early period to which the origin of the Arician priesthood must be referred. . . . The positive and indubitable evidence of the prevalence of such sacrifices in one part of the world, may reasonably be allowed to strengthen the probability of their prevalence in places for which the evidence is less full and trustworthy."

The argument rests upon a remote analogy, and for so delicate a tissue it seems to us perilously strained; remembering that a cobweb is not made stronger by the multiplicity of gossamer threads, and that a cord with so many weak strands and splices is no safe binding for a large faggot of facts. But it should be added that the question whether his points have on the whole been adequately made out, is explicitly remitted by the author of this book to the judgment of its readers.

Returning, in the last chapter, to the Arician cult, we

have still to enquire, "What was the Golden Bough, and why had each candidate to pluck it before he could slay the priest?" Now it is manifest that the replies to these questions must be founded on what, by a stretch of language, may be termed circumstantial evidence, for of what actually took place in the grove of Nemi we have not, and cannot possibly obtain, any direct knowledge; we are indeed assuming, upon a slight and shadowy tradition, that the bough was golden. Virgil merely compares his Arician bough, altogether golden, stem as well as leaves, with the misletoe, which has only whitish-yellow berries. Notwithstanding these and other preliminary difficulties, that are fairly admitted in the book, we embark upon a fresh circumnavigation of the mythologic world, and the folklore of many countries and races is ransacked in search of specimens of analogous stories or beliefs.

The custom of fire-festivals is, or has been, universal among all pagan nations, and survives in the bonfires at Hallow E'en and Christmas of our own days, while the jumping over and through the fires and the burning of effigies preserve unmistakeable traces of heathen rites. This leads us by an easy transition to the old Celtic sacrifices, the Druids, the oak worship and the mistletoe; in fact, to all customs in which either fire, tree worship, the adoration of the sun, torch processions, or the gathering of magic plants, can be detected as a principal or subordinate feature. The list is long and varied; but our readers will have perceived that the argument, after some widely ranging and circular flights, is gradually closing in upon its points of demonstration. In Sweden the mistletoe is one of four different kinds of wood used at midsummer for divining-rods to discover treasure.

> "Now, if the mistletoe discovers gold, it must be in its character of the Golden Bough; and if it has been gathered at the solstices (Midsummer or Christmas), must not the Golden Bough, like the golden fern-reed, be an emanation of the sun's fire? The question cannot be answered by a simple affirmative."

However this may be, it would seem that the effigies burned in the bonfire at spring and midsummer are held to be the images of the spirit of vegetation; and that the customs of leaping over and driving cattle through the fire are intended to secure for man and beast a share of the sun's vital energy, and to purify them from evil influence. And although "the custom of burning a beneficent god is too foreign to later methods of thought to escape misinterpretation," yet we are scarcely permitted to doubt the true character of the effigy when it is tied to a living tree and bound with it. The myth of Balder, who was killed by a mistletoe, and then burnt on a pyre, is taken as showing the connection of the two ideas; since Balder is the mythical type of the victim burnt at fire-festivals, and was therefore a spirit of vegetation. If, as is probable, this victim represented a sacred tree, then in ancient Europe that tree must have been the oak, and the mistletoe was conceived as the seat of life in the oak. Hence, when the tree god had to be killed, it was first necessary to tear out his life by breaking off the mistletoe, so that when the spirit of the oak became embodied in a man, the fancied necessity of first breaking the sacred bough still survived, and thus became one of the conditions of the combat for the Arician priesthood.*

It is with deference that I reiterate the criticism to which this method of exposition lays itself open. The theory might be said to be the outcome of skilful manipulation of a quantity of facts and fancies, selected for the purpose out of an immense heap of heterogeneous material, which have no necessary connection or intrinsic probability of relationship apart from the pattern into which they are so dexterously weaved. In other hands they might be so arranged as to exhibit a different design; they are susceptible of various equally coherent inferences and explanations; they might be cemented by other no less reasonable conjectures than those which are liberally employed in the Golden Bough to fasten together the somewhat loose materials. It is not at all improbable, for instance, that the ancient Aryans kindled and fed their sacred fires with the oak wood, if only because the oak has always furnished excellent fuel; but it scarcely follows (though our author has no doubt of it) that the man who was burned in the fire as a personification of the tree spirit could have represented no tree but the oak, if, indeed, he represented anything beyond a burnt-offering to some cruel divinity. And though it is not incredible that the mistletoe was regarded by Celtic tribes as the life of the oak, nevertheless one would have hardly expected woodland folk

* The etymological interpretation is different. Mistel, a diminutive of mist, has the meaning of vapour or gloom in Anglo-Saxon. "Since Mistel may take the sense of gloom, we see why Balder, the sun-god, was fabled to have been slain by a twig of mistletoe."—Skeat's Dictionary—*s.v.* "Mistletoe."

to think thus about an unmistakeable parasite that is found on perhaps one out of a hundred equally healthy trees in a forest, and is not found only on the oak. It is equally possible that the comparatively rare appearance of the mistletoe, which in many woods is not easily found, had something to do with its sanctity. But, "the idea that the life of the oak was in the mistletoe was probably suggested" by the position of the plant on the trunk or branches of the oak, not upon the ground; for primitive man might think that the oak spirit had sought to deposit his life in a secure place, and for this purpose had pitched on the mistletoe, which grows between earth and heaven. All this, though supported by many other curious analogies and comparisons, is avowedly mere guesswork; insomuch that if the operator had not been working toward a foregone conclusion, we cannot do him the injustice of believing that he would have cared to climb to it by a ladder of which no single step can be relied upon to bear the weight of the ascending argument. But the effect of this operation is to prejudice the judgment and scientific impartiality which is never so necessary as when an investigator is occupied with hypotheses that cannot be actually verified. He is unconsciously led to select only the facts that suit him, and among many possible explanations he chooses, not that which is plain, unvarnished, and natural, but that which will fit into an awkward angle of his puzzle map, and will best help him forward toward his preconceived solution.

Mr Frazer gives us toward the end of his book an interesting section on Totemism (a subject upon which he has made separately a valuable study), connecting this curious custom with the world-wide primary belief in a soul that is lost, goes and returns, transmigrates, survives the body's death, feels pain and pleasure, is feared or adored, is blest or curst, is originally the mere breath or vital particle, and latterly a metaphysical entity. His object is to show that Totemism implies a belief in the possibility of depositing one's soul, for safe custody, in some place, animal, or plant, outside one's body; and his view is that the transfer is usually attempted at some critical moment or period, such as puberty. Now we may agree that under the word Totemism may be comprehended many of the conjuring tricks and initiatory ceremonies by which male and female adults are inducted into the tribal circle, and are guarded against the malignant influences that wage constant war against the health, virility, and bodily functions of pubescent youth. But Mr Frazer hints at some profound and hitherto unfathomable explanation:—

> "It would be easy to prove by a long array of facts that the sexual relation is associated in the primitive mind with many supernatural perils; but the exact nature of the danger apprehended is still obscure. We may hope that a more exact acquaintance with savage modes of thought will in time disclose this central mystery of primitive society, and will thereby furnish the clue, not only to the social aspect of totemism (the prohibition of sexual union between persons of the same totem), but to the origin of the marriage system."

The conjecture may be right, and there may yet be in the sexual relations of savages some undiscovered element of illusion and disturbance. Yet for most of us it is sufficient to take account of the peculiarly capricious, involuntary, and ungovernable passion which inspires these relations, and to remember that in all ages and states of society it has provided endless employment for every species of superstition, for divinities, witches, diabolic agencies, charlatans, and quacks of every degree. It seems very unlikely that by subjecting to minute analysis the infinitely varied symptoms of this universal epidemic, we shall elicit any trustworthy addition to our knowledge of primitive ideas or institutions.

I venture to extend this observation from the particular case to Mr Frazer's general theory. It is very interesting, it is so framed as to embrace a great and valuable collection of striking and freshly-gathered facts regarding primitive belief and custom; but we may doubt whether the speculation enlarges our horizon beyond the solid landmarks already set up by the leading pioneers in this field of exploration. If, indeed, he had not tethered himself, so to speak, to one point, if he had not imposed on himself the task of showing how all his conclusions in regard to the main currents of primitive superstition bear upon the interpretation of one strange story—the Arician cult—he might have ranged much more freely over the ground which he has chosen, and he would have been less under the temptation of breaking down sound arguments by over-riding them. We are indebted to him for a material addition to the museum of folklore, for many useful suggestions and combinations of ideas, and for some very careful excavations into the hidden bases of antique ritual. If he has not succeeded in the very arduous enterprise of co-ordinating all these customs and conceptions into a system of religious development, of proving the affinities that he detects between earliest and latest species, and of making different lines of thought meet and become embodied in the Arician cult, it is, we believe, because the trustworthy solution of such problems is impossible. The stratification of religious beliefs is like the geologic record—it attests certain great periods and vast changes, but it also reflects and is varied by innumerable lesser movements, by upheavals, survivals, and catastrophes of different kinds that have marked the intellectual surface and have violently agitated the imagination of men. It represents subsidence as well as upheaval; for, although the theory of the degradation and distortion of some primeval revelation made to all nations is not tenable, yet beyond doubt we find many beliefs and traditions running downward, spreading at a level much below their source. Lofty symbols and doctrines become low idolatry; the practices of high asceticism are travestied in magical quackery. The whole panorama of religious rites and images resembles, in polytheistic countries, the entangled confusion of a primeval forest, where you see trees, brambles, and creepers of all ages and sizes interlacing, supporting, and breaking down each other; with a glimpse of blue sky above the topmost branches to symbolise the infinite ideal toward which all these earthly growths are striving and shooting up. Yet the entire forest has sprung up out of the same soil and the same general conditions of existence; and so it may be said that all these curious religious forms have a like origin, they are generated out of the common experience and common feelings of humanity. It is possible to go further, and to register the main currents of religious tendency; but after all there is a great monotony and sameness in the countless and multiform vagaries of the inventive faculty among ignorant and superstitious men. The enormous accumulations now made of folklore, fairy tales, nonsensical fables, idiotic barbarous notions, legends, myths, and mumbo-jumbo ritual, add little to our clear understanding of the working of the religious mind, and rather tend to render unmanageable the scientific handling of the subject. A large number of these stories are insufficiently verified or unverifiable by exact enquiry; they come from old books or modern hearsay. To what extent a belief or custom prevails, whether it is a genuine indigenous notion or merely a tale invented to satisfy curious travellers, whether it comes from an accident or a joke—all such questions have to be answered, and in many cases no satisfactory examination of them can possibly be made.

In substance all primitive religion, ancient and contemporary, was, and is, Nature worship, which often had, at the same time, among the same people, different significations and methods of expression. With the vulgar it meant adoration of the marvellous and incomprehensible as embodied in things and felt in dreams and visions; in the upper classes it meant adoration of the perceptible, but as yet unintelligible, forces of Nature as personified under more or less refined types or symbols; and with the chosen few it signified their recognition of the working, through external phenomena, of a divine and all-pervading energy. The development, upon this broad canvas, of certain persistent forms of ritual, worship, and dogma is an instructive study, as when we trace one dominant custom or cult, such as sacrifice or the worship of the dead, through a long filiation of institutions that are obviously allied. Animism, as an universal habit of mind among barbarous races, is a fact of first-class importance, the most rudimentary stage being, as Comte surmises, probably very little above the sense of terror at strange things or sounds that is seen in animals; and there are other great departments or stages into which early superstitions can be classified and assorted. It may be maintained, for example, with tolerable safety that no religious idea or rite has endured and prevailed widely that has not sprung out of some root of fact or supposed utility, or upon some primordial affection of the human mind, like Fear, which means the instinct of self-preservation. But all human notions at a low intellectual level are so wild and invertebrate, that we can get little out of collecting them in heaps beyond a general verification of the class or mental stage to which they belong; we cannot use them as data for working out the meaning or derivation of any particular rite or group of usages. And we must be cautious about going too far back in tracing the possible pedigree of such practices, lest we overrun the scent, miss the real starting-point, and fancy that we detect a veritably antique relic in some belief or tale that was manufactured yesterday. As for mythology, it is true that it came largely (not wholly) out of the desire to veil, obscure, and account for the real origins of religion; but for that very reason it is an unsafe guide to a clear understanding of them, and we are rather hindered than helped by those who sweep together out of many lands and libraries, and discharge upon us, all the mythic puzzles and whimsical nursery tales of human infancy. We know very well that in polytheistic countries it is the business of the mystery-men and miracle-mongers to connect all new superstitions and fresh marvels with the older popular beliefs and traditions, to identify the latest with the antecedent divinities, to find room for strange worships and outlandish liturgies. In the Golden Bough we find many examples of the accretion of the ruder worships and legends round a superior deity or ritual; it is a familiar process in the gradual uplifting and centralisation of divine attributes; and the general connection between successive phases of religious manners and practices is too patent to have escaped competent observers in any age. There are, moreover, certain conditions under which it is quite possible to work out the modifications which a cult has undergone, as where, in Italy or in India, the religious history of a country is so well known as to lend itself to fairly accurate study. But it is a hazardous method to go backward over all ages, and abroad unto the uttermost parts of the earth, in search of worships, emblems, loose priestly inventions, vulgar delusions, and all the phantasmagoria of nebulous *deisidæmonia*, in order to show ground for supposing that one explanation of an obscure story, or myth, or ritual, is more probable than another. The natural seed of religion, as Hobbes calls it, is the same all over the primitive world; but its fruits are varied infinitely by environment, by soil, climate, training, and accidental circumstance. And although the fundamental analogies can be observed everywhere, it must be doubted whether even the scholarship, ability, and insight displayed by this very interesting book, can succeed in transmuting general resemblances into particular relations.

CHAPTER IV.

ORIGINS AND INTERPRETATIONS OF PRIMITIVE RELIGIONS.*

Collection of materials and classification—Miss Kingsley an excellent collector—Her description of West African superstitions, fetish, demonology, witchcraft, poisoning—Mutual condition of West African races—The wandering soul, ghosts, and deities—Taboo—Secret Societies—Manners and morals of the people—Mr Jevons' theory—Evolution of beliefs—Primitive monotheism—Discussion of his views and methods—Taboo—Totemism—The evolutionary argument—Professor Max Müller's book—The Science of Mythology—Philological interpretation of myths—The solar hero—Physical origin of all Aryan gods—The melting down of epic scenes and characters—Concluding remarks.

THE comparative study of Natural Religion, like other branches of empirical research, divides itself into two working departments. In one of them is the collector of materials, who roams far afield and scrambles about among wild folk to gather his specimens and take note of varieties; in the other is the philosophic savant who remains at home to receive what is brought him from different countries, to classify, collate, and form his scientific inductions. Sometimes the two branches are successfully combined in one person; though we usually

---

* Mary H. Kingsley, "Travels in West Africa." Lond. 1897.

Frank Byron Jevons, M.A., "An Introduction to the History of Religion." Lond. 1896.

The Right Hon. Professor Max Müller, K.M., "Contributions to the Science of Mythology." Lond. 1897.

find that the adventurous traveller, with an eye for primitive beliefs and customs, and the gift of interpreting them, is differently constituted from the home-keeping student of results. The former has the great advantage of knowing the environment, the true connexion of one species with another, their signification among the people on the spot; while the latter, who deals with them in a library or a museum, may have a wider range of survey and a better method of classification. On the other hand, as his aim is toward bringing a heap of material into symmetrical arrangement, he is often prone to overstrain his theories, to use the same weight and measure for all his facts, to lay stress on superficial resemblances, and in other respects to suffer the disadvantages which beset every judge, however able and learned, who is obliged to take evidence at second hand.

The writers of the books which I propose to review may be taken as fairly exemplifying these two classes. Miss Mary Kingsley has explored, with great enterprise and an admirable disdain of discomfort, some regions of the West African coast that have been hitherto little visited by competent observers. She has consorted with cannibals, visited their homes, travelled in the company of the fetish worshipper and discoursed with him on sacred things; she has trusted herself alone with savage tribes, and has won their confidence. Of all these opportunities she has made excellent use. Mr Jevons, again, has equipped himself for a comprehensive investigation into the foundations of primitive beliefs by an attentive study of all recent writings upon this obscure and intricate question; he has a wide knowledge of the literature, ancient and modern, that has accumulated over it; and his design is to apply evolutionary principles (with certain important reservations) to the whole history of Religion. Professor Max Müller has long since attained a brilliant reputation and great popularity as the interpreter of Aryan mythology.

As the hearing of witnesses goes before the summing up of the judges, we may begin, logically, with Miss Kingsley's book. It must, however, be in the first place clearly understood that Miss Kingsley's travels were not undertaken exclusively in quest of the religious idea. She says, indeed, that her "fixed desire was to study fetish," but we learn that she went also for beetles and fishes; her general object appears to have been to see life in the deadly climate of the west African coast within the tropics, and to examine the social and administrative conditions under which it is endured by mankind in and about Lower Guinea. On the whole, although Miss Kingsley enjoyed the country and likes its people, these conditions seem to be unattractive. Very grisly anecdotes are told of the sudden and fatal illnesses, the rapid succession of official vacancies, the fevers, the putrescences, and the noxious animals. Scorpions, snakes, and crocodiles infest land and water; the insects are even more ferocious, proportionately to their size, than the wild beasts; and the men are no better than the animals. In regard to Sierra Leone its English bishop has recently printed the painful admission that small social gatherings are almost unknown there through fear of poisoning, which is apparently a practice universally prevalent among all classes of the native population, and operates as a check upon the excessive ill usage of wives. Miss Kingsley's courage and scientific ardour have enabled her, in spite of all these risks and of serious hardships, to mix freely with the people, to wander in magnificent scenes of mountain and primeval forest, and to bring back stores of fresh information regarding the fishes, the folklore, and the fetish. I must reluctantly leave untouched the record of her personal adventures, although it abounds with shrewd remarks and amusing incidents. In regard to the author's style, it is clear and unvarnished, though the conjecture may be hazarded that during her sojourn in a region notoriously overcrowded by spirits, she may peradventure have become unconsciously possessed by an humoristic fiend, whom in this Christian land she would do well to cast out.

The first thing, says Miss Kingsley, before starting to hunt the religious idea in west Africa, is to burn all one's notions about sun myths and the worship of elemental forces. She herself had set out in full confidence that Mr Frazer's book, "The Golden Bough," provided the "semi-universal key" to early customs and beliefs everywhere; and she soon discovered how very few of the inner mental chambers in which the wild man's fancies are bred, this key would unlock. "The study of natural phenomena knocks the bottom out of any man's conceit, if it is done honestly and not by selecting only those facts which fit in with his preconceived or ingrafted notions"—true words that should be gravely pondered by all ingenious folklorists. And she rightly enjoins upon the student, as before all things necessary, a careful reading of Dr E. B. Tylor's work, which really contains almost everything that can be soberly and safely written upon Primitive Culture. She observes that the Africans often have remarkable acuteness and a large share of common-sense, that the form of their mind is quite different from the childish stage; nor are they flighty, mystical, or dreamers. The remark is important, because nothing is more common than a comparison of primitive mankind with civilised children, whereas the only common ground is unbounded credulity; for the experiences, which shape the imaginative faculty, are in the two cases altogether unlike, and the child mostly takes his fantastic impressions from the sayings and doings of his elders. The animistic tendency of civilised man to treat a ship or a steam-engine as a living creature, whom it is possible to love or hate according to its behaviour, is much nearer the intellectual attitude of the savage to Nature at large.

Now the peculiarity of west Africa, as a field for the botanical study of beliefs, is that while almost every other part of the four continents has been more or less overlaid by some great conquering faith, in this region the indigenous superstitions grow as rank and free as the primeval forests. The proselytism of Islam or Christianity has only scattered among them a few ideas and doctrines that have been absorbed, with various distortions, into the mass of legends and practices. Probably the aboriginal African has for many generations been moving westward, under the pressure of stronger tribes, until he has been brought up against the coast line of the impassable Atlantic, in a climate where the struggle for existence is fierce and unceasing. Here if anywhere the life of man is, to borrow the words of Hobbes, "poore, nasty, brutish, and short"; and as is their life so is their religion. The people who inhabit the inland country are for the most part cannibals, among whom to kill or be killed is as much their everyday lot as among the wild animals, and of whom some tribes have become degraded during many generations of retreat before stronger enemies. May we not expect, then, to find in this very low stratum of human society any of those primal forms which the evolutionist can treat as the simplest germs of higher and wider religious conceptions, providing the materials for a connected and tenable demonstration of the growth and development of Natural Religion?

One may regret, as Miss Kingsley's collection of facts and observations is so valuable, that she has not thought it worth while to arrange and group them in more consecutive order, instead of dropping them somewhat fortuitously over her five chapters on Fetish. But she has evidently no intention of propitiating the critical spirit embodied in indolent reviewers; and as an artist she may have desired us to realise the cloudy atmosphere that overhangs the whole region of African supernaturalism. It may, therefore, be useful if, in an attempt to summarise briefly the results of her enquiries, we begin by taking, in the first place, her information regarding the kind or description of the beings, divine or disembodied, whom the African of this region fears or adores, their origins, attributes, the tokens that denote their presence, the signs of their power. The second part of our summary would then deal with the rites and customs, the rules of procedure for doing business with divinity, and the phenomena of that universal delusion, which has infested all early communities like the plague or the

Black Death, witchcraft. We have to understand that in the primitive world there are two great societies, of gods and of men, with a strong family resemblance in the matters of tastes, feelings, diet, habits, and vicious propensities in particular; having also reciprocal needs and grievances, so that they are to a certain degree mutually dependent on each other's good offices. The divine community, being much the stronger and more aggressive, is able to levy oppressive tribute upon long-suffering mankind, and even to insist upon servile obedience. Nevertheless we find that in west Africa, as elsewhere, the two societies keep up constant communication; there is much emigration to and fro; the human soul quits its earthly tenement with a distinct *animus revertendi*, the deities take bodily shape for a season; and it is plain that without continual intercourse and the interchange of dues and services, neither of them could flourish satisfactorily. It is also clear that even to spiritual despotism there must always be a certain limit, a point at which long-suffering humanity begins to rebel, as when the gods do very little for worshippers and demand too much of them.

With these remarks we may take up Miss Kingsley's account of African demonology and witchcraft. In the first place, what sort of mind is it that transforms its impressions into fearful or grotesque shapes, and peoples the surrounding atmosphere with them?

"The mental condition of the lower forms of both races seems very near the other great border line that separates man from the anthropoid apes, and I believe that if we had the material, or rather if we could understand it, we should find little or no gap existing in mental evolution in this old undisturbed continent of Africa."

It is among the negroes, therefore, that may be found "the earliest forms both of religion and witchcraft"—witchcraft being definable as the power possessed by some malevolent mortal who has acquired control over spirits; whereas religion may be roughly described in this stage as a belief in their direct supernatural action. With regard, then, to the divinities, we are told that there is somewhere a god who originally created the world and all that it contains, but who, like the Indian Brahma, takes no interest in its management; he has laid out the universe and stocked it; he has done his work, and left the administration to others; he is evidently the Final Cause invented to explain phenomenal existence, as a house implies an architect. The unfortunate consequence of his abdication is that the everyday affairs of mankind are consigned to the caprice of a disorderly crowd of spirits, very largely recruited by the incessant transmigration of souls, with diverse local origins and habitats, in the trees, the rocks, or the bodies of wild animals. There are also pure nature deities, household Lares, and mere fetish: the animistic fancies suggested by queer uncanny things. Wandering demons, like Sasabonsum and his wife, and horrid apparitions which to see is to die, are also common; while dangerous places, such as rocks, whirlpools, and swamps, are haunted, as usual, by sprites invisible. The disembodied ghost roves unresting, a mournful and troublesome vagrant, until its manes have been appeased by the proper rites, when it is relegated to the dim underground kingdom, which represents the crude indistinct notions formed by all early polytheists of some refuge, or prison house, or penal settlement for those who have finally vanished beyond the world of ordinary sense. "This place has its pleasures and pains, not necessarily retributive or rewarding, but dim . . . a veritable shadow land where men have not the joys of life, but only their shadow;" and the native proverb, which says that one day on the upper earth is worth a year in the nether world, corroborates what we know from the Odyssey of the classic Hades, where Achilles says that he would rather be a ploughboy than reign over the innumerable dead. One finds traces of the universal tradition that in old times there was closer intercourse between gods and men, who went up and down by a ladder reaching from earth to sky, until it was thrown down from above because the earth-born tried to push their way into heaven.

All this is merely the simpler sort of paganism that has prevailed in all times and places wherever superstitions have been left to grow in their natural disorderly fashion, to vary according to the environment, and to reflect through the popular imagination the conditions of human existence. There is nothing new in these African beliefs and legends; they are chiefly valuable as cumulative proofs of the very narrow grooves to which the image-making mind of man seems to be confined, of the short range within which its inventive faculty appears to work, passing the ideas from hand to hand, adapting, enlarging, and refining a few original conceptions. The typical form survives all changes, as the steel axe of the modern carpenter has not varied far from the shape of the pre-historic stone hatchet; it is obviously moulded by sensations and experiences, by moods and manner, by changing circumstance and perceptions of utility. And the process of thought moves step by step.

> "You soon become conscious of the careful way a negro follows his idea. Certain customs you can, by the exercise of great patience, trace back in a perfectly smooth line to their source in some natural phenomena, or to reasons of utility."

The killing of wives at their husbands' funeral is a fair example. The colourable object is that they may accompany him into his next existence; but a Calabar chief explained to Miss Kingsley that the custom was also a salutary check upon husband poisoning; and one cannot doubt that he is right. The progress from the rough-and-ready expedients of early society, where the same individual turns his hand to all trades, up to the specialisation of handicrafts, may be traced in supernaturalism as in political economy. Miss Kingsley tells us that the African sprites are not easily classified by their functions, although they are all to some extent limited as to the nature of their power, and work only on certain lines, so that there is no one of them who can do all things. We have here the first stages of the gradual evolution of the professional or departmental divinity.

At the bottom of all this confused jumble of gods and goblins lies, so far as I can make out, the inveterate belief in the migratory soul, whom death renders homeless until it can find another abiding-place by re-embodiment, which again is dependent upon the due performance of mortuary rites. This idea of the wandering soul is so universal, so obviously founded upon the instinctive human refusal or incapacity to accept death as the final extinguisher, that it may be taken as the ultimate ascertainable basis of religion in a state of nature. "The really important part of every funeral is the burying of the spirit, which allows it to settle down in some fresh tenement." Nevertheless, although the ghosts are all worshipped, although men and animals are offered to the souls of deceased persons, Miss Kingsley maintains, if I understand her rightly, that a clear line of demarcation exists between ghosts and gods; that the former never develop into the latter; and she warns us against confusing the offerings to the dead with sacrifices made for the propitiation of deities. At this point, therefore, she differs from the conclusions of Herbert Spencer and other authorities; nor is it easy to make out plainly from her book the grounds upon which she disentangles such a distinct and important dividing line out of the complicated medley of souls and demons, spirits and deities, with much the same habits, powers for mischief, and wonder-working characteristics, that are the objects of fear and adoration in west Africa. That famous men were constantly taking rank, after death, among the gods of classic Greece and Rome, is beyond dispute; that ancestral worship is often the first step to divine honours in polytheistic Asia, especially in China, cannot be gainsaid; the promotion of heroes, saints, and martyrs goes on continuously and manifestly. Miss Kingsley, however, is so careful and trustworthy an observer, that we must accept her conclusion, reaffirmed in her latest work, that "West Africa has not deified ancestors." It is a curious and valuable fact, proving that what is true of ancient civilised religions that have been to some degree systematised, may be untrue of worships and incoherent superstitions of African tribes, who might easily make the distinctions in practice and belief, without noticing the close filiation which connects the two ideas. It may be noticed, indeed, that in the west African Hades the souls of great men are privileged to prey upon the crowd of ignoble ghosts, although yet they seem not to return to power in the upper air. And one may throw out, also, the conjecture that in remote and obscure west Africa, men do not reach the necessary pitch of renown for mighty deeds or sanctity that qualifies them, in larger countries, for elevation after death to high place among recognised divinities.

Sacrifice and incantation are the well-known professional methods of dealing with spirits. The meat of the sacrifice is eaten, for the blood is the life offered up; and incantation may be by prayer or by mystic words and signs of the masonic order. The Taboo, or interdict laid upon certain things, is, Miss Kingsley thinks, a form of sacrifice, being a kind of religious abstinence imposed upon persons, and varying infinitely, as to the thing prohibited, with each person. Of this world-wide custom, upon the meaning of which learned folklorists have expended great ingenuity, I shall have occasion to make some observations presently. Meanwhile it is clear that the really dominant feature of west African superstitions, to which all others are secondary, and which permeates the whole religious atmosphere, is the belief in witchcraft. This is the terrible plague which is always at its worst in the lowest stages of human society, which disappears very slowly as the intellectual level rises, which has never been entirely extirpated from the most civilised communities, and which in our own day is finding a kind of scientific interpretation as a psychical force. Among early communities witchcraft is uppermost where the religion is lowest; nor is it until religion gathers strength enough to draw apart, to give fierce battle to witchcraft, and to denounce it as a black disreputable art, that there is any hope of spiritual improvement. The following extract contains Miss Kingsley's definition of witchcraft—

"They regard their god as the creator of man, plants, animals, and the earth, and they hold that having made them he takes no further interest in the affair. But not so the crowd of spirits with which the universe is peopled; they take only too much interest, and the Bantu wishes they would not, and is perpetually saying so in his prayers, a large percentage whereof amounts to "Go away; we don't want you"; "Come not into this house, this village, or its plantations." He knows from experience that the spirits pay little heed to these objurgations, and as they are a people that must be attended to, he develops a cult whereby they may be managed, used, and understood. This cult is what we call witchcraft."

In a later passage, however, we have "the origin of man's religious belief" ascribed to motives and impressions that seem almost identical with those out of which witchcraft is said to have been developed. It is generally assumed, says Miss Kingsley, in the infancy of humanity, that death is always the consequence of the action of some malignant spirit, and that there is no accidental or natural death—

"A man having thus gained a belief that there are more than human actors in life's tragedy, the idea that disease is also a manifestation of some invisible being's wrath and power seems to me natural and easy; and he knows you can get another man for a consideration to kill or harm a third party, and so he thinks that for a consideration you can also get one of these superhuman beings which we call gods or devils, but which the African regards in another light, to do so.

"A certain set of men and women then specialise off to study how these spirits can be managed, and so arises a priesthood; and the priests, or medicine men, as they are called in their earliest forms, gradually, for their own ends, elaborate and wrap round their profession with ritual and mystery."

Although this view of religious origins does by no means cover the whole ground, there is, of course, much truth in it; but the point for observation is that from these extracts we should judge Miss Kingsley's conclusion to be that witchcraft and religious rites in west Africa are originally undistinguishable. If this is correct, there can be no doubt that such a confusion of two ideas, which in their later forms not only stand widely apart, but are always irreconcilably hostile, denotes the very lowest stage of aboriginal superstition wherever it prevails. The line between abject fetishism and witchcraft may be difficult to trace in the elementary stages; yet it has been argued that from the beginning a true distinction can invariably be recognised. According to this theory the witch is more nearly allied with rudimentary science than with priestcraft: for he relies not upon prayer, worship, or propitiation of divinities, but upon his own secret knowledge and experience of the effect producible by certain tricks and mysterious devices upon the unseen powers, over whom he has attained a sort of command. Instead of serving, like the priest, these powers, he is enabled by his art to make them serve him; and it is for this reason that his practices very soon become denounced and detested by the priesthood. To the priest belong adoration and propitiatory sacrifice; if these things will not move the divine authorities there is nothing else to be done by the supplicant; but where the case can be diagnosed as witchcraft, there is a human being within reach who can be cruelly punished; and the fact that he is held personally responsible shows that the occult faculty of mischief-making is actually detected within him. When a man sets up in sorcery he becomes the scapegoat for all the ills of mankind which kings and priests cannot cure, and every inexplicable wrong is laid to his account, so that his reputation for direct wonder-working becomes fatal to him. The priest, on the other hand, is merely the steward or minister of an irresponsible and unapproachable divinity. The first step necessary in west Africa for the profession of sorcery is to entertain a familiar spirit, which is done by cutting a rude wooden human figure, into which he is persuaded to locate himself, when his services become at the sorcerer's disposal. Here we have already the tendency to obtain command over supernatural forces, instead of obedience and prostration before them; and if the witch has hit upon any very rude observations of physical cause and effect, if he knows some quackery in medicine, is weatherwise, or is cunning in what has been called "natural magic," the familiar spirit will get all the credit of his ingenuity. In the departments of love and death he has an immense practice; while all the intelligent folk know, as Miss Kingsley remarks, that "there is a lot of poisoning" in the business, as is shown by the wide diffusion among her African acquaintance of the treatment of persons bewitched by a strong emetic. But in witch ordeals your only real chance of escape is by bribing the presiding expert.*

Miss Kingsley has much to say of the secret societies, which operate in the dark, like the Spanish Inquisition, for the discovery and punishment of social and religious backsliding, and which also cover a great deal of sheer wickedness in the way of murder and cannibalism. Of course there is initiation, followed by hideous rites and the marking down for assassination of some victim, who may be a rich relative or some other obnoxious person whom it is convenient to put away under the pretext of an ordained sacrifice to the society's fetish. The worshippers of one notorious fetish are called Human Leopards,

> "because when seizing their victims for sacrifice they covered themselves with leopard skins, and, imitating the leopard's roar, sprang upon their victims, plunging two three-pronged forks into each side of the throat. There are also human alligators, disguised as alligators, who swim in the creeks upon the canoes and carry off the crew."

These associations work in the dark because their deeds are too shocking for public opinion even in west Africa, being also, of course, highly criminal within any colonial jurisdiction; and they illustrate in its lowest and most nefarious stage that spirit of license under the cloak of religious mysteries which has given such meetings an ill repute in all ages and countries. The terror caused by

* In "West African Studies," Miss Kingsley has shown that the hatred of witches is intense in societies which have no organised priesthood. I have no doubt she is right; yet I hold to the view that wherever the priest does exist, he is clearly distinguishable from the witch and his mortal enemy.

the real leopard or crocodile has invested these animals with a kind of sanctity, so that to kill them brings bad luck; and this immunity is to the advantage of the murderer in the beast's skin, against whom it is difficult to bring proof that will satisfy white man's law. The best way of putting down these hideous practices would probably be to institute a detective police with special powers, upon the plan that was successfully adopted for extirpating the Thugs, who were a secret society of stranglers and poisoners in India.

Some apology is due to Miss Kingsley for reviewing in this place only those chapters of her book which deal with the West African superstitions. It should be clearly understood that the range of her narrative and observations is much wider, and that its value consists largely in the description which she gives of the state and prospect of manners and morals on the coast, where the native tribes are gradually feeling the influence of the commerce, the colonisation, and the missionaries of Europe. Her conclusions are not hopeful, for the savage, like the wild animal, seems to degenerate as soon as he is tamed; and security is apt to breed indolence, which is fatal to the tribe, "for inactivity in Africa is death." And when you have eliminated from the indigenous religion all its superstitious terrors, the African, according to Miss Kingsley, falls away into a condition of careless self-indulgent debauchery, under which the race loses its vital vigour, and degenerates physically without much moral compensation. The prospect of punishment in a future existence is not near enough to tame the wild passions of the sinful savage; he adopts only what is pleasant to him in the new dispensation, and degenerates in consequence, because what he really needs is severe religious discipline.

"Nothing strikes one so much, in studying the degeneration of these native tribes, as the direct effect that civilisation and reformation has in hastening it. The worst enemy to the existence of the African tribe is the one who comes to it and says: 'Now you must civilise and come to school, and leave off all those awful goings-on of yours and settle down quietly.' The tribe does so; the African is teachable and tractable. . . . He treats his religion much as other men do: when he gets slightly educated—a little scientific, one might say—he removes from his religion all the disagreeable parts. He promptly eliminates its equivalent Hell, represented in Fetishism by immediate and not future retribution.

"Then goes his rigid Sabbath-keeping and food-restriction equivalent, and he has nothing left but the agreeable portions—dances, polygamy, and so on; and it's a very bad thing for him. I only state these things so as to urge upon people at home the importance of combining technical instruction in their mission teaching, which by instilling into the African mind ideas of discipline, and providing him with manual occupation, will save him from these relapses, which are now the reproach of missionary effort and the curse and degradation of the African."

. . . .

From this curious and valuable description of primitive beliefs and customs in their natural state of entangled confusion I turn to the philosophic and well-ordered survey of their origin, interconnection, and underlying psychology that is presented to us by Mr Jevons. In the opening pages of his volume we are warned that such religions as Christianity, Mahomedanism, and Buddhism have no place in the history to which the author introduces us. These positive religions, as he terms them, were designed to supersede others to which, being practised as a matter of custom and tradition, he gives the name of customary religions, and with these only he intends to deal. To this vast residuum of institutions, beliefs, and usages prevalent everywhere among wild folk and in the countries of ancient civilisation, he applies the methods of science and the principles of anthropology.

Now the instrument chiefly employed by science in the prosecution of these researches is the comparative method, which examines apparent resemblances in phenomena for the purpose of bringing out their essential differences; the record of successive differences being the history of their evolution. But in tracing the development of later from earlier forms, Mr Jevons desires to guard himself against admitting that monotheism was reached by a slow condensation out of rudimentary notions. Ideas and institutions, he observes, not only grow but decay; the Roman empire was a moral degeneration from the republic, and art often goes backward. The principle that religion is evolved may thus be accepted without rejecting the possibility that monotheism may have been the original religion, although on the other hand our lack of complete evidence prevents our assuming it to have been so.

The author's views in regard to the evolutionary process are worked out at length in his concluding chapters "On Monotheism and the Evolution of Belief." After stating very fairly the data of observation and experience which go to support the hypothesis that monotheism was evolved out of polytheism, he proceeds to argue, on the other side, that on evolutionary principles, and following the analogy of the law governing the development of physical organisms, this hypothesis is untenable. Two of the highest existing species (monkeys and men, for example) may be descended from a common ancestor, but not one from the other. To suppose that monotheism could have descended from polytheism is, therefore, in his opinion, unscientific; and, what is more, Mr Jevons holds that it would be contradicted by the actual facts of religious history, for he contends that the polytheisms known to science never pass into monotheism. And I gather that he prefers to conclude that the original ancestor of the monotheist was the worshipper of one out of a multitude of gods. The view adopted seems to be that man recognised from the beginning—subjectively, not from the external facts of which he was conscious—his dependence on a personal and supernatural Will, but found it to be impossible to identify this Will with more than one external object. Such may have been, originally, the totem or tribal god, and this single point of adoration is only lost eventually in polytheism by the confusion of deities resulting from a conflux of tribes, when each clan of a confederation worships not only its own totem god but the other clan totems. Or else the different gods are identified and their cults are fused, so that one deity is produced out of many; but in either case, whether of polytheism or syncretism, the original antecedent worship may have been monotheistic.

"The sacrifices offered to Jehovah by the Jews point back not to polytheism but to a low form of monotheism, in which each clan that offered sacrifice worshipped but one god, though that god was conceived in the form of the animal or plant which was sacrificed. This brings us to the question whether totemism, that lowest form of monotheism, is the earliest form of religion; and for the answer to that question we are reduced to conjecture."

Mr Jevons argues, also, that since of spiritual things the

knowledge comes by inward intuition, not by means of inference, deductive or inductive, so it is quite possible that a revelation of monotheism may have been made to primitive man.

It would not have been fair if, in endeavouring to review briefly an interesting book, no mention had been made of the limitations thus placed by Mr Jevons upon his application of evolutionary principles to the history of religion. But neither can I abstain from intimating the opinion that by diverging, with some incongruity, from the main lines of his argument, he has unnecessarily imported some disputable matter into his investigation of the origins and development of primitive beliefs. It was enough for him, I think, to have excluded at the outset the great monotheistic faiths from the scope of his dissertations, without entering upon theories regarding the separate sources of monotheism, which are not likely to convince the thorough-going evolutionist, while the theologian may repudiate them as offering battle to the enemy on unfavourable ground. Revealed religion will have nothing to do with totemism, or with the hazardous contention that the pagan who selected for worship one god out of a legion, carried in his breast the primeval monotheistic revelation. And the students for whom this book is professedly written may not hold fast to the rather fine distinction between this view and the Comtist induction, that the adoration of many supernatural agencies gradually concentrated upon the notion of a single omnipotent personality. To quote from one of the able essays issued under the title of "Lux Mundi" (a book with which Mr Jevons is evidently familiar)—"It is impolitic as it is unscientific to identify Christian Apology with a position" (the belief in primitive monotheism) "which may one day prove untenable." And though Mr Jevons attempts no such express identification, the drift of his argument sets plainly that way.

Apart from these speculations there is substantial value in the careful comparison made by Mr Jevons of the different shapes and species of religious belief to be found among all sorts and conditions of men, wherever the great creeds and churches have not formulated and moulded them authoritatively. His views are laid out ably and persuasively, with great wealth of illustration, and a considerable capacity for assorting and co-ordinating a vast array of heterogeneous facts. Nevertheless there are indications that the spirit of scientific arrangement, the craving of the modern mind for logical demonstration, are often too strong for him, so that he is impelled to lay down the basis of primordial ideas in terms that are, I think, too formal and definite. In the remarkable chapter, which is well worth close reading, on the "Supernatural," he contends that from the beginning man has distinguished between the natural and the supernatural, because from the first he had a clear though a very confined perception of uniformity in nature. Laws on which man could count, and sequences which he habitually initiated and controlled, were, he says, natural. It was the violation of these sequences and the frustration of his expectations that produced his original notion that the supernatural power was manifested merely in suspending or counteracting the uniformity of Nature. According to this view any unusual movement of a river, such as a great flood, was first taken to be the sign of an active water spirit, who subsequently became identified, as the river god, with the ordinary aspect and customary flow of the stream which he had been discovered to inhabit.

It is always very difficult for the civilised enquirer to follow out and define the train of logical thought which brings primitive folk to their beliefs, and I doubt whether any light is really gained by crediting them with the ideas which underlie such terms as the "uniformity of Nature," "supernatural," and "natural." So far as one can understand the savage, he makes no such distinction, and what the higher minds mean by supernatural is to him the most natural explanation of everything, usual or unusual, by which he is surrounded. He accounts for all movement by life and will; he invests even motionless objects with an indwelling spirit; he worships them all indiscriminately; and the fact that certain sequences are ordinary, and rarely if ever interrupted, does not remove them out of the divine category, for a tree or a stone may have mysterious influences; nor is there anything about a wolf, a tiger, or a snake that frustrates the wild man's expectations. The sun, the moon, the stars in their unchanging courses, are objects of his reverent adoration. And it is to a large extent his experience of invariable operation that suggests to him the presence of divinity in the case of fire, of wind, or drifting clouds. He does not worship these phenomena because they are unusual, but because they are unintelligible forces; and in his ignorance of second causes, as Hobbes says, he attributes to all these things existence; they appear and disappear;

they are animated by the souls or spirits whom he locates everywhere, and so they are gifted with the attributes of power. Undoubtedly this power is most clearly signified in things casual or unexpected, as in the case of an eclipse or a thunderstorm; but where every such sight, sound, or feeling whose cause is not obvious, from a headache to a hurricane, is thus ascribed to some capricious agency, it seems hardly worth while to provide the bewildered savage with a logical basis for his ideas by crediting him with a fundamental perception of uniformity in nature. It seems better to say at once that in his instinctive attempts to link effects with some kind of cause he infers, by human analogy, that the perpetual motion and change round him of things visible must come from the incessant activity of beings like himself, but invisible. The savage theory of causation, Mr Jevons observes truly, is not fundamentally different from the scientific; the inductive methods form the common framework of both minds. But when he goes so far as to say that "the savage would probably be able to give his assent to all the principles of Mill's logic," and that the differences between the two minds are not formal but material, he overstrains the connexion to a point where it becomes misleading and tends to darken the clear vision of actual facts. Of course the mental processes, like the brain structure, are the same in the lowest Australian as in a Newton or a Darwin, and even a monkey can reason, within his tether, from effect to cause like a philosopher. But this statement of the vague imbecile guesses of wild creatures in the rigid terms of logic will bring little help to students, who should beware of too much method; and at any rate the simple empirical habit of always attaching an effect to some immediate cause might have been touched upon with a lighter hand.

One may readily acknowledge the careful and comprehensive treatment, the skill in marshalling facts to show their interconnexion and to support conclusions, that are brought to bear in this book upon the genesis and growth of primitive beliefs. It seems to me, however, that the writer's argument is complicated by the necessity of maintaining his initial thesis that mankind has from the beginning made a distinction between natural and supernatural. "Not all spirits," it is said, "are supernatural spirits. The man who believes the bowing tree or the leaping flame to be a thing like himself does not therefore believe it to be a supernatural being;" and I understand Mr Jevons to hold that spirits of the dead are not ranked among the supernatural, that the ghost never becomes a god. The distinction seems exceedingly hard to draw, though much would depend on the precise meaning attached to the words "natural" and "supernatural"; and at any rate one may object that it is much too absolutely stated here. So also, I think, is the difference between ghosts and gods, a point quite as disputable as the converse theory, which Mr Jevons rightly rejects, that all the gods of the earlier races, without any exceptions, were the spirits of dead men divinised. It may be observed that Mr Jevons finds the dividing line between his two spiritual classes, and their separate origin, rather difficult to keep up, for he has to admit that "the spirits of the dead are occasionally credited with supernatural powers, that offerings to the dead become sacrifices to deities," that there is a tendency to assimilate the private cult of ancestors to the public worship of the gods, and that certain ancestors are, by some unexplained process, raised to the rank of gods. The evidence that such promotion does occur is irresistible, and has to be rebutted in this book by declaring that these ancestors must have been originally reckoned as divine, else would they not have been worshipped. "The fact is," it is said, "that ancestors known to be human were not worshipped as gods, and ancestors worshipped as gods were not believed to be human." How can Mr Jevons, sitting in his library, be reasonably sure of that? And is it scientific to frame such positive generalisations regarding ideas and practices which vary infinitely at different periods and places, and which are always complex, entangled, and liable to become accidentally intermixed? It is also argued that the two systems—ancestor worship and public worship—could not have existed side by side if they had a common origin, because in that case one would have absorbed the other. But I much doubt whether this general assumption is incontrovertible, and I think it rests mainly upon notions of symmetry and consistency that are foreign to primitive religions, although they prevail among highly organised creeds, which do always absorb or destroy earlier and weaker forms.

Three very instructive chapters are devoted by Mr Jevons to the subject of Taboo, a Polynesian word which has been adopted by the latest anthropologists to comprehend all the branches of what is certainly in one sense a universal institution. As thus used it includes not only that vast group of ideas and practices which attribute sanctity to certain persons, places, animals, and things tabooed, but also all ordinances of ceremonial purity or uncleanness, all prohibitory rules of caste and custom, all negative commands regulating social intercourse, especially between the sexes, and the etiquette which hedges round priests, kings, and women. The peculiarity of this code is that it operates mechanically, for any offence against it is punished inevitably, so that he who touches things forbidden is evilly infected as he would be by a virulent leprosy; and since the infection is transmissible he becomes an outcast. Any interdict laid on property or land, to preserve rights or keep off intruders, falls within this category; you can employ the taboo maker to taboo a diamond mine against inconvenient explorers; and a European ship's captain has called him in to frighten from his vessel troublesome native visitors. The whole notion of mysterious curses attaching to some original sin, or offence given to divinities, and descendible to posterity, belongs to the conception. It would seem indeed as if such notices as "No admittance except on business," or "Trespassers beware," might be classed as modern examples of taboo, if one could only persuade people that some unintelligible penalty would surely follow unlawful entry. That any breach of taboo was unintentional or well intentioned, made in good faith or for a moral purpose, tells no more in mitigation of the consequences than in cases of smallpox or diphtheria; it is simply a matter of contagion.

Now in regard to a very large proportion of cases this system admits easily either of a religious or a rationalistic explanation; it is probably the aboriginal method of enforcing respect for rules, whether superstitious or sanitary, or merely fanciful, that became current in savage societies; it contains the germ of all caste ordinances and excommunications. Where the taboo seems inexplicable and plainly irrational there is, as Mr Jevons points out, greater difficulty; though the incoherence of ideas, and the freaks of the wild ranging mind, of primitive folk, may well account for our failure to trace out a meaning. Mr Jevons decides that the sentiment, as it appears in its lowest manifestations, cannot have been derived from experience, because in many instances "it is prior to and even contradictory to experience"; though this would seem difficult to prove. His conclusion is that taboo "is an inherent tendency of the human mind," and that the belief in its contagious properties is due to the association of ideas—

"In the history, or rather the prehistory, of man, taboo was never grossly material. It marked the awe of man in the presence of what he conceived—often mistakenly—to be the supernatural, and if his dread of contact with blood, babes, and corpses appears at first sight irrational, let us remember that in these, the three classes of objects which are inherently taboo, we have man in relation to the mystery of life and death, and in his affinity to that supernatural power which he conceived to be a spirit like himself."

This somewhat metaphysical theory will not altogether satisfy those who find it hard to believe that the primitive mind is capable of travelling beyond the limits of experience, hereditary and acquired; and who think that many senseless, unmeaning and absurd applications of the taboo are little more than childish guesses, or tricks, or the survivals of some impression left by those chances and coincidences which timid superstition is constantly misinterpreting. Nothing can be more irrational, for example, than a large class of omens; or than the connection discerned very recently in Persia between a stone set up by European surveyors and the failure of rain; yet it is quite evident that these foolish random conjectures easily harden into accepted beliefs, of which the origin becomes as utterly lost as the name of the first peasant or soothsayer who invented them. And it is not clear why we should insist upon finding a deeper explanation for any incomprehensible taboo, remembering that if Mr Jevons is right, as I think he is, in observing that taboo, once established, was enforced, perpetuated, and developed as a social obligation, its earliest meaning would very soon be transfigured in the process. The mischievous and useless customs are weeded out; the prohibitions that have some sense or motive in them are retained; the taboo follows the evolutionary course of all other fallacies, and much of it was evidently bred out of the same haphazard conjecture as those which generate every kind of superstition.

In regard to totemism Mr Jevons adopts the theory of which Mr Frazer has been hitherto the leading exponent, and which we must endeavour to state very briefly. It is well known that one of the earliest forms of human society is the grouping of men in tribes or clans, of which every member is akin to the other, either by descent, real or imaginary, from a common stock or by the fiction of the blood covenant. These groups may be allies or may be enemies *inter se*; and the killing of any member by a hostile group creates a blood feud between the two tribes. But upon the totemistic hypothesis every species of animal is also regarded by man as a tribe, friendly or hostile, and in choosing an ally he naturally prefers some species that possesses supernatural powers. Every animal of this chosen species is a member by kinship of the human tribe; and every tribesman becomes a blood relation not only of the beast, but of the god incarnate within him, who is thus the ally and protector of the tribe—that is to say, its totem. From these aboriginal roots Mr Jevons traces the growth of all the widespread conceptions regarding the worship of animals and plants, the sanctity of certain species, the sacred feasts, the whole order of sacrificial rites, the slaying and eating of victims. "The mere existence of sacrifice is an indication of the former existence of totemism."

"Worship, as an act in its rudimentary stage, means only the sprinkling of blood on the altar; the blood sprinkled is that of the totem animal, and the only object of the rite is to renew the blood covenant between the totem clan and the totem species, and to procure the presence of the totem god. The idea of offering a sacrifice "to" a god is a notion which can only be developed in a later stage of totemism, when, on the one hand, the monolith has come to be identified with the god, and, on the other hand, the god is no longer in the animal."

In its primitive form the animal sacrifice and eating of the victim signified, we are told, a desire to assimilate, with the flesh, the supernatural powers of the sacred animal; the notion of the victim being eaten by the god was a later transformation of the original motive; and still later comes the idea of atonement, that one member of the tribe must die for the rest. Trees and plants were, like animals, adopted as tribal totems; and so, "it is to totemism that we owe the cultivation of plants as well as the domestication of animals." "Trivial pretexts for slaughtering victims were frequently invented," until what was at first eaten as a communistic sacrament became afterwards consumed for less mysterious purposes, with a few pious ejaculations as the sole relic of the primordial taboo.

Every consecutive link in the chain of this demonstration is carefully set out by Mr Jevons, with a powerful array of examples collected from all parts of the earth to support each position. Those who read his book attentively will admire the conscientious workmanship, the skill and diligence with which an attractive theory is maintained, and they will be impressed by the curious colligation of strange and remote fancies with ideas which have since become world-wide religious conceptions, or with industries to which, like agriculture, we are indebted for the settlement of human society. With a very moderate amplification of these evolutionary principles one might trace almost every important idea and institution to the two sources of taboo and totemism. It must be understood that no more than the outline, on a very small scale, of these interesting speculations has been here given; and with this warning it may be confessed that they suggest to the critical reviewer a certain degree of scepticism. In the history of all religions, even of those which first began among the ancient civilisations of Asia (where all the historic faiths arose), the problem of origins is obscure and complex; the psychologic situation was even there so different from our own; the accidental circumstances, the causes and consequences, which determined the line of development are so imperfectly appreciable. In the much earlier stages of the human imagination, when it was uncontrolled by reflection and reasoning, the whole superstitious atmosphere is so clouded and capriciously changeful that it is impossible, in our opinion, to be sure of discovering the elementary motives, or to give orderly sequence to a miscellaneous heap of disorderly customs. To construct hypotheses out of the materials available, to make intelligent conjectures, is legitimate and even praiseworthy, so long as the student is fairly reminded that he must look for no certitude, and that he must not allow his mind to be so possessed by a comprehensive theory as to prevent his examining facts, if he gets the opportunity, very closely and independently. There is a well-known saying of Bacon that "Method carrying a show of total and perfect knowledge has a tendency to generate acquiescence;" and for explorers in the field of folklore to be provided at starting with a master key to the meaning of all queer ideas and customs is distinctly deleterious. It is apt to produce a kind of atrophy in the faculty of genuine observation.

This caution is the more necessary, because Mr Jevons pushes his evolutionary argument very far, and indeed he has framed a considerable scheme of psychological development which embraces the whole domain of religious sentiment, from the rude natural imagery of the savage up to the lofty intuitions of devout philosophy and the mystic symbolism of the Churches. Man, he observes, began by attempting to synthesise the external and internal facts of consciousness by a reasoning process; animals were the first of the external objects that thus came to be worshipped, and totemism was the first form of that worship; the totem or tribal god being for a long time the single object of worship. "Totemism is the attempt to translate and express in outward action the union of the human will with the divine." Finally, "sacrifice and the sacramental meal which followed on it are institutions which are or have been universal . . . but before there can be a sacramental meal there must be a sacrifice. That is to say, the whole human race for thousands of years has been educated to the conception that it was only through a divine sacrifice that perfect union with God was possible for man."

These extracts may serve to indicate, of course imperfectly, the line of thought upon which "the bewildering details," as Mr Jevons truly calls them, of early ritual and adoration are arranged in this book, and the connection which he discovers between the lowest and the highest efforts of human consciousness. There is much force and attractiveness in the demonstration of instinctive ideas animating all stages of religious belief, at times taking the shape of some monstrous chimera, and latterly becoming simplified and refined into deep intellectual convictions. Nor am I in the least prepared to deny that all gradations of religion are pervaded, from the bottom to the top, by a sense of awful dependence on the supernatural powers. Whether it is possible so to co-ordinate and exhibit the filiation of innumerable facts and fancies, to appraise their value and determine their meaning, as to establish confidently the train of associated conceptions which leads up to these conclusions, is the point which may well be considered doubtful. It is hard to believe that anthropological phenomena of this class, the mental operations of primitive mankind under widely different circumstances, are as yet reducible to general laws of growth and correlation like those which can be verified by physical science. Nor is it safe to borrow the terms of that science, or to rely upon analogies which it suggests; as, for instance, when we are told that differences of belief may be compared to the variations of organisms, so that whatever varieties of belief are not favoured by their environment will perish, while the rest will survive. These are, in fact, rather metaphors than sound analogies; you could not lay out the history of religion upon such a theory, nor use it to explain either the great cataclysms which have swept over Asia, or the persistence and revivals of certain radical conceptions; while if no more were meant than that beliefs are modified by circumstances, this would be the statement of an accepted fact. That the religious idea is migratory and incessantly mutable, that the seeds of superstition are blown to and fro by chance winds, we all know. It is equally certain that similar species are always springing up spontaneously out of congenial soil, so that accident, as well as imitation, brings about unexpected resemblances quite independently of transmission by inherited descent.

The chapters in Mr Jevons' book on "The Next Life," on "The Transmigration of Souls," and on "The Mysteries," are finely written, with a true insight into the needs and propensities out of which arose and were developed ideas which have enormously influenced the mind of humanity. And he is quite right in pointing to Egypt and to India as the two countries in which the aboriginal notion of the soul's survival was purified and exalted by the priesthood into a sublime metempsychosis, with the theory of reward or retribution in the next world superadded to satisfy the conscience, and to provide the discipline of hopes and fears. But his main object in examining these subjects is to "trace the career" of totemism, beginning with the view that after death man rejoined his totem, and assumed the shape of the plant or animal which he worshipped. Both in Egypt and in India the souls of the dead were understood to migrate into animals, though gradually, we are told, the totemist faith became generalised and dissociated from the particular animal, and the soul was allowed to take any such shape, until finally the virtuous were born again into a superior beast, and the wicked got something low or unclean. Now it is very probable that man's rudimentary animism did follow some such upward course as is here laid out, while it is certain that everywhere the superior priesthood trained and pruned the wild popular fancies into decent shapes and towards useful purposes. The question is whether we can really do more than register the broad lines of evolution, or whether it is necessary to insist on the universality of such customs as the totem and the taboo, in order to interpret by reference to them a miscellaneous quantity of customs which may possibly be akin, but which may have had, for all we can tell, other motives and origins. Let us take, for example, the custom (observed also by Miss Kingsley in West Africa) of savages daubing themselves with white clay, a kind of war painting. "War," says Mr Jevons, "is to the savage a sacred function; the tribal god himself fights for his clan, the warriors are engaged in his service; as such they are taboo and dangerous, and they notify the fact by donning war paint." In corroboration of this general proposition the fact is mentioned that in Greece, when a novice was to be initiated to the mysteries, he was plastered with white clay as a cleansing process. But is it demonstrable that the ceremonious plastering had anything to do with the war painting? A passage is quoted from Herodotus, who has told us that when the Phocians consulted a Mantis upon ways and means of defeating the Thessalians he made six hundred of them plaster themselves with white clay, and sent them to make a night attack, which was entirely successful. This is regarded by Herodotus as a clever stratagem, whereby the Phocians knew each other in the darkness; it reappears in the old French wars as the *camisade*, which means that the assailants wore their white shirts over their armour for fighting at night. But Mr Jevons holds that Herodotus missed the real point, which was "that warriors should be prepared for battle by previous purification and dedication to the gods." A little straining of this theory would cover the suggestion that all military uniforms may lay claim to a long descent through war-paint and other fantastic decorations from the garb of taboo; the object of distinguishing friend from foe being regarded as modern and secondary. I must record my own impression that these hypotheses flourish better in the modern scientific hothouse than in the open air among the rough emergencies of military life. Herodotus was the best observer of all ancient travellers, and while he had a good eye for divine things in their proper place, he lived among the realities of a fighting time. Mr Jevons proceeds to remark that "the actor, like the warrior, was a sacred person during the discharge of his functions," that the satyric clowns wore goat-skins, and that the actor smeared his face with lees of wine to show that he was under the protection of the wine god—another clear case of totem and taboo. So it may have been, for all we know, nevertheless there is something far-fetched and unnecessary about such a derivation.

I have permitted myself to pass some criticisms upon the leading generalisations relied upon in this book, because the principle of evolution seems in these post-Darwinian days to have obtained almost too complete a mastery over the minds of those engaged in all branches of research. With the vast increase of data requiring some kind of systematic and rational adjustment to human capacity, the employment of this dominant hypothesis has spread from the handling of things to the assortment of ideas, and the most fascinating study is that of the religious idea. But in that study we are dealing with the strange and obscure contents of fantastic imagination, and with the most recondite problems of primitive psychology. In such a region hypotheses are as easy to frame as they are hard to verify; and I am much inclined to agree with Miss Kingsley's warning to explorers that they must not set out with foregone conclusions, but must on the contrary leave at home all such baggage, with the other ingenious luxuries of civilisation. Nevertheless Mr Jevons does not insist dogmatically upon his own views, while the lucidity of his exposition and the large repertory of facts from which he draws his illustrations are certainly impressive and possibly persuasive. The book also contains many truly philosophical remarks and reservations, and before taking leave of the author I may quote the following passage, which may be taken as explaining by analogy his general view of the evolution of belief:—

"The desire to unify our experience is a perennial need of human nature. The faith that it can be unified is not peculiar to religion, but is the base of all science. The track by which science has marched in its conquest of nature is marked by the ruins of abandoned hypotheses. One hypothesis is cast aside in favour of another which explains a greater number of facts; and though no hypothesis, not even evolution, accounts for all the facts of the physical universe (*i.e.* for all the external facts of consciousness), yet no man of science believes that the facts are incapable of explanation. On the contrary, he believes that they are only waiting for the right hypothesis, and that then they will all fall into line."

It is from this standpoint, if I rightly understand him, that Mr Jevons regards all the evidence of man's religious acts and feelings; and upon this principle he desires to establish some orderly scheme of their harmonious and consistent development. Much doubt may be permitted whether in this department of research the data are as surely ascertainable, or the inferences as verifiable, as in the purely physical sciences which rely on sight and touch, on actual experiment instead of on ancient record and incomplete observation, or possibly on hearsay. Nevertheless we may freely acknowledge and admire the philosophic spirit, the sympathetic appreciation of man's striving upward out of darkness towards light, which Mr Jevons has exhibited in his endeavour to decipher the obscure and intricate riddles of primitive religion.

. . . .

Professor Max Müller's book is the work of a distinguished scholar, who, after having devoted many years to the building up of the science of mythology upon a linguistic basis, has now resolved once more to affirm and energetically defend his main position. It has been so often and so strenuously attacked that some have imagined it to have become untenable and even to have been abandoned; but Professor Max Müller has no thought of surrender. On the contrary, he has strengthened and provisioned it with vigorous arguments and fresh evidence; while he is so far from retreating that he makes formidable sallies upon his adversaries. To attempt, in a few pages, any adequate review of such an important contribution to the literature of religious origins, would be in the highest degree presumptuous, especially as etymologic controversies lie beyond my competence. I shall therefore touch only on those points in his book which contravene or bear down upon the theories that have just been under some examination.

Although mythology does not, of course, cover the whole ground occupied by the question of religious origins, yet the interpretation of myths is so essentially concerned with the evolution of beliefs that on this subject a clear difference of system is fundamental. Mr Jevons makes no use of etymologic analysis, whereby the original and subsequent meanings of a divine name or legend can be extracted out of the comparative study of cognate languages. To Professor Max Müller, on the other hand, this method is of cardinal efficiency as a clue and a test; he maintains that the *hyponoia*, the underlying and related ideas, the way to unlock all the secrets of Aryan mythology, the solution of all its riddles, are to be found in the scrutiny of linguistic anatomy, in the rules of phonetic change, and the maladies of words. His attitude upon all these subjects, upon the modes of primitive thought, upon the fundamental analogy at the base of all religious conceptions, is too well known to need exposition here; though he has carefully restated them in the book now before us. That "the gods were originally personified representatives of the most prominent phenomena of nature," and that natural events were taken as the acts of these representatives, is the vital principle upon which he takes his stand, and whoever does not hold this faith regarding the generation of the Aryan divinities is in mortal error. As the deeds of great men were said to be god-like, so, conversely, the stories current about the Nature gods came to be told of real heroes or heroines, and as it is not possible to speak of the weather without personifying in speech the elements, so out of words meaning the sky, the clouds, rain, and thunder were evolved the great figures of polytheism; they arose, not only out of a necessity of thought, but also out of a necessity of language. The irrational and immoral characteristics of the classic deities should not, we are told, be explained as survivals from prehistoric savagery; they are distorted misunderstandings of naturalistic allegory, derived from the first abstract conceptions of physical forces; for "the foundation of all mythology was physical." It is true that other influences and impressions soon get to work upon the primary plastic material, that in later stages the authentic facts of human deeds or suffering become embedded in the primordial fiction; but those who are ready to discover historical fragments in mythology "ought never to forget that, in this marriage between myth and fact, myth comes first." It is not until a solar hero has first been created that any other real hero can be called Hêrakles, and his achievements can be sung as the achievements of Hêrakles. In short, the gods impersonated the sense of will and design stamped upon the primitive mind by the action of the elements; they were the actors in the great drama of Nature; and man's worship of them expressed his feeling of dependence upon those embodiments of the manifest yet mysterious powers which surrounded him.

So powerfully and persuasively is this comprehensive theory stated that, upon the principle of avoiding foregone conclusions as injurious to independent enquiry, one would be inclined to warn off all beginners in folklore from the study of these volumes, and to place them upon Miss Kingsley's index among the books which are dangerous for novices. In his own bright Aryan kingdom the philologist is supreme: he will have nothing to do with the outer barbarian; he takes slight account of customs and tales picked up among wild folk without any scientific knowledge of their language. Not much can be gained, in Professor Max Müller's opinion, by using such general terms as animism, totemism, fetishism, as solvents of mythological problems; and he rightly declines to trace back all theriolatry to totemism, particularly since some of the highest authorities on the myths and customs of savage races are by no means on the side of the thoroughgoing totemist. Dr Codrington, whose book is the standard work on Melanesian folklore, has collected many specimens of ancestral animals revered and spared by various families or kindred groups; and not only the practice, but the word "taboo," is indigenous in the South Pacific Islands. But in regard to the full-blown totemistic system Dr Codrington is decidedly sceptical; and for the taboo custom, which is a prohibition with a curse, he cites various examples showing its accidental and arbitrary character, and indicating that for an explanation one need go no further than the world-wide and very useful practice, indispensable to all early law-givers, of investing general rules and even casual orders with divine sanction. In short, if you spread out a custom so as to bring into affinity with it or derivation from it everything belonging to the same category of notions or habits, the whole theory is reduced to the recognition of some general instinct or universal human tendency, for which one designation or label is neither better nor more significant than another.

The ethnological school, as led by Mr Andrew Lang and Mr Jevons, would hunt an Aryan myth or custom back to a state of pre-existent savagery, discover its germs in similar beliefs or practices prevalent among Red Indians or Andaman Islanders. This is one of the capital points upon which Professor Max Müller resolutely joins issue. Granted, he says, that the Aryans must have been savages, it does not follow that the Aryan savage, in his elaboration of myths and customs, acted exactly like other savages.

"Ancient languages, ancient beliefs and customs were not formed according to rule. Even if we were to admit that all human beings were born alike, their surroundings have always been very different, and their intellectual productions must have differed in consequence. Mythology is . . . determined in its growth by ever so many accidental circumstances, by ever so many human and inhuman influences, even by individual poets and sages. . . . It forms an immense conglomerate which excludes hardly anything that has ever passed through the mind of man."

This is undoubtedly sound reasoning; and we may add the observation that it should be applied impartially to all methods of research into the origin of religious ideas. The attempt to trace out the long winding course of any particular idea or practice up to its ultimate source entangles the explorer in an intricate maze of queer habits and hallucinations, of which the nature and significance have really become undecipherable; the line is crossed, diverted, and ravelled until the clue becomes lost or erased; nor is it possible to stop at any one spot in the journey, aad proclaim that the source is found. To show that some rite or worship has a clear historical origin, or began within the memory of competent witnesses, is of no avail; the folklorist or the mythologist will so analyse and rearrange the facts as to prove that the idea underlying the story came from remoter ages, or will maintain that the true incident was caught up into the atmosphere of a solar myth, and precipitated again upon earth in the shape of a divine legend. As in the metaphysical order all religions may be melted down into pantheism; so there is hardly any institution or article of faith, or thought that wanders through eternity, that may not be gently and reverently relegated through many transformations to its far-off birthplace among the elementary fictions or experiences of humanity; it can be provided with a home in the prolific bosom of some capacious theory. Totemism has been disinterred by Professor Sayce from the ruins of ancient Babylon; and the heraldic monsters of our own day might easily claim descent from the tribal worship of animals; the story that Robert Bruce took heart to persevere in his enterprise by watching a spider at its web, may be traced, whether authentic or not, to a long-descended legend or parable. And even the horror of cats which possesses a distinguished soldier of our own day may be plausibly identified with the superstitious awe felt by earlier heroes in the presence of animals that were taboo. All warriors, indeed, are said to be themselves taboo, by reason of their sacred profession; insomuch that of late it has been gravely asserted that an ordinance prevailing among certain fighting tribes of the Hindu Kûsh, which enjoins abstinence from women during war time, is a sort of taboo; although a much more practical motive lies ready to hand.

It is easy, indeed, to show that the scientific folklorist often rides his hobby too hard and too far, and does violence to the evolutionary principle, when he uses it to prove that some modern rite or rule, which can be accounted for historically or by common sense, is allied by descent to a savage custom, nationalised and modified by changing environments. On the other hand, some of Professor Max Müller's illustrations of his general thesis, that "All Vedic gods, nay, all Aryan gods, were in the beginning physical," may still be received, even by good comparative mythologists, with respectful hesitation. That a large number of the divine shapes and legends are mainly personifications and poetic remains of natural appearances and forces is undeniable; but the determined application of etymological analysis, as if it were an infallible instrument or chemical test, produces results which strain the credit of an otherwise legitimate process. Without making any pretension to meddle with questions of high scholarship, I may refer for an example to the section in which, after pronouncing Leda to be a representative of the first grey dawn, the Vedic Sura*n*yû, and the swan to mean the sun, the writer tells us that Leda's sons, the Dioskouroi, are day and night, and that her daughter Helena can be nothing but the beautiful dawn. So the vivid scenes and characters of the Iliad melt away into mythological cloudland. Yet the abduction of women and disputes over beautiful brides have certainly been frequent causes of fighting in all rude days. We have the popular story of La Cava's ravishment, which brought the Moors into Spain. We know that a dispute over betrothals caused a long and bloody war among the Indian Rajpúts; and who is to assure us that Homer's story is not historically founded on some such very probable fact? Again, the watchdog, who guards the gate of house or village, has been known everywhere; nor does the legend which posted him at the gate of Hell seem to need any deeper explanation than universal custom transferred from the upper to the lower world. Professor Max Müller, however, insists in this book on his well-known view that the word Kerberos is connected with the name of night (Sárvarî), of which he is said to be a representative.

"If," he goes on to say, "it be asked what could be the meaning of the fight of Hêrakles with Kerberos, and of his dragging him forth from Hades if only for a short time, that is a question difficult to answer in any case. But there is no reason why it should not have arisen from some proverbial saying that the rising sun had grappled with the darkness of the night, and let it fall into the abyss the very moment he himself had risen to the sky victorious."

There is certainly no reason why such conjectures should not be hazarded; although the eminent scholar who makes them must be aware that he has thereby quitted his own special domain of high scholarship, and has generously offered battle upon the open field of ingenious guesswork and comparative probabilities, where all suggestions are unverifiable and of disputable value.

I must be content, however, with passing rapidly over a book in which the author throws down a bold challenge to his numerous adversaries, and fairly offers to renew the battle upon well-known ground. Scholarship and philology rely mainly for evidence on the past; with the present they have little to do; and the Solar Myth finds slender warrant among the ascertainable beliefs and worships of the contemporary savage. The folklorist and the traveller among wild folk undertake to compare and correct the traditions and records of the past by actual observation of primitive societies; they do not reject Vedic texts or Greek fables, they seek rather to reconcile classic paganism with modern folklore and barbarous superstitions; their ambition is to explain the grand procession of religious ideas, the long history of human credulity, upon a system that will include all periods and peoples, and will entirely exclude none of the rival theories. I must express a doubt whether any complete synthesis of religious evolution is possible, and whether the modern mind, which is unsatisfied with anything that is not consistent, precise, and logical, is a fit instrument for hewing into symmetrical shape the rude conglomerate blocks of superstition in the dark ages. In every chain of proof there are always missing links which have to be supplied at haphazard; in the piecing together of a great jumble of miscellaneous facts, there are many which cannot be fitted in, are anomalous, or even contradictory, and which must be rejected as spurious or silently thrown aside. They are naturally valued according to the use that can be made of them, so that upon this system a story extracted from some ancient writer, or the metaphor of an Indo-Aryan hymn, ranks equally with the latest myth-makings brought home by missionaries from Polynesia or Guiana.

Many high authorities will consider that these conclusions are too sceptical, and that the construction of trustworthy hypotheses upon materials carefully tabulated, assorted, and cemented, is well within the resources of science. Undoubtedly the immense information available in these days can be arranged upon general plans, and the broad lines of development followed by religious ideas can be demarcated, mainly because human imagination, like human inventiveness in dealing with things social and political, has always kept within certain definite channels. But any one who desires fairly to realise the difficulty of tracing any particular story, fact, or fancy to its actual origin, may do so by selecting some quaint custom or belief which has survived to our own day, with a clear historic pedigree, and considering what likelihood there would be of tracing it back to its real source, without the aid of authentic history. Who could ever discover, by the comparative method, the true reason why Guy Fawkes is carried round on 5th November, why the curfew tolls the knell of parting day, why oak sprigs are worn on 29th May, or even primroses on a fixed date in April? It will be as easy, in the absence of true record, to hang a far-fetched theory of religious symbolism upon the oak-sprig as upon the mistletoe. A strong savour of myth and totemism could probably be detected in all these things, and in others that might be easily added. Again, it is quite possible to bring within the sphere of taboo and totemism some of the chief rites and ceremonies of the three great historical religions, and indeed the evolution of belief is carried up to this point, in certain cases, by Mr Jevons and others. Yet if we suppose the true record of the origin of Christianity and Islam, or even of Buddhism, to have been entirely lost, what a completely false and misleading theory regarding the causes and circumstances which governed the rise and growth of these rites and creeds might have been constructed out of their inevitable connection with deep-rooted aboriginal instincts, out of fantastic analogies, and out of philosophic speculations which draw largely upon imaginative subtlety!

The attempt to solve the problem of origins requires, as Renan has said, a keen eye to discriminate between things certain, probable, and plausible, a profound sense of the realities of life, and the faculty of appreciating strange and remote psychological situations. And even with all these rare qualities, it is very difficult to attain certitude in the problem's solution. There must be always wide gaps and obscure interspaces where one can only measure possibilities, draw cautious inferences, note half-seen indications, and where after all one can but choose the least unlikely clue among many. All that can be done, for the most part, is to apprehend clearly the general course and character of prehistoric religion, to mark its outlines and prominent features, to catch its tone and colour, and so to preserve some true impression of social and intellectual states through which the foremost nations of the world have passed, and which still survive among many races for whose welfare the British people are directly responsible.

CHAPTER V.

NATURAL RELIGION IN INDIA.*

Natural Religion as exemplified by Hinduism—Meanings of the term Hindu—Hinduism apart from the three Historical religions of the world—Development of natural with supernatural beliefs—Belief in the soul's survival—Deification of humanity—Propitiation—Ritual—Pantheism—Final liberation of illusions—Recognition of Divine Unity.

I SHALL not endeavour to give, in this single lecture, any general description of Indian Religions. Nor do I propose to make any appreciable addition to the vast heap of facts and anecdotes, fables and folklore, that have been already collected in support of different theories regarding the origin of myth, ritual, primitive worships, and rudimentary belief. My present purpose is to draw attention, briefly, to the particular importance of India as a field of observation and research in identifying and tracing through connected stages the growth and filiation of some of the principal ideas that undoubtedly lie at the roots of Natural Religion. When I speak of Religion in India, I mean, for the purpose of this Lecture, Hinduism. And if I were asked for a definition of Hinduism, I could give no precise answer; I could not define it concisely

* "Rede Lecture." Cambridge, 1891.

by giving its central doctrines and its essential articles of faith; as I might do in describing one of the great historical Religions. For the word Hindu is not exclusively a religious denomination; it denotes also a country, and to a certain degree a race. When we speak of a Christian, a Mahomedan, or a Buddhist, we mean a particular religious community, in the widest sense, without distinction of race or place. When we talk of a Russian or a Persian, we indicate country or parentage without distinction of creed. But when a man tells me that he is a Hindu, I know that he means all three things together—Religion, Parentage, and Country. I can be almost sure that he is an inhabitant of India, I know that he is an Indian by birth and descent; and as to his religion, the word Hindu, though it is rather indefinite, undoubtedly places him within one of the many groups or castes that follow the ordinances and worship the gods who are recognised by the Brahmans.

I would ask you to remark that we have here at once, at the first word, a significant indication of the peculiar character and composition of Hinduism. This triple meaning or connotation of the term Hindu shows the complexity of its origin, shows how Hinduism is twisted deep among the roots of Indian society, how it is a matter of birthright and inheritance; signifies that it means a civil community, quite as much as a religious association—that a man does not become a Hindu, but is born into Hinduism.

Let me illustrate this view of Hinduism, as different in type, origin, and constitution from the other great Religions, by pointing to its position on what I may call a Religious map of the world—I suppose that in fact the geographical areas occupied by the chief religions have often been mapped out. We may put aside Africa as wholly barbarous and benighted, except where its edges have been touched by light from Asia. Then such a map, supposing that it gave only the broad outlines and divisions, would exhibit all Europe and America overspread by Christianity, and in Asia it would show that the three grand Historic Faiths or Creeds—Christianity, Islam, and Buddhism—have made a nominal partition of the whole continent, with the notable exception of one country. It would be seen that in all the three continents there is one, and only one, country of the first magnitude, only one large population of settled civilisation, that is not annexed to, or at least claimed by, one or another of these three spiritual empires; and that people are the Hindus. If we mark off roughly the spheres of religion in Asia, we may assign the north-eastern provinces of the Russian empire, including Siberia, to Christianity.* In western and central Asia, from the Red Sea and the Mediterranean to the borders of India and the Chinese empire, the religion is, speaking broadly, Mahomedan. On the other side, in eastern and north-eastern Asia, throughout China, in Japan, Burmah, and Siam, the established Church, the Faith that is incontestably predominant, though not exclusively accepted, is Buddhist. So that while in the north, the west, and the centre of Asia the people and their rulers are worshippers of one God, in the whole of

* Twenty-five per cent. of the Siberian population are Mahomedan; nevertheless Christianity dominates.

eastern Asia Buddhism, which acknowledges no supreme personal deity, still holds the chief place, and maintains a kind of high catholic dominion. The people who stand between but stand apart from both monotheism and Buddhism, are the Hindus; they are the sole surviving representatives of a great polytheistic system. We have in India a population that has been incessantly conquered politically, but never overpowered or subdued spiritually, it has expelled Buddhism, successfully resisted Islam, and has been very little affected even by Christianity Hinduism has preserved its independence between two powerful and imposing religious sovereignties—between Islam, the Faith militant, and Buddhism, the Faith contemplative, the religion of action and the religion of thought. The 200 millions of Hindus constitute the only considerable section of more or less civilised humanity that does not at this moment acquiesce in the religious authority of Buddha, of Mahomet, or of some Christian Church.

Now it must always be remembered that the Indians are not a rude and unintelligent folk upon whom great intellectual movements take little hold. On the contrary, they are the most subtle-minded and profoundly devout people in Asia. And so far am I from regarding Hinduism as unconnected with the deeper currents of spiritual ideas, that I take India to be one of the religious watersheds of the world. I mean that as from some high ridge or plateau the rivers rise and run down into distant lands, so from India there has been a large outflow of religious ideas over Asia. It has, of course been the fountain-head of Buddhism, which has flooded, as I have said, all eastern Asia; while I believe that the influence of Indian theosophy spread at the beginning of the Christian era as far west as Alexandria and Antioch. I am told that it profoundly affected the ancient religion of Persia; and it may be traceable later in the mysticism of the Persian Sufis. But while the religious thought of India has thus radiated out east and west across the Asiatic Continent, I doubt whether Hinduism, the immemorial religion of the Indian people, has in all these ages assimilated a single important or prolific idea from outside India. The current of ideas is not always above ground, it often subsides and reappears; but it seems to me to have flowed steadily out of India; until its natural course was disturbed by the violent irruption of Islam. It is in this manner that Hinduism may be said to represent high religious ground that has been for ages a dividing line between the great religious systems that have overspread the countries on either side of it. Its characteristic is the entire absence of system; it has never been under the political control or regulation of a State; it has never been organised ecclesiastically. For, in the first place, the long dominion in India of foreigners, aliens in race and religion, seems to me not only to have arrested the intellectual development of Hinduism during the last eight hundred years, but also to have kept it in a dislocated and inorganic condition. And secondly, the Hindu priesthood, though powerful, has never been able to bring within specific limits the wandering beliefs of an intensely superstitious people. The Brahmans exercise immense authority, yet they have never obtained any effective mastery over the incessant movements and changes of belief and ritual in Hinduism. The result has been that there prevails, and has always prevailed, a great incoherence and diversity in the divine affairs of India; there has been a loose and luxuriant growth of religious fancies and usages; and the religion has become a conglomerate of rude worship and high liturgies; of superstitions and philosophies, belonging to very different phases of society and mental culture. I doubt whether there is anything like it in any other part of the world. And I regard Hinduism as a survival from those early ages when in the midst of a highly organised civil society Religion was still in a state of confusion; before the rise and establishment of the great historic Churches and Creeds which have since made a partition of the old world, from Ireland eastward to the Indus. From looking closely at India as it is we can best form a notion of ancient polytheism, not such as that which in Europe we have for centuries called paganism because it lingered longest in the rural districts, but polytheism before its decline and fall, when it was the religion of the civilised world under the Roman Empire. Such is popular Hinduism as we still see it flourishing in India; and for the purposes of this lecture I propose to call it Natural Religion.

Now I do not of course use the term Natural Religion in the sense given to it by Bishop Butler, when he said that Christianity was a republication of Natural Religion. He meant, I think, religion according to right reason, framed upon the principle of accepting the course and constitution of Nature as an index of the Divine Will. The meaning that I wish to convey is of Religion in what

Hobbes would call a State of Nature, moulded only by circumstances and feelings, and founded upon analogies drawn sometimes with ignorant simplicity, sometimes with great subtlety, from the operation of natural agencies and phenomena. The presence, the doings, and the character of numerous superhuman beings are thus directly inferred from what actually happens to men in the world around them; and a mysterious kind of design is perceived in every uncommon motion, or shape, or sensation. What is it that evidently suggests the intentions and sets the model of divinity thus realised? Nothing but capricious and freely acting Nature; the religious feeling works by taking impressions or reflections, sometimes rough and grotesque, sometimes refined and artistic, from all that men hear and feel and see. This is what I desire to call Natural Religion, because it has grown up in this manner spontaneously out of the free play of man's fears and hopes, and his guesses at the truth of this unintelligible world. I mean a religion that has not yet acquired a distinctive form and a settled base, but is constantly springing up and reproducing itself under different shapes, in diverse species; and throwing out varieties of rite and worship according to the changing needs and conditions of the people. I have no doubt whatever that in many uncivilised countries something of this kind is always going on. But I believe that in no modern country has Natural Religion been as long undisturbed, or has reached anything like the height or expansion that it has attained in India. My point is that Hinduism can be seen growing, that one can discern the earliest notions, rude and vague, among the primitive jungle tribes, that one can see the same ideas and practices upon a higher level, in more distinct and reasonable shape, among the settled classes; and that one can follow them upwards until they merge into allegory, mysticism, or abstract philosophical conceptions. I think that it is possible to trace in India, less obscurely than elsewhere, the development of natural experiences into supernatural beliefs. I do not pretend that India contains any very rare or unusual kinds of ritual or worship; for nothing is more remarkable than the persistent similarity of such ideas and practices among primitive folk. What makes India so valuable as a field of observation, is that the various forms and species lie close together in one country at the same time, so that their differences and affinities can be compared. In short, I believe that India, from its position in the world, from its past history, from its present state, and because it is an antique society thoroughly accessible to modern research, presents an almost unique opportunity for the comprehensive study of the history of Natural Religion.

The time at my disposal to-day only allows me to illustrate this position by reference to a few of the most universal and prolific among primary religious beliefs. Let me take the theory that Dreams and Ghosts are the sources of the earliest superstitions—it is a theory much in vogue at the present time, though it is by no means a modern discovery. Now the evidence that can be collected and brought to bear from India on this theory is abundant and exceedingly impressive, because it brings out perceptible links and gradations between spirit worship and the adoration of the higher divinities.

Fear is a primordial affection of the human mind; and the continual terror which haunts savage men, as it does wild animals, and which is at the bottom of all superstition, seems to have been originally little more than the instinctive fright at strange sounds and sights that we can still see in domestic animals. We can judge how strong this terror must have been by noticing how long it has lasted. Just as the shying of a horse at a bush is the survival of the ancestral instinct that made his far-off progenitors shun anything strange and therefore dangerous, so, I think, the unreasoning horror that is apt to come over people at the image of a ghost, or even at a ghost story, is traceable backward to the times when our ancestors felt themselves to be surrounded by capricious or malignant beings. The fear of ghosts is the faint shadow still left on our imaginations by the universal belief of primitive folk that they were haunted by the spirits of the dead.

Now the essential characteristic of ghosts is given better by the French word than by the English—it is a *Revenant*, one that returns. And if I were asked to make a conjecture why this notion of the return or reappearance of a dead man's spirit is so widespread, I should reply by pointing to the one fundamental fact, the first and most formidable law—that comes home to all men and partly I suspect to some of the higher animals—the endless succession in Nature of birth, death, and revival. I do not think it possible to overrate the deep impression that must be engraved on the minds of the early races of mankind by the continual perishing and reproduction of all animate things. To man in his wild state the same life appears to stir in everything, in running water, in a tree, and in a creature; it ends and disappears in everything at times, but it reappears again constantly, in shape, movement, and outward character so similar as to seem identical; conveying the inference that something has gone and come again; there is nothing around a savage to suggest that the animating principle of vitality suffers more than suspension or displacement. The analogy of Nature affords him no presumption that death means extinction, while his imagination supplies him with constant evidence to the contrary.

But however this may be, one thing seems sure, whatever may be the reason of it, that although the fact that all men die rests upon the most direct, conclusive, and unquestionable evidence, constantly renewed, yet no race of men ever seems to have accepted death as the certain end of the dead man's personality. Among primitive folk the presumption seems to have been exactly the reverse; they are all convinced that his soul has only gone elsewhere; they do not regard life as extinguished; they look for signs and tokens of it somewhere else; and they are incessantly haunted, asleep or awake, with the apparitions of familiar forms or hints of a familiar presence. This incapacity or desperate refusal to acquiesce in the finality of death powerfully affects all the primitive races of India; and it is my opinion that the notion of the survival, reappearance, and transmission of the soul or spirit runs like a spinal cord through the whole connected series of the beliefs that are comprised in Hinduism. It pervades, I think, all classes of Indian society; it is the chief motive of ritual, it explains the origin of many divinities, and it underlies some of the cardinal doctrines of high Brahmanic orthodoxy. The notion is seen very plainly in the least advanced societies. The Khasia Hills, for example, are peopled by a very simple folk, whom until lately the propagation of Brahmanism had scarcely reached. In those hills, when a man dies far from home, his friends tie threads across the streams near his village, in order to provide the spirit with a bridge on his return journey; and I mention this particularly because the custom may throw some light on the well-known inability of Scottish elves and sprites to cross running water.* Among the Khasias also, when a man dies abroad, a cock is killed that the bird may wake the ghost early each day on his travel homeward; and as far as I could make out when I visited the country, the indigenous religion consists almost wholly of the worship of the spirits of the dead. Now the beliefs of the Khasia folk are merely a sample of the ideas universally prevalent, among the aborigines of India, regarding the returning spirit. If again we go among the general settled population of Hindus, we find the same feelings persistent among them. The lament at a Hindu funeral says, "That which has spoken has gone—the Spirit has departed"—and at the same time there runs through their obsequies the notion that the wandering soul of the dead person must be provided with a new refuge, must be harboured, and comforted. As bodily death is a giving up of the ghost, he must be provided with a fresh tenement, or at least with some temporary

* "If you can interpose a brook between you and witches, spectres, or even fiends, you are in perfect safety." Note to Scott's "Lay of the Last Minstrel." The notion may be that they need some help to bring them across it.

accommodation; and here comes in the very general custom among certain classes of Hindus, after a cremation, of picking up at the funeral pyre some small object in which the soul is supposed, by a fiction, to have taken refuge after the body has been burnt, and of carrying it back to the dead man's house.

You will observe that the belief in survival involves the necessity of giving the homeless spirit some local habitation; he must take up his abode in something animate or inanimate, in a tree, an animal, or perhaps in queer-looking stocks and stones. He is thus likely to be haunting places in some shadowy or substantial form; he may be helping his friends and plaguing his enemies; his presence can be discovered by the breaking out of a disease, by an odd accident, or by the strange behaviour of an animal. One remarkable case is worth mentioning to an English audience. Some fifty years ago a very high English official died in a fortress, at a place that is one of the centres of Brahmanic orthodoxy; and at the moment when the news of his death reached the Sepoy guard at the main gate, a black cat rushed out of it. The guard presented arms to the cat as a salute to the flying spirit of the powerful Englishman; and the coincidence took so firm a hold of the locality that up to a few years ago neither exhortation nor orders could prevent a Hindu sentry at that gate from presenting arms to any cat that passed out of the fort at night.

My conjecture is that a great part of what is called Animism—the tendency to discover human life and agency in all moving things, whether waving trees or wandering beasts—begins with this ingrained conviction that some new form or habitation must be provided for the spirits of dead men. I do not pretend that in India the whole worship of trees and animals can be traced to this habit of the mind, but I believe that the widespread idea of possession by spirits or demons, particularly the very common notion that the soul of a wicked or miserable man is inside a wild beast, does come largely from the imaginary necessity of finding lodging and employment for ghosts.

Nothing indeed is more common in India than the belief that the spirits of dead men have passed into certain animals, and I could give some curious instances of the manner in which this passage of the spirit through an animal shape affects the subsequent development of a deity, who often retains in his attributes, symbols, and mythology, the recollection of this earlier stage of his metamorphosis. But this is a side line of my main subject, and anticipates a later stage of it. I can only say here that in India the worship of animals becomes crossed and intertwined at a very early stage with the worship of spirits, in a manner very difficult to unravel; that there is good evidence that as the ghost developed into a god, he retained some characteristic of the animal whom he may have at one time inhabited, which animal often became in a later stage one of the god's temporary embodiments. A serpent, for example, is unquestionably dreaded, and therefore worshipped, as a dangerous and mysterious beast; and for that very reason he may be also treated as the embodiment of a malignant and subtle spirit recently passed away from among men. Later on the sacred snake is regarded as the shape into which some sage or semi-divine person has become transformed. And ultimately it becomes the emblem or allegorical symbol of a great god. I repeat, that at the bottom of all these imaginary changes lies the belief in survival, the notion that death is transmigration, and that man is encompassed by the restless and roving spirits of the dead, who have human wants and affections, and superhuman powers. All these fancies appear to me to become grouped and interlaced in the word superstition—a word that may have originally meant something like survival—and out of this atmosphere of ghostly terrors, griefs, and wonder the rudimentary deities seem to me to be continually issuing.

It is certain that in India one can distinctly follow the evolution of the ghosts of men whose life or death has been notorious, into gods. Wherever in India the beliefs can still be found in an elementary or indigenous state, wherever they appear to have grown up spontaneously, some of the principal deities can be identified with the spirits of departed humanity. When I lived for some years in a province of central India that had been very little touched by external influences, I had many opportunities of personally verifying this fact. In the outlying districts one could find everywhere the worship of the spirits of men who had been distinguished for valour, wisdom, piety, or misfortune, for a notable life or a tragic death. Their Manes were propitiated; and if their power to harm or to help increased, their tombs might become shrines or temples; and the offerings to the dead might develop into sacrifices. The report that a god has lived on earth as a man, the fact that he has been perfectly well known in the neighbourhood, are no prejudice whatever to his subsequent dignity; though as his wonder-working reputation rises, his earthly history becomes usually more dim and mystical; the legend comes in to disguise his mortal origin, and he veils himself more and more under divine attributes. If we look steadily at these processes, visible in the clear daylight of the present time, they may well seem to reflect, as in a mirror, the fables and mythologies of the antique world, and to throw a ray of light on their origin; while the reality of the thing is brought home to us by the fact that the spirits of more than one Englishman, and of one Englishwoman, are now worshipped in India. General Nicholson, who was killed in the storming of Delhi, had a sect of worshippers; and in south India they adore the spirit of Captain Pole, who was mortally wounded and died in a forest; the people dug his grave, built his shrine, and employed a local priest to devise a form of worship that was certainly going on within the last few years.

But the authentic transformation of the disembodied spirit into a superhuman being is contested by no one; the difficulty is only to disentangle the ghost, the divine ancestor, and the incipient deity with his attributes or special powers. They seem to be often blended, and their earthly and unearthly characters remain for a certain time interfused. We had last year a census of all India; and I noticed in an Indian newspaper of March last that one Hindu householder filled up his schedule by returning, as Head of the Family, his household deity, whose profession he described as subsistence on an endowment, while the question whether the divine personage was or was not literate was somewhat indirectly answered by entering him as Omniscient. At a later stage, when the divinity is once clearly established, his special attributes or department may be determined by an accident. We may take, as an example, the history of Hurdeo Lala, who was, not very long ago, poisoned in central India by his brother through jealousy. This was a sensational murder, not unlike that of Hamlet's father; and whereas in England he might have been commemorated by a tragic drama, a mournful ballad, or by a figure in a wax-work exhibition, in India temples were erected to him. Some time afterward, when the cholera broke out suddenly and fiercely in a camp that was pitched close to his shrine, it was ascribed by public opinion to the displeasure of his injured ghost, who was thus credited with the power of letting loose epidemics; so Hurdeo Lala became the special god of cholera in that region. It is in this manner that dim shapes and mere superstitious dread gradually give place to the distinct image and definite attributes of divinity.

Thus it seems to me, if I may here briefly recapitulate, that everywhere in India the natural propensity to adore curious, terrible, or beneficent things has become crossed and mixed up with the habit of detecting human spirits everywhere. This leads to the deification of humanity; which is throughout so much the strongest element in the shaping of superstitious imagery that it gradually absorbs all other elements. And thus the detection of divine power or purpose in plants and animals, in stocks and stones, in plagues and diseases, has a tendency to coalesce and harden into the worship of some glorified man, who may have the place as his sanctuary, the plant or animal as his embodiment, or the plague as his attribute. The adoration is paid both to the object, and to the spirit that has become accidentally connected with the object, and the two lines of worship take human shape eventually.

It is true that the deification of notables does not go on in India in so regular and recognised a fashion as in China, where the gods and their ritual are under State patronage and authority, and where promotions from the lower to the higher grades of the Pantheon are often announced in the Official Gazette. In India, Religion has always been, as I have said, independent of State supervision, and is only imperfectly controlled by the priesthood. The minor Indian spirit is left to rise by his own merit and by popular suffrage; the foreign governments that have so long ruled in India are either hostile or indifferent—and in these latter days the gradual spread of wider knowledge of the outer world, the general stir and movement of civilised and peaceful life, the spread of education, are undermining the whole fabric of these beliefs, and driving them into obscure corners. In the course of one or two generations they will probably dwindle down to the condition of paganism or heathenism; they will be regarded as the quaint, old-fashioned superstitions of the wolds or the remote rural districts; and thus the embryonic stages of the generation of gods will gradually disappear. The origin of the divine species, the descent of the deities from man, may then come to be vigorously disputed by scholars and antiquarians; the saints and heroes will become fabulous and manifestly unreal, and their true evolution will be explained philologically, or demonstrated by the science of comparative mythology.

At present, however, the deification of ghosts can be unquestionably established by the collection of plentiful evidence in India. Of course I do not pretend that it covers the whole ground, or that it is more than one of the sources which have produced the confused multitude of deities that are worshipped there. And I am well aware that the genealogy of deities has been traced back to ancestral and spirit worship in various countries. Nevertheless we have never before been able to take such a comprehensive survey of the actual process; and the value of observations taken in India is that it gives us not only the earliest but the latest stages of deification, and shows us the connected series. We have at the bottom the universal worship of spirits partly ancestral and commemorative, in part propitiatory; we see them gradually transmuted into household gods, local deities, and divinities of special forms, attributes, and departments; while at the top we have the full-blown adoration of the lofty Brahmanic deities who preside over the operations of Nature and the strongest passions of mankind.

The verification of such an important phase in the Natural History of polytheism seems to me not the least curious result of that remarkable contact and contrast between ancient and modern ideas and institutions, that is represented by the English in India. To us, whom political circumstances have brought more closely than any other modern nation into relation with archaic beliefs, it is of particular interest that we should find in India a strong corroboration of the theory that was adopted, from a point of view different yet not altogether dissimilar, by those who stood face to face with the decaying polytheism of the Roman empire. It was positively affirmed by the Christian Fathers and apologists that the gods of classic paganism were deified men. Tertullian challenges the heathen to deny it; and Augustine vehemently asserts it. "For with such blindness," he says, "do impious men, as it were, stumble over mountains, and will not see the things which strike their own eyes, that they do not attend to the fact that in all the literature of the Pagans there are not found any, or scarcely any, gods who have not been men to whom when dead divine honours were paid." *

You will remember that I began by throwing out the conjecture that the original bent or form of Natural Religion had been moulded upon the deep impression stamped on primitive minds by the perpetual death and reappearance, or resuscitation, of animate things. And I argued that the incessant presence of this visible operation, aided by the natural feelings of terror and regret, had generated in the imagination of the earliest races their intense conviction that the death of man is only the transmigration of his soul, that he only suffers a change of shape or abode. I suggested that this had contributed to produce spirit worship generally, and had led to the adoration of the more illustrious spirits, who were invested with superior powers, and became gods. Where now, in the upper grades of Hinduism, may we observe the full growth and maturity of these primordial

* *De Civitate Dei.*

ideas? We see them, I think, magnified and reproduced upon a grand and imposing scale, in the supreme divinities of Hindu theology, in Vishnu and Siva; for Brahma, the creative energy, is too remote and abstract an influence for popular worship. Siva represents what I have taken to be the earliest and universal impression of Nature upon men—the impression of endless and pitiless change. He is the destroyer and rebuilder of various forms of life; he has charge of the whole circle of animated creation, the incessant round of birth and death in which all Nature eternally revolves. His attributes are indicated by symbols emblematic of death and of man's desire; he presides over the ebb and flow of sentient existence. In Siva we have the condensation of the two primordial agencies, the striving to live and the forces that kill; and thus, philosophically speaking, we see in this great divinity a comprehensive transfiguration of that idea which, as I repeat, I hold to be the root of Natural Religion. He exhibits by images, emblems, and allegorical carvings the whole course and revolution of Nature, the inexorable law of the alternate triumph of life and death —Mors Janua Vitae—the unending circle of indestructible animation.

Vishnu, on the other hand, impersonates the higher evolution; the upward tendency of the human spirit. He represents several great and far-reaching religious ideas. In the increasing flux and change of all things he is their Preserver; and although he is one of the highest gods he has constantly revisited the earth either in animal or in human shape. What are the modes and ascending flights by which the spirits, who have been deified for their valour, sanctity, or beneficence, are brought into relation with this supreme conception of divinity? They rise by the medium of the Avatárs, the descents or re-appearances of Vishnu, who personifies the doctrine of successive divine embodiments, which is one of the most important in Hinduism. Most of the famous saints, heroes, and demigods of poetry and romance, with many of the superior divinities, are recognised as having been the sensible manifestations of Vishnu; their bodies were only the mortal vesture that he assumed for the purpose of interposing decisively at some great emergency, or whenever he condescended to become again an actor in the world's drama. It must be clearly understood that this theory of the divine embodiment is one of the most essential and effective doctrines of Hinduism; it links together and explains the various phases of the religion, connecting the lower with the higher ideas, and providing them with a common ground or method of reconciliation. It serves to show, for instance, that the sacred animal of a wild tribe is merely the great Brahmanic deity in disguise, or it may prove that the worshippers of some obscure or local hero have been adoring Vishnu unawares. It thus accommodates and absorbs the lower deities; and while it draws them up to the sky and completes their apotheosis, it also brings the higher gods constantly down again from heaven to take part in human affairs. We thus find running through all Hinduism, first the belief in the migration of spirits when divorced from the body, next their deification, and latterly their identification with the supreme abstract divinities. But these supreme divinities reappear again in various earthly forms; so that there is a continual passage to and fro between men and gods, gods and men. And thus we have the electric current of all-pervading divine energy completing its circle through diverse forms, until we reach the conception of all Nature being possessed by the divinity.

We are now on the limit of that which I take to be the intellectual climax of the evolution of Natural Religion—I mean the doctrine of Pantheism. The adoration of innumerable spirits becomes gradually collected into the main channels and runs into the anthropomorphic moulds of the higher polytheism, which again is still further condensed into the recognition of the Brahmanic Trinity under multitudinous shapes, signs, and attributes. And as all rivers end in the sea, so every sign, symbol, figure, or active energy of divinity, is ultimately regarded as the outward expression of that single universal divine potency, which is everywhere immanent in the world, which in fact *is* the World.

I must guard myself from being understood to hold that the deification of humanity accounts for all Hinduism; for in India every visible presentation of force, everything that can harm or help mankind, is worshipped; at first instinctively and directly, latterly as the token of divinity working behind the phenomenal veil. We have of course to take into account the direct adoration paid to the mountains and rivers, to the Sun and the Moon, to the Sky and Winds, and to such abstract personifications as the goddess Fortune. And into the allegorical and mythological branch of this vast subject I cannot here enter.

It is now time for me to turn to another side of Hinduism, to its Ritual, which is in its early stages a vast method of propitiation, and latterly a lofty kind of ceremonial liturgy. My view is that just as the higher polytheism is connected by descent with the aboriginal veneration of disembodied spirits, so likewise much of the ritual can be followed back, in India, to primitive obsequies, to methods for laying the ghost, for feeding, comforting, and conciliating him. Many years ago, on my road home to England, I travelled straight from the depths of central India to Paris, and on the Boulevards I came suddenly to a stand before a fashionable mourning warehouse, which had in large letters on the plate glass the motto, *Le deuil est un culte*—Mourning is Worship. As this was precisely the conclusion that had been suggested to me a month earlier, by the sight of the funeral rites of the Bheels, a wild folk in the jungles, I was startled by finding it proclaimed in Paris as an advertisement of crape and black silk. And I began to consider whether this might not be the attenuated survival of a remote but once universal idea. For the ceremonies, the honours and attentions paid to the dead, among primitive societies in India, seemed to me intended to please and provide for the ghost; and some trace of this purpose may be discerned in almost every stage or gradation of funeral services among Hindus, from the lowest to the highest, from the offerings made to the dead and the wailing prayers of the rude tribes, up to the formal oblations prescribed by the Brahmanic High Church. You may have heard, for example, that the right to inherit property is by Hindu law co-extensive with the duty of making certain periodical offerings to the ancestral spirits.

I agree, therefore, that mourning in its original meaning partook largely of the nature of worship. I think the prayers were not for the dead man but addressed to him, that the funeral service was usually an offer or an attempt to do him service. And I find reason to believe that whenever a spirit became gradually translated to some higher degree of divinity, the earlier propitiation of the wandering ghost passed into a form of worship, that the offerings at the grave or shrine became sacrifices in the temple. Now I submit to you the general remark that in no existing religious system does sacrifice play such an important part, occupy such high ground, as in Hinduism. In the ancient world it may be said to have been almost an universal practice, the most essential of all religious observances. In the modern world it has almost entirely disappeared. It lingers in Mahomedanism as a figurative or commemorative act; in Buddhism the offerings are not propitiatory; they are pious gifts reverentially presented, chiefly as alms to the priesthood. But in India we can still see with our eyes the performance of sacrifices in almost every stage or step of an ascending scale; there is every variety of offering; the wild tribes slaughter buffaloes to the goddess Devi; the altars of Siva, in the heart of Calcutta, stream with the blood of goats; and although human sacrifice and self-sacrifice by suicide have now been everywhere suppressed, yet traditional remains of these customs still circulate in the outlying parts of the country. The Brahmans do their best to discourage and refine these savage rites, but as in the matter of the ruder gods so in regard to their ritual, the priesthood has never been strong enough to purify and regulate all the discordant usages of a most diversified society. It has thus come to pass that some very rough and barbarous rites are practised side by side with the pure and lofty ceremonial of the Vedic devotions. The idol may be the god itself, may be the consecrated image in which the deity is present, or may be merely the token or point for prayer and meditation; and according to the votary's conception of the god so is the intention and meaning of the sacrifice. The lowest conception seems to be that of providing food or service for the ghost, the highest is of a sin offering, or mysterious atonement.

Human sacrifice is one of the earliest forms of the rite. How did it first begin? Some very ingenious and intricate explanations of its origin have recently been suggested; I myself doubt whether we can go back with any certainty beyond the motive of pleasing or paying due honour to the ghost of some powerful personage. Perhaps the earliest notion to be found now authentically existing, not in India, but upon the Indian borderland, is that of despatching slaves or companions to accompany a dead chief on his journey into the next world—that is, into his new state of existence or abode. The tribes of our North-East frontier still make occasional raids upon the villages of the plain for the purpose of capturing Bengalees, whom they slay at the funeral of a chief in order to provide him with a retinue. In the case of prisoners taken in war there may also be the desire of finding a plausible, what we might call a sanctimonious, pretext for getting rid of them by slaying them on the altar; for nothing is more common than to find a sacred duty used to veil some motive of direct human interest or utility. However this may be, there is strong evidence connecting human sacrifice in India with funeral obsequies; and the view which I venture to put before you is that by the same process of development which converted the spirit into a deity, the slaying of slaves and captives to attend the departing ghost becomes the offering up of victims to powerful gods. There is no doubt whatever that human sacrifice has been held, is held, in India as elsewhere, to be a sovereign remedy for appeasing the wrath of the gods. Most of us have heard of the Meriah sacrifices among the Khonds, who periodically slaughtered human victims. There is moreover a well-authenticated case of an English official finding a victim tied up before a shrine during a sharp epidemic of cholera; and there was another mysterious incident not very long ago at a temple in that city which is chiefly given up to the worship of the great god Siva. I may mention, also, that certain unaccountable and apparently motiveless murders, very like those which some years ago frightened London, have occasionally been committed; and were probably due to the accomplishment of a vow made, like Jephtha's, to be fulfilled if a prayer for some great favour were answered.

But systematic human sacrifice, except among a few savage tribes, must have disappeared long ago from India. Such traditions of the custom as remain, point to the idea of resorting to it only on some great emergency or mysterious difficulty indicating divine displeasure. There is one world-wide and inveterate superstition belonging to the sacrificial class, of which we have many vestiges in

India—it is the belief that a building can be made strong, can be prevented from falling, by burying alive some one, usually a child, under its foundations.

Grimm, in his "Teutonic Mythology," gives stories showing the prevalence of this custom in North Europe before the Teutonic tribes were Christianised. And the tradition still overshadows the imagination of primitive folk in India. I recollect that when one of the piers of a railway bridge was washed away by a flood in central India, there was a panic among the tribes of the neighbouring hills, who were possessed by the rumour that one of them was to be seized and buried in the basement when the pier should be rebuilt. The ghost of such a victim becomes naturally deified. On the bastion of many of the forts in that country is a sort of mimic grave or shrine, sacred to a dead man who is said to have been sacrificed long ago to keep up the wall of a fortress, and who has now become the tutelary spirit of bastions. But the Moghul emperor, Shah Jehan, was humane enough to bury goats instead of men under the walls of his fortified palace; and there has probably been a steady transition to milder forms of consecration. We still, in England, bury something, though only a few coins, under a foundation-stone; and without pretending to connect this formula with any ritualistic origin, indicating propitiation for the building's safety, I may say that theories have been strung together on quite as far-fetched and as fanciful lines of association.

But sacrifice may also be voluntary, upon public or private grounds; and religious suicide has always had much vogue in India. There is a story of the commander of an army, who turned the adverse tide of battle by causing himself to be beheaded in front of his troops as a sacrifice to the gods. And though in military history I have discovered no other instance of a general who won an action by losing his head at a critical moment, yet the legend illustrates the persistence of the central idea that great emergencies demand supreme propitiatory acts. I admit, however, that to the sceptical mind, which discerns under every observance the germ of utilitarian motive, the story may present itself as no more than a pious invention to sanctify the sudden violent removal of an incapable or unlucky leader.

Let me now refer to the highest form of human self-sacrifice, the latest to disappear in some parts of India. I mean the custom of Suttee. In the burning of Hindu widows on the funeral pyre of their husbands, we may perceive two or three motives intertwined; we have, first, the primordial idea of sending a wife to accompany her husband into the next world, secondly, the much later doctrine, that for a widow to die in this manner with her husband is an act of the purest and noblest devotion, and lastly comes in the irrepressible utilitarian motive of liberating a great man's estate from the very serious burden of dowry for several widows. Some years ago a Hindu nobleman, with whom I was acquainted, had to support twelve of his father's widows; and those who have seen in Rajputána, on the marble tombs or cenotaphs of the chiefs, a long row of the figures of the wives and slave girls who were burnt with some great Rajah three or four generations back, might easily appreciate the danger to which the temptation of putting away defenceless women might expose widows in the dark ages of India.

These things were done, however, as Macbeth says, in the olden time, "ere human statute purged the gentle weal"—that is, before Governments were strong enough to support the higher morality of India in suppressing them. The savage forms of sacrifice are now extinct, but the later and milder varieties of immolation and offering exist in great abundance, far greater, as I have said, than in any other civilised country. The Ritual is the outward and visible sign of natural piety; for piety, as we are told in a Socratic dialogue,* is a sort of science of praying and sacrificing, of asking and giving. This definition, given at Athens more than 2000 years ago, exactly fits in with the apparent object of the ritual of Indian polytheism. Indeed its whole aspect is to me that of an open market or bazaar, in which these dealings are carried on under every kind of ensign, by every kind of device and method of intercourse, among an infinite number of establishments and profession.

For the characteristics of Natural Religion, the conditions of its existence as we see it in India, are complete liberty and material tolerance; there is no monopoly either of divine powers or even of sacerdotal privilege; since the Brahmans, though a most exclusive caste, are not an exclusive priesthood. No deity is invested with a supreme prerogative; no teacher proclaims himself the sole proprietor of the secret of the divine will; the army of the gods is not a fixed establishment; nor has the State ever asserted authority over the public worship. In India the British

* Euthyphro.

Government is more absolutely disconnected with the country's religion than in any other part of Her Majesty's dominions; it interposes only when barbarous customs fall within the range of the ordinary penal code; and in fact, the whole art and practice of Hinduism still lies open, as it has always done, to the changing influences of social and political environment.

It is this unrestrained indulgence of the religious propensities, this immemorial immunity from authoritative limitation, that has made India so important a field of study, especially for those who desire to understand the ancient polytheisms. For in the gradual transformations of the divine figures is seen the free and natural working of the radical ideas that seem to have inspired the earliest forms of superstition everywhere, and to have determined their subsequent expansion. As with the gods, so with their ritual; one may see in India the stages and transitions; one may fancy that their pedigree can be identified, may find corroboration of the hypothesis that most of these customs and practices can be traced to a few primary sources.

What does Hobbes, in the "Leviathan," call the Natural Seed of Religion? "And in these Foure Things (he says), Opinion of Ghosts, Ignorance of Second Causes, Devotion toward what men fear, and Taking of Things casual for Prognostiques, consisteth the Natural Seed of Religion, which by reason of the different Fancies, Judgments, and Passions of severall men, hath grown up into ceremonies so different that those which are used by one man are for the most part ridiculous to another."

These words, quaint and stiff as they are, appear to me

to cover most of the ground out of which polytheism in India has grown up, and, what is more, can be still seen growing. I do not mean that the process of transformation is always upward—I think that the strong tendency of beliefs and customs to improve is counteracted by another tendency toward degradation. I could give examples to show that a pure and exalted religious conception very often suffers decay and corruption, that spiritualism relapses into idolatry. But this is because the upper Hinduism has never been organised authoritatively, has never acquired the concentrated and sustained leverage that enables a powerful Church to lift the lower beliefs permanently up to the higher level. In Europe and western Asia the lesser worships and loose invertebrate beliefs have been systematically extirpated by Christianity and Islam, whereby the whole religious landscape has been entirely altered. The establishment of Churches and uncompromising Creeds, with the enormous support given to them for centuries by autocratic and orthodox Governments, has laid out the ground of Religion like a stately and well-ordered domain. Even under the Roman empire Religion was largely the concern of the State, the city, or the nation; and in modern Europe the sense of uniformity, discipline, and symmetry in matters of faith and worship, has become deeply impressed on our minds by long habit and the force of law. Popular Hinduism, on the contrary, is left to multitudinous confusion; for it defies limitation, and it is obviously useless to stamp as pure and genuine any particular image or doctrine of divinity, if a great many others may issue and pass current simultaneously. And this state of things seems likely, to judge from the past history of religions, to continue so long as Hinduism remains without any central influence or superior control, but goes on reproducing itself and spreading from the natural seed. In short, the whole panorama of religious ideas and practices, in polytheistic India, may be compared to the entangled confusion of a primeval forest, where one sees trees of all kinds, ages, and sizes interlacing and contending with each other; some falling into decay, others shooting up vigorously and overtopping the crowd—while the glimpse of blue sky above the tree tops may symbolise the illimitable transcendental ideas above and apart from the earth-born conceptions.

For it must always be remembered that the dominant idea of intellectual Hinduism, the belief which overhangs all this jungle of superstitions, is the Unity of the Spirit under a plurality of forms. Every religion must be in accord with the common experiences and needs of the people; but if it is to keep its hold on the higher minds it must also rest somewhere upon a philosophic theory; and Pantheism is the Philosophy of Natural Religion. The identity of all divine energies underlying this incessant stir and semblance of life in the world is soon recognised by reflective minds; the highest god as well as the lowest creature is a mere vessel of the Invisible Power; the god is only a peculiar and extraordinary manifestation of that power; the mysterious allegorical Trinity, Brahma, Vishnu, Siva, at the summit of Hinduism suggests and personifies its regular unchanging operation. It is of little use for those who attack Hinduism to insist that the mythology is a romance, or a disease of language; that the divinities are phantasms, that the idols are merely carved stones or cunning casts of clay. The higher Brahmans would probably agree that the popular polytheism is not much more than a symbolical representation in visible forms of the divine power that is everywhere immanent in Nature, and indeed identical with it. They might say that the anthropomorphic divinities are expressions of the various inscrutable powers that affect mankind; and that Infinite Unity cannot possibly be brought into relation with human affairs; but that no religion can flourish which does not concern itself or conform with the ordinary needs and circumstances of the world we live in. In this world of sensation the soul is locked up as in a prison; nor can it escape by the worship of gods, or by the help of any philosophy that relies upon experience. The only sure way of liberation is not by ascending an illimitable staircase which is always within the phenomenal circuit, but by purification of the soul from the illusion of the senses: until the whole fabric melts away like a vision, and the soul, being emancipated, attains to clear intellectual apprehension of divine knowledge.

In the meantime Pantheism is not an abstruse theologic doctrine; it is ingrained in the minds of all thoughtful persons; the inner meaning lies everywhere close below the outward worship, and it comes out at the first serious question. Queer idols and grotesque rites are to be seen everywhere in India, yet if any one were to challenge the priest or the worshipper to justify or explain them, he might very possibly receive an answer that would startle him by its subtlety, and by the momentary disclosure of some profound meaning underlying the irrational and superficial observance. And so Pantheism may be regarded as the final stage in the fusion and combination of the multitude of forms and conceptions bred out of vagrant superstitions; it does not stamp out or abolish them; it hardly cares to improve them; it explains and finds room for them all.

Thus forms and ceremonies, prayer and sacrifice, are useful only within the limits of this visible world, which is for gods as well as for men the sphere of action and concern. The highest devotion of Hinduism has for its object spiritual knowledge, the rescue of the soul from the ocean of illusory ephemeral existence; and this liberation is attained by the soul's passage through the vicissitudes of innumerable lives. Even here it is possible, I believe, to discern the remote influence of the persistent analogy from Nature; for there is no extravagance in supposing that the great Hindu dogma of the transmigration of souls still prolongs metaphysically the rule of change and transition by which the whole apparent universe is, to the Indian, so manifestly governed. The material conception of the homeless, wandering ghost, whom death is constantly dislodging, who may become a god, and again become a man, reappears in the moral doctrine of the laborious travel of the soul through many forms, through a labyrinth of painful and purifying existences; it is the promulgation of Natural law in the Spiritual world. According to this doctrine every human being has suffered a long series of births and dissolutions, his present condition being the necessary consequence of his precedent doings or experiences. And the range of his diverse existences stretches from a vegetable to a divinity; for gods also are subject to the law which governs the world of sensation. The same soul that moved in the flower may reappear in the god; and we can here perceive that this doctrine mysteriously points to or shadows out the inner meaning of the connection or common basis that underlies and holds together the lower and higher forms of external worship.

Every successive death does indeed interrupt consciousness; but so does sleep; and as in the visible world our birth is but a sleep and a forgetting, while we nevertheless inherit the qualities, good or bad, of our progenitors; so between each stage of its journey the soul loses all remembrance of the past, yet its next life is influenced by the merits or demerits accumulated in previous states. I venture to suggest that the upward striving of Nature through the modifications of forms and species is reflected, as in a glass, darkly, by this vision of spiritual evolution that gradually liberates the soul from the bondage of conscious existence, that purges it from the periodical returns of life's fitful fever, and brings it to final release by absorption into the one Essence. Then at last it is seen that all the changes of mortal life are merely illusions of the Sense; that as Lady Macbeth has said, the sleeping and the dead are but as pictures; and that this manifold working of Nature is but a kind of embroidery on the curtain which hangs before the illumination of true spiritual knowledge.

"And as," says one of their text-books, "by spreading out a picture, all its figures are rendered plainly visible, so the apparent existence of the world is due to Máya—that is to say Illusion. With the destruction of this Illusion by knowledge phenomena are reduced to Unreality—just as the figures in the picture disappear when the canvas is rolled up."

I have thus endeavoured to give some general outline and measure of the vast difference in religious ideas and observances that separates the lower from the higher beliefs in India. It is the difference between the primitive belief in the survival and constant re-embodiment of the human ghost, and the philosophical notion of the soul's passage through a cycle of existences until it is absorbed into Spiritual Being. It is the difference between the superstition that every moving thing or wandering animal is possessed by a peculiar spirit, and the discovery that all nature is imbued by one divine energy. From the feeling that a god is phenomenally everywhere, the train of thought advances to the conviction that God is phenomenally nowhere, to the idealism that regards the whole world as a subjective creation of one's own illusive fancy. Although these differences are extreme, and cover from point to point the whole range of natural theology, yet they are not treated in Hinduism as mutually hostile or inconsistent; the higher ideas and observances tolerate, adopt, and interpret the lower; the worshipper at an ordinary temple, a man who adores a shapeless image, may, probably does, hold the highest Unitarian doctrines. His mind finds no difficulty in reconciling shifting multiformity at the base of his religion, with changeless Unity at the summit. No one, certainly not I, can pretend to give a clear demonstration of the whole line of connection, or to follow the processes of imagination and thought which lead from the belief in millions of gods to the recognition of one Universal Spirit, or to the final conclusion that He is Unknowable. I can only say that the impression produced upon myself, after long personal observation of Religion in India, is that the whole of this marvellous structure comes by what, for want of a better term, I must call natural growth.

CHAPTER VI.

HISTORY AND FABLE.

Early relations between Fable and History—Common source of both—Changes of the standard of credibility—Gradual dissociation—The Myth—Its origin and contents—Heroic tradition—Separation of Fiction and Fact—History draws apart from and disowns Fiction—Fiction still leans on historic fact—The Historical Romance—Defoe, the modern mythmaker—The Gothic romance—Revival under Scott—Contemporary historic novels—Esmond, Romola, John Inglesant.

In glancing over the books which provided light reading for our forefathers, we cannot fail to perceive the great change that has come over the important department of national literature which may be termed Fiction, whereby the Romance has become the Novel. The fact is obvious enough, yet to show adequately how and why this has come to pass, to investigate the psychological causes, would be a task far beyond the limits of a short chapter. The modern novel has a very ancient descent, and has sprung from many intricate roots in diverse countries. It would be most interesting to trace its origin, to describe the changes in its form and character, and to show their connexion with the general course of intellectual development and the extension of accurate knowledge.

But since the growth and gradual modification of Fiction is a subject leading out into a vast field of discussion, I can only venture, at this moment, upon taking one of the many paths which cross that field in all directions. The line therefore which this chapter will attempt to follow is that which appears to connect the domain of Fable with the domain of History, in order to illustrate, if possible, the extent and manner in which fable and fiction have at different times employed themselves on the basis of historic fact. For imagination is constantly working upon authentic incident; and tradition enlarges the real personage up to the limits of accepted probability.

The mainspring and source of all fable and fiction that deal with famous events and persons of a past time, are to be found in our immemorial anxiety to know, or at any rate to imagine, something of what happened in old days, and to revive, if possible, scenes and characters that played their part on the stage, now dark and silent, of the world long ago. Somehow the future, with all its bright promises for this world or another, is not, to many of us, so attractive as the past: we know nothing of what is to come, but though we know little more of what happened in far distant times, of that little we are always trying to collect and interpret what fragments can be picked up here or there. The remainder we supply by guesswork and imagination. It is this enquiry, this regretful looking back to the dim past, this delight in ancient legend and tradition, this fanciful guessing at what cannot be known, that nourished in old days the spirit of imaginative fable, just as it now stimulates the collection of folklore, the scrutiny of old records, and as it has sustained up to our own time the fading delight in Romance. Much also has always been, and is still, due to the enormous influence of the religious sentiment, the lingering trust in supernatural interposition, the belief that in old days Divinity was nearer, was more manifest, spoke more clearly to human beings. In an unlettered and primitive age men accepted as true and authentic everything that was handed down and repeated to them of the deeds of gods and heroes; and thus the hazy atmosphere of the marvellous and miraculous obscures all early origins of race or religion, and clouds the beginnings of history. Soon the splendid visions which surround the youth of man begin to fade into the common daylight of growing civilisation; the standard of what is credible goes on changing; we take fewer things for granted and demand more proof of them. Thus the dry land of authentic History emerges slowly out of the sea of Fable, until gradually things which appeared natural and acceptable to the elder generation become incredible or suspiciously improbable to ourselves; the love of wonders and of things that pass man's understanding gives way to a demand for the intelligible, for the reasonable, for what seems likely to ordinary every-day experience. The delight in awe and astonishment is superseded by a taste for accurate thought and rigorous evidence. In short, whereas at their birth History and Fable were twin sisters, so like that one could hardly distinguish between them, in their after life the resemblance rapidly decreases until it disappears altogether. History becomes serious and accurate, Fable becomes artistic and romantic; they become greatly estranged though they are never entirely disjoined, for there is always a certain quantity of fable in history, and there is always an element of history in one particular sort of fable. We think that this kinship between history and fable may be traced through many centuries of myths, legends, romances, and historic novels, with various changes of relation down to our own day. And we propose to attempt some explanation of how this came to pass by a very rough survey of the general line and successive stages of the transition.

To begin with the Myth, which was originally a name for those common stories of the deeds and adventures of gods and heroes which were spread all over Greece in the earliest days. These popular tales were at first universally believed; History and Fable stood on the same level of probability. Then, after a certain time, when the marvels and miracles in these stories were gradually seen to be extremely improbable if not incredible, the attempt began to be made to sift out what was likely to be true from what was likely to be false, to separate history from fable. Long afterwards, in our own day of scientific research, the idea sprung up that there is no truth at all in most of the myths, that a good many of them are entirely fabulous with no mixture whatever of history. Thus the attempts to explain these old stories have given birth to many theories and diverse methods of interpretation. One school of interpreters, of great authority, has declared that all tales of wonderful adventure or of the doings of divine personages are mere imaginary fabrications with no basis of fact, that the figures are mere phantoms of the sun and mist, and that the incidents were created out of unconscious allegory. According to this doctrine, when a primitive man saw light striving with darkness he called it a fight between gods and demons, or when he saw the sun setting behind dark clouds he figured to himself a hero dying conquered by enemies, or when he looked at the blushing dawn he made a story of some beautiful bride. Into this controversy we have neither time nor space for entering. We can only here indicate our opinion that the sounder conclusion, which is supported by much recent research and actual observation of the growth of myths in countries where an analogous state of society still survives, is that a very large proportion of the old fables have grown up round a kernel of truth. The kernel may be sometimes small, and the tree very large—there may be all the difference between the acorn and the oak. The point for which we here contend is that the early Fable was no mere fanciful invention, spun by some one out of his own brain, but that it almost always had an invisible root in some underlying fact, that it was an imaginative amplification of some real incident. The heroic myth repeated and preserved the far-sounding echoes of the noise made by some famous chief or warrior in the primitive world; it reflected the great shadows thrown upon the mists of tradition by some figure that had impressed its personality upon primitive men. And since the supernatural was in those days merely an enlarged copy of the natural, the divine myth represented no more than a later chapter of the same story, a further development of the Fable working upon true events and persons. It has been, we know, the universal practice in modern as in ancient days, in China and India as in Greece or under the Roman Empire, among all polytheistic nations outside the pale of Christianity and Islam, that were not utterly barbarous, to make gods out of men, to promote to the rank of divinities saints or heroes whose exploits or sufferings have impressed with awe or wonder the popular imagination. It is a matter of common observation that among the lower and more ignorant races at the present day the ghost of a man who was notorious in life is usually worshipped after death; he becomes a demon or a demigod to be propitiated or adored. His posthumous career as a divinity often becomes much more important and eventful than his mortal existence; it is confused and magnified mythically. Thus a man who has made his mark upon his generation, who overtops the rest by bravery, piety, or some peculiar power of mind or body, becomes among unlettered folk the source and subject of legends, which rescue and transmit to posterity all that can be saved out of the flood of deep oblivion that has submerged the pre-historic ages of humanity.

Such, then, are the earliest relations between History and Fable. They begin with a common fund and joint stock of legends, traditions, and wondrous tales, with stories of the wandering of tribes, the adventures of heroes, of the terrible or splendid achievements of gods and men. At the commencement of their long partnership Fable is the prominent member of the firm; for though History supplies a small but solid capital of fact, it is the enterprise and versatile inventiveness of Fable that advertise the wares, put them into circulation, and attract customers. Not only are fact and fiction so intermixed as to be indistinguishable, but it is probable that in many cases the maimed and scanty facts would not have survived at all if Fable had not published an enlarged and illustrated popular edition of them. On the other hand, it must not be supposed that these tales were credited among the earlier races in the serious, matter-of-fact, absolutely historical sense in which we of these days accept a properly verified narrative or record. Beyond the sphere of scientific research and established churches, the belief in things sacred and profane is still loose, easy-going, and carelessly indulgent. Our own English philosopher, Hobbes, writing in the seventeenth century, defines Religion as consisting of Tales publicly allowed, and Superstition of those not allowed; but such distinctions as these belong to a much later stage of civilisation, when the sphere of belief has become authoritatively limited. So also at a time when the canons of historical criticism had not been invented, when between the true and the apocryphal elements of a story no clear dividing line could possibly have been drawn, it is likely that the whole mass of legends obtained from readers or listeners the same kind of willing acquiescence and provisional acceptance that any one might now give to some remarkable tale, purporting to be true, the particulars of which he might have no means of verifying. The conclusion of ordinary folk would be that such a story must have a good deal of truth in it, and we may guess that the mental attitude of our remote forefathers toward the historic fable was of much the same kind.

Having regard, therefore, to the true observation of Renan that all History begins with Romance, we may venture to add the suggestion that Romance has its source in History. Among unlettered people in all ages and countries Fable has given the poetical and fanciful rendering of great events; it is the popular and pictorial edition of their annals, the primitive form of a biographical series. So far, indeed, as yet are the true and the imaginary elements of a story from being disentangled, that there are no tests by which they can be extracted, and to the popular appreciation there is no difference between them. We have to remember, moreover, that in earlier times the actual difference was really much smaller than it would be in these modern days; for in an age that was full of violent incidents and sudden tragedies, when men lived in constant peril, and when the greater part of the world was unexplored and mysterious, the ordinary existence of mankind was often what we should now call romantic, agitated by passions, dangers, and hazardous uncertainties. The range of possibilities was so wide as to provide ample room for fabulous invention—seeing that what is possible is always credible—and to render detection very much more difficult. Every one has noticed how any stirring or extraordinary event—a war, a great national disaster, a terrible crime or catastrophe—will at once excite and revive the latent spirit of myth-making among the people of our time, will for a moment confuse the boundaries between fact and fiction, and will suspend the faculty of discrimination.

But as the world grew calmer and more settled, literature and the advancement of learning gradually brought in the historic feeling, the desire for precise knowledge, the search for some test that might distinguish fact from fancy. The sphere of the knowable and credible assumed some distinct limitations, excluding the outer darkness of mere conjecture; the slow expansion of experience gave precision to thought, and some fixity to standards of probability. And since the general tendency of these intellectual changes was to mark off a separate domain for History—for the exploration, that is, of the true facts that might be found embedded in the conglomerate mass of legends and traditions—it followed naturally that Fables began on their side to take up their own ground, and to draw slowly together as a separate department of literature. This process of dissociation and separate development may be said to have gone on in Europe throughout the period during which the nations were emerging out of the dark ages. Its effects showed itself plainly upon the sacred legends, the marvellous stories of saints and martyrs, which begin to disconnect themselves from the heroic legend, form a class apart, fall under the control and censure of the Churches, admit very few fresh accretions, and show a disposition to subside into passion plays, or finally into allegory. In these symptoms we may, perhaps, trace the tardy and reluctant retreat of the confused army of fables before the disciplined advance of regular history.

We have now, therefore, passed clearly out of that long period when history and fable were so blended, and resembled each other so closely, as to be practically indistinguishable. In the succeeding stage of their immemorial partnership, the grand outlines of history have become more or less settled, and the authentic existence, the general character and career, of the celebrated men whose names have been transmitted to posterity—whose figures have thrown a long shadow over succeeding generations—are at least incontestably ascertained. So far they are no longer subject to the caprice of Fable; yet the true particulars of what they did, their real features, and the precise nature of the events and circumstances in which they took a leading part, are only known in bare outline. These outlines are still filled in, the victories, conquests, and personal exploits are still magnified and illuminated, by the free use of the fabulous art which supplies imaginative details and the romantic colouring. The existence, for example, of Charlemagne, of Roland and Oliver, his famous paladins, and of the Spanish Cid, has by this time become matter of fact, has been definitely placed within the recognised province of history; and they are thenceforward preserved like disinterred statues in the national museum, where the rubbish will in time be cleared away from them, and their true proportions set out and displayed. Nevertheless, Charlemagne and the Cid continued through centuries to be the figure-heads for whole shiploads of legends, which were as good as real history for the people at large. When, in mediæval Europe, annals, chronicles, and biographies of great men first began to be composed, the writers did their best to collect genuine material: but they inevitably included a great deal of fabulous stuff, and they put down much that was obviously apocryphal, or at least unverifiable. Yet the historic sense was evidently prevailing, for these chroniclers undoubtedly meant to write history; they spared no pains to extract the nuggets of fact from the mass of tradition and hearsay; they desired earnestly to part company with the fables and legends which had by this time become grouped under the form of Romance. It will be easily understood that the delimitation between these two great provinces, History and Romance, which have since become separate independent kingdoms, went on with much difficulty and delay, if indeed it has ever been finally completed. For a long time there was no formally acknowledged frontier, but on the contrary a wide debateable borderland; and each made constant incursions into the other's territory, to carry off anything worth laying hands upon.

The romance, therefore, like the primitive myth, is essentially Fable built up on fact, with this modification that the main facts of the romance are solid foundation stones, immovably laid down by authoritative History. So long as the records of the past are dim, confused, slight, and untrustworthy, they are constantly being transformed and twisted by the force of the prevailing popular sentiment. Accordingly, although in the early mediæval romances of Europe the events and personages are usually authentic, yet the true stories of kings and warriors, of saints and martyrs, are enlarged and re-arranged for the delight and astonishment of a credulous multitude in the various countries through which they circulate. History generates fable; and then again the group of fables, having acquired credit and currency, become embodied into the uncritical history of those ages, so that history and romance, borrowing material freely from each other, still remain blended and interfused throughout the greater part of the middle ages. Such chronicles as that of the Cid, or such a metrical romance as the "Song of Roland," are evidently the popular and poetic renderings of real history, of history that has taken the only shape in which it could make any impression upon the mind of the people. One can see that the sound of a great reputation spread abroad into all lands, and gave rise to a cycle of fables, as a huge stone makes a number of widening circles when it drops into a pond. The myth of Alexander the Great, which is said to have originated with a fictitious history produced about the fourth century A.D., travelled with numerous ramifications all over Europe. The myth of King Arthur was expanded and multiplied in the same manner. In the former case we see a famous and genuine story distorted and misplaced; in the latter we have a collection of legendary tales pointing backward to a lost history. The "Chansons de Geste," again, which embody the myth of Charlemagne, afford another striking example of the fantastic superstructure that the mediæval romance could erect upon an historic foundation. All the main events and personages have been recognised as the property of history, but the writers assumed full liberty of executing upon this base such variations as might please them; and the battle of Roncesvalles is as mythical in characters and incidents as any that was fought under the walls of Troy.

Whereas, however, we have no sure proof that Troy town was burned, or that Achilles existed, we do know that one Hroland, a prefect of the Britannic March, lived under Charlemagne, and that a battle was lost by the Franks in the pass of Roncesvalles. By this time History has so far shaken itself loose of Fable as to be able so far to fix and identify certain events and persons, that neither Roland nor Oliver can be melted down into solar heroes. The principal landmarks and commanding points of the historical position are now firmly occupied, although Fable still lays claim to at least co-ordinate authority over all the open country and the debateable borders. No one as yet thinks worse of the historian who fills up his outlines with picturesque and probable details; and, while he borrows freely from fabulous sources, the early romancer may do what he likes with Alexander the Great or with Virgil, with King Arthur or Charlemagne.

In short, the partnership of History and Fable during the middle ages was undivided, and to a large extent unlimited. The great fountain and reservoir for the supply of narrative or the composition of stories was still that broad ocean of floating traditions and changeable legends, which as yet submerged the lower part of the slowly rising continent of recognisable fact. The historic warrior still performs fabulous deeds, and the real battles are frequently decided by superhuman interference. We may suppose that it was long before any, save a very few learned men, cared to enquire how far the romance did or did not purport to be an authentic account of what really happened, and we may be certain that the general mass of hearers or readers continued still to be very indifferent upon the question. It seems clear that Sir Thomas Malory's compilation of the Arthurian legends was regarded by the ordinary reader of his time as historical, for Caxton relates that he was much pressed to "emprynte the noble history of the Saynt Graal and of that most renowned crysten king, Arthur," but that he long hesitated because of the opinion that all such books as had been made of Arthur had been "but fayned and fabled." Here we may see history and romance just beginning to draw apart and to disentangle themselves.

Yet we may doubt whether in the much later time of Shakespeare his audience knew or troubled themselves to ask whether King Lear or King John was the more genuine personage of the two; nor is it certain that Spenser's "Faëry Queen," or even Milton's "Paradise Lost," was at first treated as a work of pure imagination beyond a limited literary circle. In fact, the Paradise Lost, which represents the latest stage of the divine myth, has largely coloured and confused the ideas of English folk in regard to the orthodox narrative, and to the exact proportions of scriptural and poetic inspiration in this magnificent poem.

Nevertheless the time came, though one must not attempt to define the precise epoch, when History is seen to have formally dissolved partnership with Fable, and to have set up her own rules and tests of what she claims or rejects. When a narrative of past events could be so far classed as authentic, that the attempt to introduce arbitrary details and variations, to place the real figures under the magnifying glass of romance, would be resisted and disallowed, the watershed and dividing line between these two main currents of literature has been perceptibly demarcated. Not only is their union now in process of disintegration, but the widening divergence of aims and methods brings about a kind of antipathy on one side, for History is inclined to treat her ancient associate as a troublesome parasite. But though History now disowns Fable, Fable clings persistently to her inveterate connexion with History; she cannot yet afford to dispense with the aid and countenance of so respectable a dealer in hard facts. The old business, if we may continue the commercial metaphor, is still carried on, and has indeed had a long and successful career, under the title of the Historical Romance, upon the system of constructing stories that are compounded of historic material, that are deliberately fabricated by the writer, but are only by degrees, and in quite modern times, put forward openly and exposed to the public for sale as fictitious.

The phases through which this new development of the ancient art of story-telling has passed, illustrate curiously the subtle modifications of taste, of mental appetite, of literary craft and resource, that have been produced by the moral and material changes of national life and character which succeed each other from generation to generation. History, as we have said, has disowned Romance on the ground that she is not to be trusted, is too much given to speculation, overdraws upon her credibility, and therefore must set up for herself. But Romance is still reluctant to venture forth alone; she even hesitates to admit that she is constructing a fictitious story upon historic material; she falls back upon the device of counterfeiting the genuine products of History. One very curious example of this balancing attitude, of this reluctance to lose the powerful impression of reality, may be seen in the works of Daniel Defoe, who wrote romances which he foisted upon the public as genuine memoirs, biographies, or narratives, and which constitute a singular link in the chain of the transformation of the romance into the historic novel. In short, he was a fabulist who knowingly fabricated history.

It has often been said of Defoe, and rightly, that he is the direct literary ancestor of the modern realistic novelist. It may also be affirmed that he can claim descent from and a strong family likeness to the primitive myth-makers. We have seen that the heroic myth was formed by imagining for some hero an appropriate career, or by enveloping some prehistoric war or adventure with a cloud of picturesque circumstances, interweaving facts with fable so harmoniously that they have ever since remained indistinguishable. To the myth-maker this process was of course entirely legitimate, for he was in no way troubled by any sense of difference between what did happen and what might have happened. Very much after the same fashion did Defoe take some well-known personage whose biography he invented, or whose memoirs he fabricated; or else he embroidered upon such a famous incident as the Plague or the Civil War, winding round his hero a tissue of plausible details, and filling up the real outline of his pretended narratives with coherent and life-like circumstances. He treated in this way kings, highwaymen, pirates, soldiers, and sailors—the popular characters of the day, trading upon their notoriety, taking the precise measure of the credulity of his readers, and carefully working out his mosaic upon the strongest features or types of a class or period. "Robinson Crusoe," "Captain George Carleton's Memoirs," now generally believed to be spurious, and the "Memoirs of Colonel Newport," are perfect specimens of the modern myth, in which fact and fiction are so interweaved as to produce narratives which were successfully imposed upon the whole world as authentic. It has taken all the acuteness and careful microscopic apparatus of the latest criticism to discover the deception, which could never have been detected at all if the stories had appeared a century earlier. The main difference between these works and the early fables is, in the first place, that Defoe was knowingly deceiving his public while the fabulist was not; and secondly, that while the myth-maker or romancer often employed unnatural exaggeration of real events, the secret of Defoe's art lay in his trick of reducing all his incidents to a natural scale, in his use of a quiet and level style of plausible narrative, commending itself to common sense, and conveying the impression of scrupulous exactitude in small particulars.

We may reckon, however, Defoe's works as the last examples of the long and inveterate confusion, unconscious or intentional, between History and Fable. We are now in the midst of the eighteenth century, a period of sceptics and critics, and the historical romance is assuming its modern shape of avowed Fiction, borrowing characters and events from the history of past times, and artistically working them into an imaginary narrative. It is curious to observe how at this stage the romance does outward homage to the rising sovereignty of realism, to the increasing demand for historic probability, not only in outline but in particulars—by new devices and theatrical contrivances of language, costume, and sentiment. The dramatists of the English Renaissance, who put early romance upon the stage, had been content that their characters should speak in the vulgar tongue, quite independently of the time or country to which the plot or scene belonged; so that Shakespeare's Greeks and Trojans use good racy English, Macbeth never attempts a Scotticism, nor does even Dryden's Aurungzeb, the Mogul Emperor, who appeared much later, imitate the metaphoric and quasi-biblical style of false Orientalism. The writers of that period thought no more of local colouring or archaic diction in their plays or romances than the sixteenth-century painters cared for Oriental costume in such a picture as Paul Veronese's "Marriage in Cana of Galilee." They were intent on plot or character; and they disdained the accessories which are now so much in demand with a critical public.

It was the later eighteenth-century romancer who first attempted to introduce his notions of what might be appropriate in manners, garb, and language, into a description of bygone periods. That a monarch, or a crusader, or a monk, should discourse like men of the writer's own day, seemed undignified and manifestly inartistic, an anachronism to be corrected by the display of erudition. The dialogue of the historical novel thereby fell into a sort of stilted jargon, larded with quaint phrases and strange oaths supposed to belong to the particular period under treatment, or at any rate not modern; and the ordinary vernacular was carefully eschewed. Whether this queer dialect was ever really spoken by mortal man at any period whatever is exceedingly questionable; it seems to have been compounded of obsolete words and turns of phrase picked up indiscriminately out of old plays and chronicles, and of such obviously stage properties as "Unhand me, Sir Knight," "By my Halidome," "Marry good morrow to thee," and the like, while the use of Thou and Thy instead of You and Yours seems to have been thought an excellent way of giving to conversation the flavour of age. Then, again, the rising sensitiveness to anachronisms and incongruities produced a demand for local colour, theatrical scene-painting, and archaic costume. This was supplied by drawing upon false antiquarianism, ancestral wardrobes, old armour, dungeons, tournaments, feudal castles with their portcullis and barbicans, and a good deal of sham fighting. The author tried to persuade himself and his readers that this kind of varnish gave his picture a genuine historic character, and made it something like a true reflection of a past age. Horace Walpole's "Castle of Otranto," written in 1764, is a remarkable instance of this phase. In his first edition the author follows the practice in vogue among myth-makers of the transitional period; he endeavours to delude his readers into the belief that his fable is true. He does not, however, rely, as Defoe did, upon consummate skill in fabrication; he adopts the easier trick of pretending to have found an ancient black-letter manuscript, writ in the purest Italian. In his second edition he throws off this cloak, and stands forth boldly as one who has produced a new species of romance by judiciously crossing the ancient with the modern kind. In the former kind, he observes, all was imagination and improbability; while in the latter, "the great resources of fancy have been dammed up by a strict adherence to common life." His own simple rule was Nature, even in "the deportment of servants." "I am content," writes Walpole to a friend, "if I have amused you by tracing with any fidelity the manners of ancient days"—as if Gothic castles, trap-doors, skeletons, a monstrous helmet, and all his mysterious horrors could represent anything in the world except a wild and fantastic extravaganza or pantomime. Yet in the early days of George III. this "Gothic Romance" struck polite readers with awe and admiration; and its author claimed special credit for having discarded the improbability of the old fables, whereas his own stories were in their own manner quite as improbable. He said that he had made his men and women talk as they might naturally do in extraordinary and dreadful situations, such as the sight of a horrid spectre, or in a moment of terrible peril; but as neither Walpole nor most of his readers had ever had the slightest experience of any such situations, it is manifest that his imitation of natural horror and dreadful situations was mere guesswork.

Similar changes followed in the drawing of characters. The mediæval romances had breathed the simple spirit of chivalry, devotion, and love, as we find it, for instance, in the "Morte d'Arthur," the story of the Knights of the Round Table. Their characters were straight and clear personifications of one or two single ideas, like the figures of saints and knights on the early stained-glass windows. Then had come the much more complex creations of the Elizabethan drama, when the kings and barons, the ladies and their lovers, express in the language of the author's day the feeling, passions, and moods that belong to human nature in all times. But to the later eighteenth-century school of historic romance it seemed to be an offence against polite taste, a breach of the unities, that the men of old time should so nearly resemble the writer's contemporaries; and this anomaly he tried to correct by a strong infusion of what he fancied to be mediæval manners and ideas. The consequence was an awkward jumble of artificial sentiments with modern ideas and conjectures, like an ill-arranged collection containing a good many counterfeits. The pursuit of Probability and Consistency in Art only led the writers of this period deeper into the Improbable and the Unnatural, for the plain reason that they were writing of times and describing situations of which they really knew little or nothing at all; they were travelling far outside their own experience, and they were copying from clumsy casts of originals that they had never seen. And it is interesting to observe how this crude notion of conformity to nature, which has since dominated and moulded the whole art of novel-writing, influenced the writings of Mrs Radcliffe, —a lady who at the end of the last century wrote romances seasoned with mysterious and gloomy horrors, pictures with black veils, howling winds, secret prisons, skeletons, and rusty daggers. After perplexing and terrifying her reader through many chapters, she considers herself bound to provide at the end a natural and reasonable explanation of these portentous puzzles, and she always winds up with the triumph of respectable virtue.

We may say, therefore, of the Historical Romance in this stage, that it was something like an artificial myth; a myth that had not grown, but had been deliberately fabricated. It was a completely fabulous story of past times invested with a false air of plausibility, a hollow nutshell with its withered kernel of truth inside. That it still clung feebly to the skirts of history is shown by the device, which has lasted up to our own day, of setting out with a preface in which the author pretends to have found an ancient manuscript in a hidden chest, or to be merely editing papers confided to him by an old Italian monk. The romance did not even yet stand forth boldly and candidly as a purely imaginary conception, although of course it was so understood to be by all intelligent readers. The prehistoric myths and the early romances had been conventional in the sense that the folk accepted marvels and miracles, gods and giants, with a kind of half-belief—such things were likely enough when the tale was of old times—and the eighteenth-century romance, so long as its scenes were put a few centuries backward, flourished upon a mutual understanding of the same sort. The truth is that the whole method now rested upon convention, upon a tacit agreement between the author and his public that they should accept, in the book or on the stage, certain assumed notions regarding men and manners of which little or nothing was really known exactly. They were false tokens which were allowed to pass in circulation as genuine ancient coins. The main point was to avoid being commonplace and modern; and thus exaggerations, absurdities, and a whole store-room of musty and rusty things and phrases, were brought in to produce the necessary illusion and the appropriate effects. A horse, for instance, must always be called a charger or a steed, a sword went by the name of falchion, a girl was a damsel, a servant was a trusty henchman, and so on.

But although the romance of past times had fallen low towards the end of the eighteenth century, at the beginning of the nineteenth it suddenly rose to high-water mark, as an artistic creation, under the hands of Walter Scott. Romance has now finally abandoned the expedient of simulating history, and, instead of attempting to pass off her conceptions as genuine, she is content to take real personages and events as an acknowledged loan of material for the plastic art of undisguised fiction. By his picturesque descriptions, the force and individuality of his characters, his spirited battle-scenes, his men in armour and buff jerkins, and his thorough mastery of antiquarian lore, Scott did actually give life and reality to stories about the middle ages, and threw a luminous glow over certain obscure epochs of history. His plots were so good, his actors were so full of individuality, that his readers were abundantly satisfied. No one then cared to make the objection, which would certainly be made in these very exact and critical days, that the state of society in the eleventh and thirteenth centuries must have been essentially different from the splendid creations of Ivanhoe or the Talisman, that Scott's Richard the Lion-hearted and his Knight Templar are magnificent but fantastic, or that Saladin had nothing Arabian about him but a turban and a scimitar. In Ivanhoe the knights in the famous tournament at Ashby dash full tilt at each other with the furious gallop of modern race-horses. If they had actually done so, both riders must have inevitably broken their necks at the first shock; but this troubled no one's delight at the vivid picture. Nor were the readers of Scott's metrical romances startled even at the grotesque image of knights carving at the meal with gloves of steel and drinking red wine through the helmet barred. The convention still existed, the fabulous element still dominated, there was a common understanding that matter-of-fact criticism would be out of place, and that a certain magical illusion might still hover over past times, when things might happen and deeds might be done which would appear absurd or preposterous apart from the enchantment of distance. The peculiarity of Scott's work is that it contains an unusually large proportion of real history; as for instance in Anne of Geierstein and Quentin Durward, where the great battles and leading figures are all taken from the contemporary chronicles. Yet Scott, who knew well that a novelist must not write history, took considerable liberties with the real order of events; and thus his mediæval romance is a direct lineal descendant of the heroic myth, it is history disguised by artistic re-construction; it is a fictitious narrative embroidered upon the canvas of fact. The distinction lies in this, that in the myth the substantial facts cannot, never could, be verified, whereas in the later historic romance they are easily distinguishable.

But by this time the old partnership of History with Fable was almost dissolved; and Fable was receiving peremptory notice to quit the historical domain. There was a growing disposition to treat the handling of ancient records and mediævalism generally for the purposes of romance as unjustifiable; for, if the true circumstances were accurately known, the romance perverted them, and if they were not known, the romance was sure to be unreal and probably absurd. Not even the erudition and transcendent genius of Scott could raise his Norman barons, gentle ladies, knights-templar, or Saxon thanes much beyond the level of very carefully costumed characters in a brilliant masquerade; and masquerades were now going out of fashion. To reproduce the real unvarnished crusader, or outlaw, or peasant of England who lived five or six centuries ago, was felt to be beyond the most consummate literary skill, at a time when the critical, exacting, naturalistic feeling of our country was protesting more and more against conventional and counterfeit workmanship, however good of its kind.

The long series of romantic story-telling was now evidently approaching its close. In the novels of Bulwer Lytton, who was in some respects the last writer of the true historic school, we may perceive a vain attempt to bring about some reconciliation between history and romance, by accommodating his fiction to the precise and earnest notions of the rising generation. When he took us back to the Norman conquest and the wars of the Roses, he endeavoured to persuade us that such stories as Harold and The Last of the Barons were written not merely for entertainment but for instructive and useful purposes. He pleaded, to use his own words, that Historic Fiction might be employed to elucidate fact, by increasing the reader's acquaintance with the habits and modes of thinking which constitute the true idiosyncrasy of the earlier ages. To this end he charged his tales heavily with philosophic views of the course of history; and his personages, instead of minding their own affairs, can be detected acting or conversing with the transparent intention of impressing upon the unwary reader some rather dubious modern theory as to social evolution, such as the gradual formation of the English middle class, or the dawn of scientific research. Here we have that very recent invention—the Novel with a purpose—applied to history. But this somewhat maladroit method of propitiating the stern spirit of Realism only exposed him more fatally to its indignation. It was impossible to argue seriously that imaginary conversations between Saxons and Normans, or the fanciful love-passages between Harold and his mistress Edith, would throw any true light on the manners and motives of warriors and statesmen in the eleventh century. Nor could anything save amusement, with a touch of the ludicrous, be gained from the scene in The Last of the Barons, where the early man of science exhibits a rude steam-engine to Edward IV., which explodes in the royal presence. These ingenious illuminations of past ages were soon seen to be glaring fallacies, unendurable in an age which demanded accuracy in its history and probability in its novels; and the project of infusing new vigour into the antiquated romance by pretending to make it instructive, only betrayed its decay and accelerated its dissolution. The taste for imaginary scene-painting, for conventional portraits of knights and fair ladies, for old armour newly furbished up, and the stilted jargon that did duty for old English, was passing away; and the whole phantasmagoria which Bulwer tried to foist on his public as a vivid reflection of a vanished society was irrevocably disappearing.

The school of conventional art closed finally with G. P. R. James, whose model seems to have been Scott's Quentin Durward, and Harrison Ainsworth, who worked upon the horrors of history, the torture chamber, the headsman, and the burning of heretics. In the case of James his monotony of treatment, and in Ainsworth's case his crudity of invention and colouring, have relegated both these authors, once as popular as they were prolific, to the limbo of the unreadable. Bulwer, and even Scott, survive chiefly by reason of those stories which dealt with contemporary, or recent, or very well-known periods. Nothing could long sustain the interest and simple pleasure taken by the general reader of sixty years ago in the artificial myth, in the attempt to show off history by a kind of literary magic lantern, to supplement our ignorance of a remote unlettered time by mere arbitrary inventions. The training of our mental apprehension, the extended knowledge of the real world in different stages of social evolution, the spread of accurate observation around us, and the increased precision of historic criticism, have been cutting away the slight ground still occupied by the old-fashioned romancer; burlesques and parodies have been trampling him underfoot; until the latest generation looks back upon him as an antiquated impostor.

The severe and laborious historian now rejects all aid from the romancer, and has not only dissolved partnership, but declares any connection with him to be fatal to his credit. And though History does not always refuse to the Novel a small loan of useful materials, yet if historic events and personages are not yet banished absolutely from the land of fiction, they must belong to periods well surveyed and traversed in all directions, well furnished with documents, pictures, and memorials of every kind, so that all details and characteristics can be rigorously scrutinised, and no liberties can be taken either with personalities, language, or transactions. These conditions are usually found too hard for the modern myth-maker: the cool scepticism and pitiless criticism of the present generation disconcert his aims and damp his ardour; they are to him what scientific analysis is to some sacred book, they dissipate the inspiration. And even if all these conditions are fulfilled, all these exigencies satisfied, the effect produced is often little more than a sense of elaborate effort, leaving an impression similar to that made by architecture carefully copied in every detail from the antique. The historical novelist of our own day does not mix his styles, he has abandoned the old jargon of Bulwer or James, he has abjured dungeons and spectres, his heroes deliver themselves like men of the world; but if he ever attempts to go back upon those obscure periods of history which were the favourite hunting-grounds of his predecessors, his work runs a high risk of failure. The earlier romancer said: "We know nothing accurately about the eleventh century, so I may indulge my imagination at pleasure, using the general historic outline as the frame of my picture." In the case of the modern novelist, the precise and realistic criticism of modern readers warns him off from attempting to delineate the manners of the crusaders or society under the Plantagenets or even the Tudors, because everything except a bare outline must necessarily be conjectural, probably false, and certainly unhistorical. So the use of historic material is permitted only on condition that it shall not be tampered with, and that the fictitious embroidery shall be strictly in accordance with the ascertained and verifiable pattern of manners or transactions in some familiar period well lighted up by contemporary records. In fact, the Romance has by this time fairly become the Novel, a tale of real life, adjusted to the actual ordinary train of human events. And the same rules prevail whether the scene be laid in the reign of Queen Anne or of Queen Victoria; the plot must be probable and circumstantial; the fictitious incidents must be so interposed as to supplement without superseding the delicate and sparing use of history.

Such work can only be produced by artists of the first order; and consequently we find that only three writers of our own day have attempted it with indisputable success. Thackeray's "Esmond" is a rare and striking example of what can be done by a writer who has mastered the secrets and correctly apprehended the limitations of the art of historical novel-writing; he has really accomplished what Bulwer Lytton professed in vain to do, the illustration of a famous chapter in our national history. Remembering that Johnson's dictionary defines Romance in its primary sense to be "a military fable of the Middle Ages, a tale of wild adventure in love and chivalry," we can measure the progress made in refinement of taste and literary workmanship. The great wars of Marlborough are illuminated for us by the side-lights which Colonel Esmond's carefully arranged narrative of his personal experiences throws upon the battles, the camp life, the manners of the army, and the character of its various leaders. The tone and composition are subdued and realistic; the air of a modest memoir is sedulously preserved, except in certain passages where enthusiasm seems to break irrepressibly through the natural reserve, and Marlborough's godlike serenity amid the din of battle extorts Colonel Esmond's reluctant admiration:—

"Our chief, whom England and all Europe, saving only the Frenchmen, worshipped almost, had this of the godlike in him, that he was impassible before victory, before danger, before defeat

Before the greatest obstacle or the most trivial ceremony, before 100,000 men drawn in battalia, or a peasant slaughtered at the door of his burning hovel; at a monarch's court or a cottage table where his plans were laid, or before an enemy's battery vomiting flame and death and strewing corpses round him, he was always cold, calm, resolute, as fate . . . having, as I have said, this of the godlike in him, that he could see a hero perish or a sparrow fall with the same amount of sympathy for either. . . . He would be haughty, be humble, threaten, repent, weep, grasp your hand, or stab you whenever he saw occasion. But yet those of the army who knew him best and had suffered most for him, admired him most of all. And as he rode along the lines to battle, or galloped up in the nick of time to a battalion reeling from before the enemy's charge or shot, the fainting men and officers got new courage as they saw the splendid calm of his face and felt that his will made them irresistible."

Here, in the historic novel of the present day, we have the spirit and the theme which inspired both the heroic myth and the mediæval romance — the glorification, almost the deification, of a famous warrior and leader of armies. Thackeray is doing for Marlborough what the Homeric legend did for Agamemnon or Achilles, and what the Spanish romances did for the Cid, he is clothing the authentic or traditional figure with intense life and semi-divine attributes. The passage has the quality, so rare among latter-day novelists, of vibrating on the nerve and stirring the blood, like those old ballads that have handed down to a calm world the clash of arms and the true image of fighting men.

The second writer of our own day who has succeeded in the historic novel is George Eliot, whose Romola takes us back to Florence at the end of the fifteenth century. Modern taste dislikes and distrusts, as we have said, remoteness of time and place; nor can even George

Eliot's consummate management of detail, or the care with which she had evidently studied her period, or her forcible delineation of civic life in the full glow of the Italian Renaissance, entirely win the confidence of her readers, or inspire strong permanent interest. Her method is indicated in the opening pages of her book.

"As we may be sure," she writes, "that in 1492 the sun rose upon a Florence resembling in broad outline of landscape and architecture the city that shone in the early dawn of yesterday, so the great river-courses which have shaped the lives of men have hardly changed, and those other streams, the life-currents that ebb and flow in human hearts, pulsate to the same great loves and terrors. As our thought follows in the slow wake of the dawn, we are impressed with the broad sameness of the human lot, which never alters in the main headings of its history."

The idea is, we see, to locate a story of human love, passion, and suffering—feelings which never change, though they may become less common—amid the environment and tragic circumstances, the paganism and monkish fanaticism intermixed, of Florentine society four hundred years back. The historical facts are very skilfully worked up out of authentic documents; nevertheless we attribute the book's success not so much to the mediæval painting, or even to the terrible picture of Savonarola's mental anguish and fiery death, as to the careful preservation of modern feeling, of what may be called naturalistic treatment, in the fine literary style, the philosophic sentiments, and the handling of character.

The last of the three successful novelists to which we have alluded is the author of John Inglesant. The scene is laid in the seventeenth century, during the Civil wars and Cromwell's Protectorate, and upon this ground the author has constructed what he terms a Philosophical Romance. It is, however, an excellent specimen of consummate art in the latest style of the historical novel. No better example could be found of the vivid interest and sense of actuality that can be given to a fictitious narrative by the skilful introduction of real events and characters. The battle of Edgehill, for example, is so described as to present the illusion that one is reading the account of an eye-witness. And the thread of John Inglesant's story is interweaved upon a tapestry that exhibits wars, intrigues, courts, scaffolds, portraits of kings and popes of priests and assassins, in order to set out in relief the character of a man who in the midst of all this turmoil is little moved either by love of life or fear of death, but is intent mainly on things spiritual and on his search for the Divine illumination.

Another singular quality of this book is that it brings back again the supernatural element once so common in romance; and this is done with such reserve, with such fine shadowing of a mysterious inexplicable incident which might or might not be an illusion of the sense, that the incident of Strafford's ghost visiting Charles I. falls into just accord with the tone of a seventeenth-century narrative, without jarring upon the sensitive incredulity of a nineteenth-century reader.

We have now run very rapidly along the whole line of filiation by which, according to the view here suggested, the latest historical novel claims kinship with and a kind of lineal descent from its antique forefather, the myth. At one end we have the primitive myth-maker enveloping a true story in imaginative circumstances, making no distinction between real and imaginary, so that the whole is equally true to his hearers and probably to himself. At the other end of the line we have John Inglesant, the beautiful and artistic representation of the scenes and manners of a past day, worked up out of close and sympathetic study of the authentic documents in which those scenes and manners have been preserved. No one can tell how much is real and how much is fable in the myth; in the novel this may be ascertained easily by any careful reader. Yet although the constructive methods of the myth and the nineteenth-century novel are very different, the result is much the same; for to those who knew nothing about English history John Inglesant might be either a true chronicle or a complete fiction. And indeed, to some of us who are saturated with modern scepticism the question may occur, whether the rough old myth was not, after all, nearer the actual situation than the most finished and carefully studied historic novel. For the old Fabulist lived in a society very similar to that which he was describing in his heroic legend; he painted from what was actually going on all round him, merely throwing in broadcast the marvels and miracles of tradition, or adding them at discretion to enhance his effects. But the modern novelist works upon records and documents, upon the literary materials left by a distant age; he attempts to portray the attitude and feelings of men in situations quite unfamiliar to himself and to his generation, and in an age that is distant. One is inclined to doubt whether mere Art can possibly possess the spell which calls up the dead men and vanished scenes of the past, whether they are not all lost irrevocably. How near is the very best acting of Richard II. or Julius Cæsar to the real men and their ways? How near indeed is the most authentic history? remembering that it is quite impossible to winnow the ancient records so as to separate with any certainty the hard grain of fact from the chaff of fable. Even the picturesque historians who undertake to accomplish this feat are taking too much upon themselves, and some of them are not very far behind the old myth-maker in imposing upon their audience enchanting pictures of what probably happened, as if they were photographs taken on the spot. It is true that the romancer's device of pretending to find ancient manuscripts in family chests is obsolete; and that we are now ransacking the public record offices, in Spain and elsewhere, for authentic documents that have long lain hidden. But yet the manner in which these papers are occasionally handled is apt to revive the half-suspected odour of Fable which still hangs about some of the most delightful of our recent histories.

CHAPTER VII.

PERMANENT DOMINION IN ASIA.

Mr Pearson's prediction that China would become a dominant military power—Mr Curzon's views to the contrary—Question whether European dominion in Asia will expand or eventually contract—Chinese emigration—Have conquering races been accompanied by their women?—If not, is assimilation with subject Asiatic races possible?—Effect of assimilation and non-assimilation or permanency of dominion—The case of China—Political position and prospect of the Chinese empire—Present condition of Asiatic States—European domination in Asia—Administration from a distant metropolis—Difficulty of acclimatisation—The religious question—Possibility of China's revival.

In Mr George Curzon's admirable book on "The Problems of the Far East" (Japan, Korea, China), the twelfth chapter is entitled "The Destinies of the Far East," a very attractive subject of political speculation, which is rising rapidly into prominent importance. The empires which, outside Russia, divide the dominion of Far Eastern Asia are Japan and China. For Japan Mr Curzon predicts a very considerable development of position and power, especially in regard to checking the spread of European influence on that side of the Pacific Ocean; although, writing before the war began, he held it to be a necessary condition of Japan's free expansion that "she should not come into sustained collision with her old and hereditary antagonist China." But China is the country whose destinies stand in the foreground of the discussion; and Mr Curzon takes occasion to contest the conclusions of the late Mr Charles Pearson, who in his work upon "National Life and Character" prophesied that the Chinese would become a dominant military power in Eastern Asia and beyond. Looking to the quick and incessant multiplication of the Chinese people; to their habits of emigration; to their capacity for acclimatisation in all adjacent countries; to their potency of industrial expansion and political organisation, Mr Pearson concluded that they would spread out and consolidate a great semi-civilised empire. On the other hand, the European races, he thought, would not only fail to establish any permanent dominion in tropical Asia, but their position as rulers of Asiatic territory and masters of the sea-borne trade would before long be seriously endangered.

In opposition to these views Mr Curzon maintains that China is more likely to be conquered than to conquer, an opinion that events seem at present disposed to verify; and he evidently perceives that she is seriously threatened by Russia. As to Chinese emigration, he observes that it need cause no anxiety to the countries whither they resort, because the Chinaman is a tractable settler, who leaves his womankind at home, intermarries very readily with the races among whom he finds himself, and owes his success as a colonist to the facility with which he takes advantage of good European administration. Mr Curzon adds that the Chinese at home have displayed their greatest strength not by conquest, but by their power as assimilating conquerors.

At the present moment the expansion of European dominion (not the spread of European races) into countries outside the temperate zones, into Africa and Asia, is operating with accelerated rapidity. Mr Pearson's view is, nevertheless, that this outflow of enterprise must soon come to a standstill, and even that a reverse movement must set in. Mr Curzon, on the other hand, may be reckoned among the prophets of expansion.

As Mr Curzon's book deals exclusively with Japan, Korea, and China, his criticism of Mr Pearson's general argument is necessarily confined to that part of it which relates to the prospects of China; for it is a curious fact that of Japan Mr Pearson took no notice. Mr Pearson on the other hand used China merely as one prominent example of his main theorem—that whereas it is a commonplace to assume that the enterprising European races will continue to expand until they possess the earth, as a matter of fact the permanent limits of their predominance are unchangeable, except so far as they may contract. Now, I believe Mr Curzon to have proved undoubtedly that Mr Pearson's special knowledge of China was seriously deficient; that he knew little of its interior economy, its constitutional weakness, the military incapacity of its government, the instability of its dynasty, and the incoherence of the various races which form its population. Every day corroborates Mr Curzon's judgment that there is nothing to fear at present from China as a fighting power. Whether Mr Pearson's defeat upon this particular part of the field has substantially damaged his main position is a further question, which seems worth raising here because some of Mr Curzon's arguments and observations lead towards much broader issues than that of China's immediate future, and in fact touch upon the difficult problem of discovering the essential conditions which favour or frustrate the spread of ruling races and the building up of a permanent dominion.

For example, Mr Curzon, in the course of his argument that the Chinese custom of leaving their women at home and taking wives from the people among whom they settle renders them practically harmless, incidentally throws out the observation: "I doubt, indeed, whether emigrants have anywhere established a permanent dominion who did not bring their wives with them." But this is a very far-reaching and important generalisation, bearing directly upon the whole question of the future spread of European conquest. For which are the countries where dominion has been established on the system of family emigration? It seems probable that Mr Curzon had in mind the founding of colonies in North America and Australia, within the temperate zones, where the first thing needful was to plant homesteads and to drive off nomad savages, and where the emigrants from England and Holland settled with their families. Among all kinds and degrees of dominion, the most permanent is certainly that which is founded by clearing away forests and wild folk, and entering upon the land to people and possess it. But almost all the regions suitable for this sort of colonisation has already been occupied, and nowhere (except in parts of South America) has it as yet been found practicable for Europeans outside the temperate zones. The consequence has been that, as enterprise and conquest overflow into less habitable climates, the migration of European races cannot follow the extension of their dominion. It is true that Englishmen usually take their wives with them into the countries where they reside temporarily as merchants or administrators, and that this may be reckoned as a minor element of their success in maintaining political ascendancy; for they avoid intermixture with the native races. These cases, however, have little bearing upon the point under discussion. Mr Curzon's words, taken in their large and literal sense, imply that permanent dominion has rarely if ever been established by the migration of foreign races who have not been accompanied by their women; in other words, that where men only migrate, the dominion which they establish is very seldom permanent. And it is very interesting to enquire how far this opinion can be substantiated by historical facts.

In examining this position we ought first to determine what should be understood by permanency. Over the greater part of the world, and during most of its history, all dominion has been transitory; nevertheless it seems reasonable to let any dominion rank as permanent which covers a long and important period in the annals of a country. Now, it cannot be supposed that the migrations of the Asiatic tribes in the first centuries of the Christian era, which overthrew the Roman empire, constantly changed dynasties, occupied territories, and set up more or less durable rulerships in the early ages of Europe or in Asia up to modern times, were usually accompanied by their women in their conquering expeditions. They were great tribal agglomerations, among which some of the nomads were followed by their families; but so far as we know the women of subject countries were part of their plunder; they carried off wives and concubines, they intermarried and enslaved. In Spain the Goths and the Moors, the Ottoman Turks in Asia Minor and South-Eastern Europe, the Moghuls in India, the Spaniards in America, were emigrants who founded empires and kingdoms that lasted for centuries; but it is very questionable whether they imported their own women, at any rate until the dominion had been completely assured; and it is certain that all these ruling races intermarried or intermixed freely with the subject people. In South America the early Spanish conquerors often parcelled out the lands of the natives and took the native women to live with them, the Indians being rather eager for than averse to the connexion; and it is said that for the offspring of these mixed households the fathers were very careful to secure participation in their own rights and privileges. For a long time very few European women reached the interior of the Spanish territories in America; and the pure Spanish families were to be found either on the sea-shore or on some of the highlands where, as on the Indian Himalayas, the European race can live comfortably, though it does not thrive or reproduce itself vigorously. The Creole, bred in America of pure Spanish parents, was not much more considered or trusted by the governing caste than the half-breed. The Mamelukes in Egypt form a peculiar case, for although they settled in the land and ruled it tyrannically for several centuries, they did not intermix with the indigenous people, but continually imported their women, as slaves, from Georgia, Circassia, and other countries whence they themselves had originally been carried off. The existing distribution of races throughout the world, their characteristics, with their development or depression, are in fact due in a great measure to the crossing of stocks that up to modern times may be said to have been one of the invariable consequences of victorious emigration.

On the whole, therefore, if the case of the English and possibly the Dutch colonies proper be set aside, it seems doubtful whether permanent dominion has anywhere been established by emigrants who have brought their wives with them. It has always, except in these colonies, been established by conquering races who intermarried and interbred into the subject population. For migration implies settlement in the new country, and to this end a ruling race is obliged to mingle into the indigenous peoples, to adopt in a large degree their manners and habits of life. Religion, on the other hand, has usually followed the flag, has been propagated by conquest, and has shared the fortunes of the political supremacy. If a ruling race had attempted to intermarry strictly within its own folk, such exclusiveness would have tended toward the formation of a caste, which, being compact and united in interest, might long preserve an ascendancy; but its dominion would always rest not so much upon a broad popular base within the country as upon the maintenance of communication with the metropolis. This is, indeed, the actual situation of European dominion in climates unfavourable to European settlement, where the conquerors cannot make for themselves a permanent habitation; and it tends to produce a dilemma. If the superior nation keeps the blood pure by avoiding intermixture with the general population, its dominion depends on communication with the fatherland; and Pearson denies that under such conditions permanency is possible, though the experiment has yet to be conclusively tried, for a firm enlightened administration, looking always to the welfare of the people, may solve the problem. If, again, the European does not maintain his exclusiveness in an unfavourable climate, the half-breeds which are produced and cross with indigenous stocks, are prone to deteriorate until they merge into the native population; and even families of pure European descent, if they settle down and try to acclimatise, show a tendency to diminish and become unproductive.

The foregoing argument, if correct, points to the conclusion that for a ruling race in Asia the capacity of assimilation with the indigenous population without losing vigour is of essential value. Now Mr Curzon tells us that China has always assimilated her conquerors, yet he appears to hold that it does not add to her national strength or to her power of resisting what is most dangerous to Asiatic dominion, the intrusion of Europeans.

"So far from taking naturally to a career of conquest, it is rather in her power of assimilating those by whom she has herself been conquered that China has displayed her greatest strength. Two and a half centuries ago the millions of Chinese succumbed easily to the assault of a few hundred thousand Tartars, whose yoke they have ever since contentedly borne. Four centuries earlier they had in similar fashion accepted a Mongol master. What the Mongols did, and what the Manchus did, I fail to see why others shall not do after them, whose power, as compared with theirs, is in the same ratio as a field-gun to a Roman catapult, or a repeating rifle to a crossbow."

In this passage we have at any rate two instances of fairly permanent dominion established by emigrants who intermixed with the subject people, and whose empire was until the other day both flourishing and formidable. As the Mongols and Manchus came from adjacent countries, they probably brought with them some families, but the stability of their rulership evidently rested not upon exclusiveness but upon assimilation; and we may also infer that populations which, like the Chinese, possess this aptitude for absorbing stronger races are sure to have been fortified by the process. Mr Curzon suggests, however, that the coming race of conquerors is the European, whose success will be easy in proportion to their military superiority. Yet it is not likely that Russians or Frenchmen, even if they subdued the country, would submit to the necessary assimilation. Wives they might be expected to bring; but they would probably find that their own pure-bred children could not thrive in the climate, and that domiciled European families tend to die out in the third generation. A breed like that of the French or Spanish Creole in America cannot prop up a dominion in China. If, therefore, the Manchus were succeeded by a dominant white race, the Europeans would be casual and temporary residents as soldiers, merchants, and administrators, sojourning, but never settling in the country. Now the cardinal point of Pearson's thesis is that under such conditions no permanent dominion can be founded, in spite of repeating rifles and breechloading artillery. That does not depend, he would say, upon superiority of armament or discipline, for these things can be imported or manufactured, and a stable empire cannot rest upon bayonets only. Nor does it depend upon the woman question, for it would not strengthen the new-comers to take wives in the country, while to bring them from home implies a refusal to associate with the general population. Permanency of dominion depends on that very capacity of assimilation, of becoming acclimatised and settling down in the country without losing the qualities of rulership, which has been the characteristic of dominant Asiatic races all over the continent from the Bosphorus to Pekin. And since China has this faculty of assimilating vigorous invaders—a faculty that probably has much to do with her empire's immemorial antiquity—any race which aspires to permanent rule in that vast territory must not only conquer, but also inhabit and intermarry; and this the European cannot do. Meanwhile, as arms can be bought and armies organised, the time may come when the transformation of the Japanese into a formidable civilised war power can be imitated on a larger scale by the Chinese. We may admit that Pearson's lack of local information led him to take insufficient account of "the Chinese system of government, short-sighted, extortionate, universally corrupt"; but to this objection it may be answered that such evils are remediable, and that to the ordinary European observer the Japanese government of thirty years ago seemed no better.

Mr Curzon observes, again, that Mr Pearson's daring forecast has been framed in an epoch which has witnessed China's territorial decline. "It is entirely during the last half of this century that Tonkin, Annam, and Cochin China have been wrested from the grasp of China by

France, that Siam has repudiated her allegiance, that Burmah, once a vassal, has been absorbed into the British system, that the Amur and Ussuri provinces have been ceded to Russia," and that Japan has now lopped off Korea. But excepting the northern districts that have been ceded to Russia, these acquisitions made by France and England were independent States that paid only a formal tribute to Pekin, and had long ago separated themselves from China, if, indeed, they had ever formed a substantive part of the empire. They all have a seaboard and great rivers which afford an easy waterway inland, so that when they were attacked by the maritime powers of Europe, China was incapable of protecting them. If they had indeed been integral parts of the empire, instead of distant tributaries, it is very doubtful whether England and France would have ventured to wrest away the territory by main force. Their loss, therefore, is no very remarkable symptom of China's weakness, while the gain to their present masters is in some respects questionable; for whether the European rule will be found worth the trouble and cost of maintenance beyond a certain distance from the sea-shore remains to be tried by experience. All this South-Asian country is peculiarly unsuited for habitation by Europeans, who are obliged to keep up their governmental agency by frequent relays of fresh officials and regiments. So Mr Pearson might reply that the European domination is not more likely to be long-lived in these provinces than was the Chinese, since the Europeans can only govern from a distance through local agency—a system that lacks the elements of durability, because no fusion or association of races is possible—while pacification and orderly government only increase the pressure upwards against alien and isolated rulers. It is still an open question whether either France or England has done wisely in pushing upwards from the maritime provinces at the mouths of the great rivers into the heart of Indo-China; nor is it for these inland portions of their Asiatic dominions that durability can be most confidently predicted. By commerce, by communications, by contiguity with the Russian Empire in central Asia, by a certain affinity of origin and mind, India is year by year brought closer to Europe, with whom she has always had historical and ethnic connections. For eight hundred years she has been ruled by races from the north-west; and one might fairly maintain that this ancient Aryan land has been definitely acquired to western civilisation. But the Indo-Chinese region has never hitherto fallen within the range of European politics or relations: it lies apart under the lee of the great eastern Empire, and its natural attraction would be toward the orbit of China. There is a constant inflow of Chinese, who form an important and active element of society, with some of the qualities of a superior race.

Mr Curzon observes that extension of race is not the same thing as extension of empire, and that physical multiplication may even be a symptom of political decline; yet this latter phenomenon must at least be exceedingly rare. No one would deny, on the other hand, that physical multiplication, which means the settling and increase of an invading race in a conquered country, has always been one important and powerful mainspring of political ascendancy, and it is clear that even the pacific overflow of surplus population into lands possessed by weaker races is a considerable danger to them.

"The extinction of China is impossible and absurd. A population of 350,000,000 souls cannot be extirpated or bodily transferred. On the contrary, I believe it will increase and swell and continue to overflow. But in this movement I detect no seed of empire, and I foresee no ultimate peril to the white race." In this passage Mr Curzon may be directing his argument mainly against the view that the emigration beyond sea of the Chinese, and the rapid rise of their wealth and numbers under a civilised government, may lead to an extension of their dominion which might trouble European powers. So far as this view relates only to the multiplication of the Chinese in such isolated settlements as Borneo and Singapore, or in temporate regions beyond sea, it seems to be incontestably right; but the passage cited touches upon a larger problem, of much greater importance to foreign rulerships in Asia. What, one may ask, is to be the future political destiny of this population of 350,000,000 Chinese, which is likely to increase and overflow? China has lost her outlying dependencies; but from this kind of loss many a nation, including England, has been able to recover. The Russians are rending away territory on her far north-eastern border; while other European powers are taking up ground and spheres of influence on her sea-board; but a native dynasty may still preserve China's integrity and independence in the rich and populous central provinces. Let us assume that this may last for at least another century. Will not the teaching of misfortune, the experience of perils and defeat, increased facilities of armament, and a closer acquaintance with the methods of European administration, lead to some kind of revolution or change of system that may perforce bring in a more efficient government for the strengthening of the Chinese empire? The great viceroy, Li Hung Chang, actually attempted to re-organise the Chinese military forces by sea and land; and, although he failed through the utter rottenness of the whole administration, his attempt may soon be repeated less unsuccessfully. China, writes Mr Archibald Little, is politically weak through the corruption of its government and the unwarlike character of its people; and his remedy lies in calling in European organisers and a trained European staff for the army, which he believes must come ere long. There are at present no signs of such a reform; but, on the contrary, the government has been seized by conservative reactionaries; yet it is difficult to suppose that this vast and intelligent people, with the example of Japan before their eyes, are likely to remain much longer under the oppressive burden of an antiquated and discredited official hierarchy.

And if some kind of revolution brings in a more efficient government, may not the seeds of empire germinate until the existing balance of power becomes materially altered in eastern Asia? It would be hard to prove that the continuous progress of great Asiatic peoples toward a higher level of intelligence, toward organised administration and effective war power, does not tend to affect the position of the European rulerships in Asia in regard both to domestic institutions and external relations. Peace, prosperity, education, and acquaintance with European models lead to the concession, within a dependency, of political rights that have to be reconciled with the reservation of political supremacy. And without, beyond the frontiers of the European domain, the situation will have materially changed whenever an adjacent power on the Asiatic continent shall have successfully followed the example of Japan in adopting the western system of great standing armies, which is usually the earliest improvement that an able despot borrows from civilisation. In some ways such a neighbour would be more troublesome and disquieting than even a European rival, for his policy would be exclusively Asiatic. The fundamental interests of England, France, and Russia lie at home; nor have any of these nations ever gone to war with one another on an Asiatic quarrel unless the situation in Europe had already provided strong independent motives for doing so; and if these motives are absent they keep the peace in Asia. Whereas a great non-European power would be hampered by no such checks or deterrent considerations.

It must be admitted that we have never yet witnessed the revival of any Asiatic power that has once fallen under the dominant influence of civilised Europe, which seems to have a paralysing effect upon indigenous political growth. Looking back over the course of the world's history during the nineteenth century, one would have said that its general drift has been to draw all Asia gradually under the political tutelage, if not the dominion, of Europe. In the West the great historic kingdoms of Turkey and Persia have been shorn of territory and reduced in strength; their integrity and their independence have alike suffered diminution. Throughout the whole of the nineteenth century the European powers have been alternately propping up Turkey and pulling away her outlying provinces; the empire's life has been saved by periodical amputations. Persia is isolated externally and left to misrule internally, with the result that she is suffering from depopulation and impoverishment of national wealth and character. In central Asia the barbarous khanates, Khiva, Bokhára, Kokhand, have been absorbed or subdued by Russia. Afghanistan, preserved as a barrier between Russia and India, has come under the protectorate of England; and the three empires, Russia, China, and India, have made a partition of the great Pamir region, with its ridges, valleys, and barren table-lands. From Persia eastward to the confines of China and Siam all southern Asia is possessed or protected by the English. The French have assumed sovereignty over Tonkin, Annam, and all the eastern provinces of the Siamese kingdom. One would infer that there is a tendency toward the extinction of minor States and the aggregation of immense territories under European sovereignties; that the ancient kingdoms of the East are crumbling through decay and dry rot produced by a system under which they can neither be repaired nor pulled down, and that the people are losing their vitality under the discipline of European control. Where rulers are exempt from the ordinary vicissitudes of Asiatic sovereignty, where insurrection or foreign invasion is no longer to be feared, the natural remedies for bad or feeble government disappear. So also do the natural conditions that develop and bring to the front strong rulers and establish powerful dynasties. Never more will Egypt be governed by a Mehemet Ali who could neither read nor write, but who extirpated the Mamelukes, founded a dynasty, and would have overturned the Sultan's throne at Constantinople if the great European powers had not interposed with their fleets and armies. When Ismael Pasha fell into the net of European money-lenders his kingdom lost its independence, and if the existing system continues, his successors will have been as completely emasculated as if they had been relegated to the harem. It is the pressure of the western powers that has been keeping within bounds both the might and the misrule of kings and ministers over the greater part of Asia; it is their superintendence that has prevented commotions, changes of dynasty, wars, disruption of territory, irruption of stronger races, and all the violent collisions which have hitherto made or unmade kingdoms. Most of the frontiers have been laid down under European supervision, and none of them could be seriously violated without interposition from the same quarter; for the adjustment of all international relations is virtually managed by European diplomacy. The sea-coast is entirely commanded by the powerful navies of the West, and except in Japanese waters the whole sea-power is in their hands. In proportion as any government has run into debt with European financiers, or has permitted the investment of foreign capital within its territory, this political superintendence becomes more stringent, self-interested, and inquisitive. After this manner and for divers reasons, the European powers maintain a police which keeps the peace except when they themselves find cause for breaking it, and insist on the immobility of all frontiers except their own.

On the other hand, where the European has taken actual possession of a country, and directly administers it, there is progress. India which is governed by Englishmen, and fed by English capital, shows an extraordinary increase of riches, population, and intelligence that are producing an upward pressure upon the superstructure of foreign rule, insomuch that frequent alterations are required to adjust the stability of the edifice. And all over central Asia the Russians have substituted profound tranquillity and the rudiments of civilisation for barbarous anarchy and the predatory life of nomad tribes. Such is the unnatural and artificial condition of Asia up to the Chinese border. Every part of it, whether decaying or reviving, lies under the shadow of Europe, and the whole region has exchanged the old state of chronic warfare, dynastic insecurity, and perpetual shifting of frontiers, for submissive acquiescence in the ascendancy of the white races. And such, it has been confidently asserted, will before long be the condition of the whole continent, whenever the Western shadow shall have lengthened until it falls over China.

But we have now begun to comprehend the immense difference between western and eastern Asia, between the historic kingdoms that have been known to us for ages—belonging, it has been supposed, to one immutable type—and those which have lain so long beyond the sphere of political observation, avoiding all contact with Europe except by trade at the seaports, unaffected by disturbance from the West, and sheltered on the East by a broad ocean. It is not much more than a century since the Europeans began to encroach seriously upon Asia, and before that time the Asiatic founders of permanent dominion came from the north-east. The old migratory hordes that swept across Asia into Europe and planted dynasties in the West were Turks and Mongols; the only great empire that has existed in India before our own was founded by Moghuls; in Persia and Turkey the ruling families belong to a Turkish tribe of north-eastern origin. The Arabs did indeed overrun western Asia, but though they changed its religion, they established no durable rulerships. It would seem as if the true reservoir of Asiatic forces lay among the population of a region with which Europe has only very recently come into effective contact. Now that our political explorations have reached the further side of the continent, we are discovering, not without anxiety, that by forcing open the gates of commerce with the industrial races of Asia we have let out upon ourselves a flood of formidable competition. It is clear that the yellow race have not been overtaken by the depression that has been spreading over the Asiatic kingdoms in the West, nor have they yet passed under the dominant influence or the administration of Europe. On the contrary, they are so using their intercourse with European nations as to appropriate our inventions and extend their commerce without forfeiting their independence; and up to the outbreak of the Chinese war they had avoided that most perilous snare, the European money market. In this manner Japan has achieved a transformation that is without precedent in the history of Asia. The war between China and Japan will have forced most of us to modify our fixed ideas regarding the immemorial unchanging East, as it used to be called in prose and poetry; and for China it may prove to be the beginning of the new era in which the militant, industrial, and administrative inventions by which Europe has hitherto prevailed easily over Asia will be turned against their inventor. Instead of the decrepit dynasties or barbarous chiefships which Europe begins by controlling, and will possibly end by consuming, we have seen the only two independent Asiatic powers falling into violent collision; we have a young, active, and ambitious government assaulting an unwieldy old-fashioned empire whose weight had for centuries steadied all eastern Asia; kindling again the fire of war and conquest which has been smothered out in the West, and acting without regard for the interests or wishes of the European powers, who stood by awaiting the outcome.

What is likely to be the effect upon Japan and upon China of this unexpected eruption of the old Asiatic volcano? Japan will probably become a first-class naval power in the China seas, to the infinite advantage of her commercial enterprise and foreign trade, which are driving European goods out of the markets of the Far East. In regard to China, for the moment it looks very much as if Japan had only broken down the Manchu dynasty to let in the European, a very disadvantageous result for Japan. China has been humbled, has lost Korea and Formosa, and has submitted to a heavy indemnity; but on the other hand it may be that nothing less than this violent shock could have roused her government from the deadly lethargy into which it has been sinking. Such a blow may break down the monopoly of the literary officials, may bring out any latent vigour or leadership that can be found among China's immense population, and may thus enable her, if she recovers from it, to guard against being a second time caught unarmed and half asleep. If the result is to substitute a strong government for a supine one, and to make China lose no time in arming herself at all points, it is certain that the three hundred millions of industrious and ingenious people who inhabit her fertile lands provide ample resources for the erection of a formidable military empire. This may come to pass in a generation or two, if China holds together and avoids financial embarrassment, and then will Pearson's prophecy have been so far fulfilled that the European will be barred out from conquest, and will have another formidable commercial rival in eastern Asia, while in all those provinces that have been recently detached from Chinese suzerainty, his position will be much less comfortable than it is at present. The sense of nationality will be created or confirmed, as it usually is, by the stress of international conflict; or at any rate the dislike of foreigners will be intensified within the empire. The new spirit may even spread abroad over neighbouring countries where a kind of national feeling is already being stimulated by foreign rule.

The speculation, therefore, which the recent war suggests is that, if the rude lesson given by Japan to China teaches her to set up armaments on the European scale and pattern, we shall have in the East two powers very different from the worn-out monarchies of western and central Asia, and intrinsically stronger than any foreign rulership can be that has occupied a country where it cannot acclimatise. And since one of the principal factors of European conquest, eastward and westward, has hitherto been superiority of arms and discipline, so it is now important to observe that Europe has latterly opened a huge workshop and magazine for the supply of arms and ammunition to the rest of the world, from savage African tribes to great Asiatic governments. The mutual jealousy of European powers induces them to check each other by supplying arms to any tribe or potentate who may be thereby encouraged to oppose the progress of a rival. This flourishing business is neither creditable to Christendom, nor will it, I believe, bring anything but eventual disadvantage to the cause of western commerce and civilisation generally, or of permanent dominion in the East. It can hardly fail to go a long way towards diminishing the odds against Asiatics (always superior in number) in combating the trained soldiers of Europe; particularly since, as trade extends with the facility of penetrating everywhere, there will soon be no possibility of controlling the supply. It will strengthen the hands of able despots who can set up and manage a standing army to be used at first for crushing out local liberties and tribal independence, and afterwards for signifying to any European rulership on their frontier that it has no longer to deal with feeble, or ignorant, or submissive neighbours. The present attitude of Abyssinia is in this respect significant. Neither France nor Italy cares to meddle with her, and it would be totally impossible now for England to repeat the expedition of 1868.

It seems to me, in short, that those who believe the tide of European predominance in Asia to be still rising must take into account the growth of various forces and circumstances which hold it in check and throw it backward. The paramount fact that all the temperate zone is virtually occupied by firmly planted nationalities or strong governments, has altered and is transforming the course and character of the vicissitudes of dominion. The old conquests, wherever they were permanent, rested upon multitudinous invasion, upon intermixture of races, and upon acclimatisation. The armies or hordes subdued a country, settled down among the people, intermarried with them, imposed new customs and creeds or adopted those of the subject races. All this blending of blood, of manners, and of religions produced material and moral acclimatisation, whereby the ruling or foreign element usually consolidated its dominion. Where there was no great difference between the conquering and the subject races, this process went on easily enough; where the difference, particularly in climate, was great, it went on slowly, and the rulers maintained their military superiority by constant importations of their own folk. There has always been an indraw from the cool uplands of central Asia, which breed martial tribes, into the low-lying fertile regions inhabited by industrious but comparatively unwarlike populations. The weak and wealthy countries have attracted hardy men from the comparatively barren highlands, whose dominion has lasted until the original stock had so far deteriorated that it could not resist the vigour of a new invasion. The history of Europe shows that this natural succession of tribal conquests formerly went on to some extent in our continent, although the general uniformity of climate does not give us such well-marked phenomena. In Europe, however, the era of migrations and invasions on a large scale has long passed away. Throughout the greater part of Asia also it would seem to have closed, for the weight of European ascendancy fixes down the kingdoms and prescribes limits to their territories; and the beginning of this immobility of the populations is indicated by the Indian census of 1891. Formerly there was a continual influx into India from the North-West, as is proved by the variety of origins clearly perceptible in the North Indian people; but as these were all military immigrants following in the wake of conquests, and as the era of invasion by land has closed for the present, we find by the census of 1891 that there is now very little immigration from outside India. Among a population of 300,000,000, no more than 660,000 were born outside the country, and this number includes 115,000 Europeans and Americans, almost all of whom are merely sojourners in the land. The proportion of *bonâ fide* immigrants into India must in fact be very small.

But this same ascendancy which has closed the migratory period has substituted a new species of dominion for the old rulerships that rested, as I have said, on invasion, settlement, intermarriage, and acclimatisation. The new European dominion rests on no such foundations: it relies entirely on superiority in arms, on skilful administration, and on commerce. The fundamental characteristic which differentiates it from Asiatic and American dominion of the old type is that the European possessions in Asia are retained as dependencies of an alien race and a distant metropolis. For the Asiatic conqueror always established a separate rulership, unless he could incorporate his conquered lands into a mere adjacent province of his native country, being usually incapable of governing from a distance. The secret of the long dominion of the Arabs in Spain, the longest in the whole record of foreign dominations, is probably that it was an independent dominion of a settled race. It would have been impossible to hold Spain as a province of some great Arab empire in North Africa. And we may guess that one reason why Alexander's generals founded durable dynasties in Syria, Egypt, and even in remote Bactria, may have been that the great conqueror's death broke up his vast conquests into separate local sovereignties, which could never have been held together as provinces of a Macedonian empire.

Instead, therefore, of the system of successive independent sovereignties, we have now the system of dependencies, ruled from a distant metropolis. Now we know that whenever a dependency has been actually colonised by emigrants of the ruling race, the connection with the metropolis grows weaker and weaker, until, as in North and South America, it is violently broken. It is true that in Spanish and Portuguese America it lasted three hundred years; but that dominion was largely of the Asiatic type: it drew much strength from intermixture of races and partial acclimatisation. The new species of European dominion in Asia strikes no such root into the soil. The old dominions, moreover, had another method of planting themselves in a foreign soil that has been necessarily abandoned by the civilised rulers of the present day. For Europeans who go out to govern a modern Asiatic dependency usually take with them from home their wives and their political principles, and among those principles they always export the rule of strict religious neutrality. On the other hand, the old-fashioned invaders and *conquistadores* very rarely brought their wives—they were wont to leave morality, whether public or private, at home—but wherever a dominion was founded there the religion of the conquerors was sedulously propagated. The Mahomedans stamped the faith of Islam into all their subject peoples so deeply that except in Spain it has never since lost ground. The Spaniards, who in the fifteenth century had just succeeded in exterminating Islam at home, set themselves deliberately to obliterate the indigenous beliefs in America, and their success has been complete. All Mexico and South America were compelled into the Roman Catholic faith by the Spaniards and Portuguese: the native worships were relentlessly trampled out; the monuments and records were destroyed; the rites were transformed where they could not be wholly eradicated. Religious authority became incorporate in the Church of Rome, which thus acquired enormous power over the domesticated Indian races, whether pure or of the half-blood. And the political value justly attached to this spiritual dominion may be measured by the fact that up to very recent times the superior priesthood was carefully restricted to home-bred Spaniards—even the Creoles, or pure Spaniards of American parentage, being altogether excluded; while as the whole ecclesiastical patronage lay, not with the Pope, but with the king's government at Madrid, it could be the more easily used as an engine for political control. No one would deny, and no one should attempt to excuse, the abominable persecution of which both Islam and Roman Christianity were often guilty. But it is impossible not to admit that in many instances the successful propagation of a superior or stronger creed has been favourable to political amalgamation, nor can there be any doubt of the intense fusing power that belongs to a common religion. In our day the decree of divorce between religion and politics has been made absolute by the judgment of every statesman, above all for Christian rulers in non-Christian countries; nevertheless the religion of the Spaniards was a part of their policy in the New World, and this of course is still true in regard to Mahomedans everywhere. There have been many periods, and there are still many countries, in which an army composed of different religious sects could hardly hold together. And it is certain that for ages identity of religious belief has been, and still is in many parts of the world, one of the strongest guarantees of combined action on the battle-field. It has often shown itself far more effective, as a bond of union, than territorial patriotism; it has even surmounted tribal or racial antipathies; and its advantages as a palliative of foreign ascendancy have been indisputable. The attitude of religious neutrality is now manifestly and incontestably incumbent on all civilised rulerships over an alien people; it is a principle that is just, right, and politic; but there is nothing in its influence that makes for that kind of assimilation which broadens the base of dominion. Religion and intermarriage are the bonds that amalgamate or isolate social groups all the world over, especially in Asia, and their influence for or against political consolidation has lost very little of its efficiency anywhere. Mr Pearson went wrong, unfortunately, in affirming "that British rule is tending to obliterate the religious differences between Mahomedan and Hindu" in India.

These are, I think, some of the general reasons why the present predicament of the Chinese Government—weak, unwieldy, battered by Japan, and perhaps on the brink of some tremendous disaster—does not yet warrant the conclusion that Pearson's prediction is receiving signal disproof, still less that his general theory as to the profound instability affecting the rulership of races that cannot acclimatise is shaken. It may be that Russia will eventually take from China some more territory on the Amoor or in Kashgar, and that France will cut off slices from the southern provinces; although the dominion of the French in the neighbouring country of Annam is not yet very prosperous. And those who are attempting to raise the cry of Asia for the Asiatics seem to need reminding that the greatest Asiatic power is Russia, whose dominion has the immense advantage of being an unbroken territory from Petersburg to Vladivostok, subject to no abrupt variation of climate, and with a population that blends and graduates from the European into the Asiatic. Nevertheless, as one does not sell the bear's skin before the beast is slain, so to discuss expectations of the European inheriting from the Manchu is at least premature; for there is still room for the contingency that from war may eventually come the regeneration of China, and in that event the European powers who shall have been rending the skirts of her empire might find their tenure of any such acquisitions neither cheap nor comfortable.

At the present moment Russia and France appear to be joining hands with the object of establishing an ascendancy over China; and our own diplomatic action points towards a policy of alliance with the Japanese sea power. For such a policy there is much to be said; yet we must not forget the very large extent to which England is interested in the maintenance of the Chinese Empire, whose frontier runs for several thousand miles with our Asiatic frontier. On the whole, we can never look for a better neighbour than China has been to us—exclusive, uncommunicative, but pacific and incapable of aggression—and the substitution of France or Russia for China on some section of this long border-line would benefit us not at all. It is true that a numerous and well-armed Chinese force just across our Burmese border might not precisely suit us in every respect. But a strong and warlike Celestial Empire would be much more inconvenient to France, and even to Russia; for probably Russia's views would be best promoted by preserving China, like Persia, to stew in her own juice, and to decay until she can easily be dismembered, or until she dissolves naturally. It is to be feared, however, that the reformation of China is still so far beyond measurable distance as to be out of the range of effective political discussion, except for the purpose of reminding those whom it may concern that, if the Japanese war does prove to have been a turning-point in Chinese history, there is still a possibility of its leading toward revival instead of to decadence or disintegration.

THE END

INDEX

PRINTED AT THE EDINBURGH PRESS, 9 AND 11 YOUNG STREET EDINBURGH.